# McDonnell
# DC-9/MD-80
# & MD-90

*Above:*
**The General Electric GE36 Ultra High-Bypass (UHB) engine on flight test aboard an MD-80 in 1987.**

*Overleaf, top:*
**Inex Adria Airways took delivery of its first DC-9-32 on 25 April 1969.** *Paul A. Tomlin*

*Overleaf, bottom:*
**Ghana Airways became only the second DC-9 customer in Africa when it took delivery of this Series 51 in July 1978.**

*Front cover:*
**British Midland Airways was the first UK operator of the DC-9 when it put its first aircraft into service between London and Teesside in September 1976.**

*Back cover, top:*
**The Texas International fleet of DC-9s, including this DC-9-31, provided 95% of total seat capacity on its extensive route network.**

*Back cover, bottom:*
**Double rows of DC-9s at the Douglas Aircraft Co's final assembly building at Long Beach, California.**

# MODERN CIVIL AIRCRAFT:10

# McDonnell Douglas

# DC-9/MD-80 & MD-90

## Günter Endres

LONDON

IAN ALLAN LTD

# Contents

First published 1991

ISBN 0 7110 1958 4

Published by Ian Allan Ltd, Shepperton, Surrey; and printed by Ian Allan Printing Ltd at their works at Coombelands in Runnymede, England.

*Below:*
**Austrian Airlines DC-9s being worked on at the airline's maintenance facility at Vienna-Schwechat Airport.** *Austrian Airlines*

*Below right:*
**Bonanza Air Lines was the second customer for the DC-9, introducing two Series 11s on its Phoenix-Las Vegas route on 1 March 1966.**

To Vanessa,
whose dedication, unstinting effort at the computer and loyal support provided a solid base from which to work. It is her book as much as it is mine.

# Introduction

The McDonnell Douglas DC-9/MD-80/MD-90 family, manufactured at Long Beach, California, is one of the world's most popular twin-jet airliner, with more than 1,800 delivered at the end of 1990. The DC-9, which made its maiden flight on 25 February 1965, was the last civil airliner designed exclusively by the Douglas Aircraft Co before it became part of the McDonnell Corporation in 1967. The early DC-9s and DC-9 Super 80s retain the famous DC (Douglas Commercial) designation, though the latter were retrospectively given an MD prefix in 1983.

Twenty-five years have now passed since the first member of the family made its debut. In that time, DC-9s have logged a total of some 40 million flying hours and carried 2.5 billion passengers over 15 billion miles, while in 10 years the MD-80 fleet worldwide has already reached six million hours and has carried more than 570 million passengers over a distance of 3.5 billion miles. Both types have to date been operated by more than 120 airlines across the world and a large number of corporate owners, private companies and organisations. The latest addition to the family is the MD-90 series, due to enter service late in 1994, ensuring that the success of the McDonnell Douglas twin-jet airliners will continue well into the next century.
Günter Endres

## Acknowledgements
In the preparation of this book I have been fortunate to be able to call on the kind and knowledgeable assistance of many people including Geoffrey Norris and Marion Osborne, McDonnell Douglas representatives in London; and my friends David Dorrell, Mike Stroud, Hector Cabezas in Frankfurt, Professor Johannes Zopp in Vienna, Peter Zsille in Budapest, Rickydene Halliday and Captain Dave Carter for reading through the manuscript and making useful suggestions. To all the airlines who took the time to provide the requested information, a special thank you. Unfortunately, there were many more who did not.

# 1 A Difficult Gestation

The McDonnell Douglas DC-9/MD-80 family is the world's best-selling twin-jet transport aircraft, with total orders, options and commitments received by 31 March 1990 amounting to 2,840 aircraft. It was the last civil airliner designed exclusively by the former Douglas Aircraft Company whose famous DC (Douglas Commercial) series from the DC-1 onwards needs no introduction.

From the early 1950s, Douglas embarked on a search for a short-to-medium range jetliner to partner its long-range, large-capacity DC-8, then under development. A number of different concepts under the tentative designation of DC-9 were examined, and one of the proposals actively put to several prospective airline customers was for a medium-range, four-engined design with a passenger capacity of some two-thirds that of the DC-8. This proposed aircraft, closely comparable in size to the later Convair 880, in commercial terms one of the least successful jet aircraft, found little favour with the airlines approached and was quickly discarded. In order not to lose out entirely in the medium market stakes, Douglas entered into an interim two-year contract with Sud-Aviation on 10 February 1960, establishing complete technical co-operation between the two companies, in effect merging the DC-9 and Caravelle programmes in favour of the French airliner. Douglas was appointed general sales and technical agents for most parts of the world, with the exception of Western Europe and the various French-speaking areas, but with a firm eye on the potentially vast American market. A Caravelle III was 'americanised' as the Series VIIA with the installation of General Electric

*Below:*
**The first two DC-9s being rolled out at Douglas' Long Beach facility. The lead aircraft made the first ever flight of the new twin-jet on 25 February 1965.**

CJ805-23C turbofans and other details to meet US airworthiness requirements, and this first flew from Cincinnati on 29 December 1960. Douglas was to build the engine pods and establish spares manufacture and management centres on the east and west coasts of America. It also had the right to build the Caravelle under licence at its Long Beach facility, if orders were to exceed the Toulouse plant production limit of 7-8 aircraft per month. This never looked likely and only one order, partly financed by Douglas, was placed in September 1961 by TWA-Trans World Airlines for 20 of the Caravelle 10A development with 15 options, for delivery in 1963. This order was later cancelled and, although specifically tailored for the US market, the General Electric-powered Caravelle failed to win any sales and the contract was terminated. Chastened but undaunted, Douglas at least learned from its experience and went quickly back to the drawing board to study a considerable number of options and configurations of a wholly original design, working in close consultation with airlines, whose specific requirements enabled Douglas more clearly to define and shape the aircraft that was eventually to take to the skies.

With the long-haul market satisfied by the Boeing 707 and its own DC-8, and the needs of the medium range met by the Boeing 727 and to a lesser extent the Convair 880, Douglas concentrated its efforts on the requirements of the short-haul operators, whose needs had hitherto largely been ignored. Airlines like the US local service carriers, who were ready to replace their ageing piston-engined aircraft, but who wanted to bring the speed, comfort and operating economies of the larger jetliners to their main short-haul sector routes. Thus the DC-9 was to be the main American contender in a specific field at that time dominated by European-build jet aircraft in the shape of the British Aircraft Corporation One-Eleven and the French-designed Caravelle, both rear-engined twin-jet machines. Dominated is perhaps overstating it, since the shortcomings of both European designs ensured that success was strictly limited. However, their important contribution to the development of short-haul jet aircraft must be acknowledged. Nevertheless, it provided Douglas with the opportunity to improve on and eliminate to a large extent the failings of the European competition, and it was a considerable disappointment to the manufacturer that in spite of the enormous advantage of the later design, no orders had been received for the DC-9 by 8 April 1963, when it announced that production of its second jetliner would proceed. When design study data of the DC-9, then known as Douglas Model 2086, was released in 1962, it offered a 63-seat aircraft with

a 69,000lb (31,298kg) gross weight, powered by either two Pratt & Whitney JT8-10A-6 of 10,500lb (47.72kN) thrust each, or two 10,400 (46.28kN) thrust Rolls Royce RB163-2 engines. Preliminary work on a revised design was initiated later that year. Fabrication started on 26 July 1963 and assembly of the first aircraft was begun on 6 March 1964.

The definitive DC-9, therefore, was designed with more powerful rear-mounted turbofans, electrically-operated integral air stairs, a built-in APU (Auxiliary Power Unit) which gave it minimum dependence on airfield facilities and made for quick turn-round, a comfortable five-abreast single-aisle seating arrangement, and the capability to carry a fair amount of cargo under floor in addition to baggage and mail. Other design parameters included good short-field performance and an MGTOW (Maximum Gross Take-off Weight) of less than 80,000lb (36,287kg), a limit then imposed by the FAA (Federal Aviation Agency, later the Federal Aviation Administration), enabling the use of a two-man flight crew. Douglas also placed major emphasis on minimum maintenance, to levels well below those achieved by other airliners. In many ways similar to the One-Eleven, it too featured a moderate wing-sweep and T-tail configuration. A high maximum landing weight was also adopted to enable the aircraft to fly sev-

*Above:*
**Air Canada was one of the earliest DC-9 operators when it took delivery of a DC-9-14 in April 1966.**

eral segments without refuelling, an important consideration taking account of the 'bus-stop' type operation of local and regional airlines whose routes often included flight sectors of less than 100 miles (160 km). Douglas also had the foresight of designing the DC-9 with considerable 'stretchability' and the capability of ready adaptation to meet a wide variety of customer requirements, which was to prove one of the principal factors in the later success of the aircraft. All this added up to a performance edge over the Caravelle, which had higher operating costs and only limited underfloor cargo capacity, and to a much greater growth potential than the One-Eleven, which was handicapped by the thrust limitation of its Rolls-Royce Spey turbofans. It also stole a march on the slightly more advanced Boeing 737, which did not enter airline service until two years after the DC-9.

## Into the Air

In May 1963 a month after the go-ahead, Douglas received a first order from Delta Air Lines for 15 aircraft, with another 15 on option. This was followed during the same year by orders from Bonanza Air Lines and Air Canada for three and

six aircraft respectively. Sales were disappointingly slow, though this was largely the result of the airline industry finding itself in the midst of a severe recession. Fortunately, the situation improved radically in 1965, with a substantial increase in traffic pushing airline orders up from 58 to 228 in the 10-month period between the initial flight and the time the DC-9 entered service with Delta on 8 December 1965, an altogether healthier picture and confirmation, if somewhat belatedly, of Douglas' design philosophy.

The DC-9 took off on its maiden flight from Long Beach to Edwards Air Force Base on 25 February 1965 under the command of George R. Jansen, assisted by test pilot Paul H. Patten and flight engineer Duncan Walker. The first flight lasted 2 hours 13 minutes, during which the structural stability and aerodynamic behaviour of the aircraft, together with the functioning of on-board control systems, proved satisfactory. Take-off weight was 77,160lb (35,000kg) and the speed was taken up to 285mph (460km/h). Designated DC-9-10, it was powered by two 12,000lb (53.38kN) thrust Pratt & Whitney JT8D-5 turbofans and was destined for eventual service with Trans-Texas Airways. As with its previous designs, except for the DC-1 which served as the prototype for the bigger DC-2, Douglas did not produce any prototypes but used production aircraft for flight testing. By June, four additional Series 10 aircraft were flying and participated in the trial and certification programme, which was speedily and successfully completed with the award of the FAA Type Approval on 23 November that same year, less than nine months after the first flight. Altogether five aircraft, therefore, participated in the test programme, four of which were packed with test equipment, whilst the fifth was completely fitted out for passenger service. A total of 12 pilots and 40 engineers were employed in the evaluation process, working under the leadership of John C. Londelius, Director of Flight Development, and John P. Hann, Flight Test Project Engineer. With the exception of specifics, the procedures and methods of flight testing and certification are similar for all transport aircraft, and Douglas' rich experience helped considerably in speeding up the process towards certification. Putting together a sensible programme using the PERT critical path method, began long before the first flight, when every test requirement was analysed for content and flight duration and grouped to ensure the most efficient series of tests for each aircraft. Many tests and measurements were repeated in different aircraft as an insurance against possible delays which might have put off the granting of its certificate of airworthiness. Aircraft No 1 was used primarily for examining the flight characteristics of the DC-9, functioning of all on-board control and stall characteristics. Main task for the second test aircraft was the assessment of aerodynamic stresses in the structure for different flight parameters, to provide a direct comparison with values obtained from wind tunnel trials. On-board systems were also thoroughly tested. The third aircraft was put to testing projected flight performance and engines, together with the operation of the reverse thrust braking system. Aircraft No 4 was fitted out with pneumatic and electrical systems, communications and navigation equipment, anti-icing installations and air conditioning and pressurisation systems. The noise level in the cabin was also monitored. The fifth aircraft served to demonstrate the type's suitability and reliability for the transport of passengers under the most demanding service conditions in compliance with FAA requirements.

*Below:*
**Double rows of DC-9s at the Douglas Aircraft Co's final assembly building at Long Beach, California.**

## Phased Test Programme

The test and certification programme of the DC-9 proceeded in three phases with a certain amount of overlapping in the later stages. These were the actual flight testing by the manufacturer, a so-called development period, and the airworthiness flights by the FAA. During the works trials, the complete performance envelope of the aircraft was explored step by step, ie altitude and speed were gradually increased, as was the aircraft weight, which ranged from the minimum to beyond the upper design limits. Once the DC-9 had confirmed its flying characteristics, the programme graduated into the development phase, during which Douglas had to satisfy itself that its latest jetliner met all projected design criteria and especially its performance guarantees quoted to customers. Where necessary, improvements and corrections were made at that stage. Within the framework of these trials came such checks as take-off and landing field requirements, stability at differing weights and centres of gravity at all flight altitudes, and landing with different flap and reverse thrust settings. All trials were undertaken under normal and abnormal operating conditions, for example simulating an engine shut-down at the critical point on take-off, or flap malfunction on landing. Passenger comfort was also high on

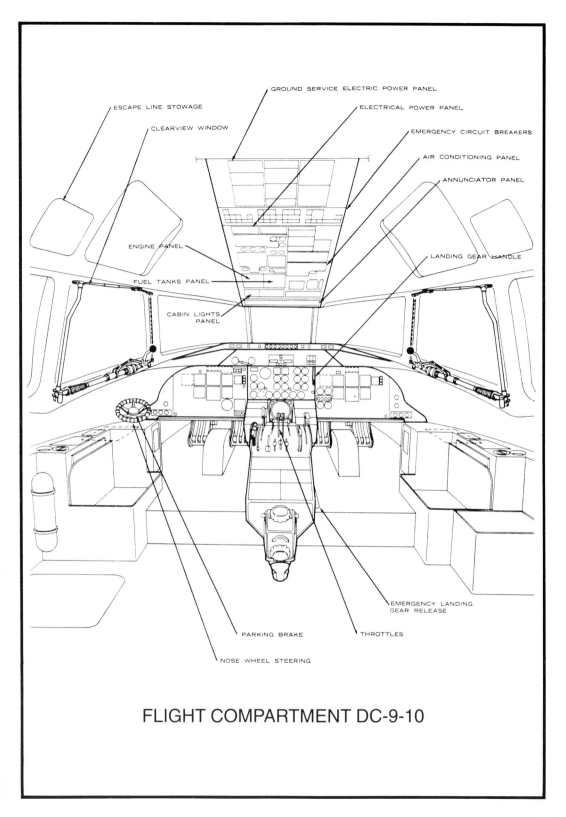

FLIGHT COMPARTMENT DC-9-10

11

the list, making sure that noise levels, pressurisation, air conditioning and cabin temperatures complied with all requirements. Above all, the development phase had to prove beyond reasonable doubt, that in spite of all possible breakdowns and emergencies, the DC-9 was still capable of safe operation. Finally, FAA pilots put the aircraft through its paces once again, before pronouncing it fit for regular commercial passenger service by granting it a Type Approval.

## The DC-9-10

A smaller Series 5 had been projected, but was not proceeded with. This had a fuselage 9ft 6in (2.90m) shorter than the Series 10, and provided accommodation for 60 passengers. Engines were to be the same JT8D-5, with a maximum gross take-off weight of 70,000lb (31,750kg). Thus the initial production model was the DC-9-10, of which a total of 137 were eventually built for US and foreign airlines.

The Series 10 comprised several different models including all-passenger versions and two convertible passenger/cargo variants. All have the same external dimensions, but differ in engine configuration and MGTOW. High-density passenger accommodation is possible for up to 90 passengers with reduced facilities. A more typical layout provides for 80 passengers at a 36in (86cm) seat pitch, without penalty on performance. Main external dimensions are 89ft 5in (27.25m) span, 104ft 5in (31.82m) length and 27ft 4in (8.33m) height.

**DC-9-11** Powered by two Pratt & Whitney JT8D-5 turbofans with a static thrust each of 12,000lb (53.38kN) and MGTOW of 77,700lb (35,244kg).
**DC-9-12** Powerplant two 14,000lb (62.28kN) thrust JT8D-1 or JT8D-7 engines, MGTOW 85,700lb (38,873kg).
**DC-9-14** Powerplant two 12,000lb (53.38kN) JT8D-5 or 14,000lb (62.28kN) JT8D-1 engines, MGTOW 86,300lb (39,145kg).
**DC-9-15** Powerplant two 14,000lb (62.28kN) JT8D-1 or JT8D-7 engines. MGTOW 90,700lb (41,141kg), increased fuel capacity.
**DC-9-15MC** 'Multiple Change' convertible model produced for Trans-Texas Airways. Powered by JT8D-1 engines, with an MGTOW of 90,700lb (41,141kg). Convertibility achieved with folding passenger seats stored at the rear behind cargo.
**DC-9-15RC** 'Rapid Change' passenger/cargo model, which went into service with Continental Airlines. It has the same MGTOW as the -15MC, but is driven by JT8D-7 engines. Change to cargo is achieved by means of removable seats on pallets.

*Below:*
**Aeronaves de Mexico has been operating DC-9s since 1967 when this Series 15 aircraft was delivered.**

Both convertible models have a strengthened main cabin floor and feature an 81in×136in (2.06m×3.45m) upward-hinged cargo door, installed on the forward port side of the fuselage. To accommodate the cargo door, the fourth and eleventh windows were removed.

## Technical Profile

The Douglas DC-9 is a low-wing cantilever monoplane of conventional all-metal construction. The wing is designed as a torsion box with three spars inboard, two spars outboard and spanwise stringers riveted to the skin, forming an integral fuel tank. Mean thickness/chord ratio is 11.6%, aspect ratio 8.25 and sweepback 24 degrees at quarter-chord. Ailerons are hydraulically controlled, each being made up in two sections with the outer used at low speed only. Flaps are also hydraulically actuated and are double-slotted, covering 67% of the semi-span. Leading-edge slats are featured on later models only. The design also includes wing-mounted speed brakes and a single boundary layer fence (vortillon) under each wing. Wing-tips are detachable. Thermal anti-icing is provided on leading edges. The fuselage is of semi-monocoque, fail-safe construction and forms a pressurised cabin, excluding only the landing gear wells and the area aft of the rear pressure bulkhead. The rear fuselage carries the tail unit, which is a cantilever structure with hydraulically-actuated, variable-incidence tailplane mounted at the tip of the fin to form a T-tail. Elevators are manually controlled with servo-tabs, whilst the rudder has hydraulic control with manual override. Trailing edges on all control surfaces are of glass-fibre material.

Power is provided by two axial-flow, two-spool turbofan engines, attached to pylons with anti-vibration mountings, one on each side of the rear fuselage section. The special flexible system also prevents ingress of fuel, oil and hydraulic fluid. The Pratt & Whitney JT8D, which was first tested in April 1961, has a 13-stage split compressor, an annular type combustion chamber, and a four-stage reaction impulse turbine. The engine is equipped with an annular bypass duct which runs the full length of the engine. Largely of steel and titanium construction, the JT8D engine was originally available in three configurations, the JT8D-1, -5 and -7. Physically, the -1 and -5 variants are identical, the only difference being in engine trim, which changes the thrust rating. The JT8D-7 has slight internal differences. The JT8D-5 is rated at 12,000lb (53.38kN) maximum thrust at sea level, while the JT8D-1 generates 14,000lb (62.28kN) of thrust, also on a standard day at sea

*Below:*
**TWA cancelled its order for the Sud-Aviation Caravelle in favour of the DC-9-14. N1054T was the fourth aircraft out of 20 to be delivered to the airline in 1966.** *John Stewart*

level. The -7 has a similar rating, but this can be achieved on a hot day. The engine is fitted with a 40% target-type, hydraulically-actuated thrust reverser for ground operation only, an air turbine starter drawing air from the aircraft pneumatic system or an auxiliary power unit, a hydraulic pump, a constant speed drive, and a 40kVA generator. Standard fuel capacity is 3,700 US gallons/3,080 Imperial gallons (14,000 litres). An AiResearch gas turbine auxiliary power unit (APU) was made available as a customer option to provide an on-board source of pneumatic and electrical power. The APU is located on the bottom centreline of the aircraft in the unpressurised fuselage section beyond the rear pressure bulkhead. While on the ground, this independent energy source ensures the operation of the air-conditioning and pressurisation systems, as well as engine starting and switching on of on-board electrical systems. In flight, the APU regulates temperature, air flow, pressurisation and icing protection. The APU can be operated unattended, because automatic shut-down features are incorporated in the event of system malfunction.

The landing gear is of the retractable tricycle type, consisting of a two twin-wheel main landing gear and a twin-wheel steerable nose gear. The main gear retracts inboard and up into the fuselage, and the nose gear forward into the nose section. Doors fully enclose the gear in the retracted position, but also close automatically after the gear is sufficiently extended, to provide a smooth aerodynamic surface. Power is drawn from the main hydraulic power system, which also activates the door latches, bungee cylinders, brakes and nose-wheel steering system. Emergency operation is accomplished through the use of an alternative control lever, which releases the gear and permits it to free-fall to the down-and-locked position. Electrically-controlled anti-skid units provide a locked-wheel protection feature to the brake system.

Accommodation is provided for a crew of two on the flight deck, plus cabin attendants. The main cabin can seat 56-58 first class passengers in a four-abreast configuration, or up to 90 tourist class passengers five-abreast. The cabin is air-conditioned and fully pressurised to an equivalent altitude of 6,000ft (1,830m) at a cruising height of 30,000ft (9,145m). There is provision for a galley, and toilet facilities are located at the rear of the cabin. Passenger access is via a door 2ft 9½in x 6ft 9in (0.85m x 2.057m) at the front port side of the fuselage, with electrically-operated built-in airstairs stored beneath the floor, which can be

*Below:*
**Saudi Arabian Airlines bought three new DC-9-15s in early 1967, but never ordered any of the later models.**

*Above:*
**A Finnair DC-9-14 flying over one of the country's 1,000 lakes. This particular aircraft was previously operated by Southern Airways and delivered to the Finnish national airline on 24 January 1971.**

In June 1966 the FAA certified three Category II all-weather landing systems for the DC-9, comprising the Collins FD-108 and Sperry AD-200 flight director systems, and a coupled approach utilising the Sperry SP-50A autopilot.

deployed and retracted from inside the cabin as well as from the ground. An optional hydraulically-actuated ventral stairway could be installed at the rear, controlled from both inside and outside the aircraft. On unavailability of power, stairs can be extended by free-fall and retracted by means of a hydraulic hand pump, located in the main well. Servicing and emergency exit doors can be found on the starboard side opposite. Freight and baggage for the under-floor holds are loaded through inward opening doors forward on the starboard side and at the rear door on the port side. Convertible DC-9-15RC and -MC models have an upward-hinged cargo door, installed on the forward port side of the fuselage. Both forward and rear cargo compartments are pressurised and maintained above freezing, whilst the forward compartment is also heated to permit the transportation of animals. Cargo flooring and supporting structure has been designed for a maximum floor loading of 150lb/sq in (1.035N/sq mm).

**In Service**
The DC-9-10 entered scheduled service with Delta Air Lines on 8 December 1965, less than 10 months after its maiden flight. A total of 137 of this, the smallest version of the DC-9, were eventually produced for customers in the United States and abroad, which included four US trunk carriers, seven US local service carriers, one US supplemented airline, seven foreign airlines and two private operators.

Launch customer, Delta Air Lines, which also led the way with the DC-8, was, as already mentioned, the first major US carrier to bring the benefit of jet speed, comfort and reliability to the smaller communities on its vast network. Within months, TWA, Continental and Eastern had followed suit, the four trunk airlines accounting for just over half of the total production. TWA's order for 20 aircraft, placed in July 1964, was notable in that it replaced a similar order for the French Caravelle, cancelled two years earlier. It was also the first purchase from Douglas since the days of the piston-engined DC-4. The first local service carrier to operate the DC-9 was Phoenix-based Bonanza Air Lines, which introduced jet appeal on its principal Las Vegas route from 1 March 1966. Bonanza, incidentally, first signed a letter of intent for the One-Eleven, but subsequently cancelled this in favour of the DC-9. Hawaiian Airlines started DC-9 service on 1 April, Ozark Air Lines on 8 July, West Coast Airways on 26 September, Trans-Texas Airways (the only company to acquire the convertible DC-9-15MC) on 30 October 1966, followed by Southern Airways on 15 June 1967. Allegheny Airlines tested the market with a single aircraft from 1 September 1966, before going on to operate a large fleet of the later models of the Douglas twin-jet. The first foreign carriers to add the DC-9 to their fleets were Air Canada, KLM Royal Dutch Airlines and Swissair, all committed, long-standing Douglas customers. Air Canada was first, including the DC-9 in its schedules from January 1966, with KLM next from April, and Swissair following on in July 1966. Other DC-9s went to the Middle East and Central and South America, with the last Series 10 aircraft being accepted by Aeronaves de Mexico on 27 March 1968.

The DC-9-10 proved very popular and reliable in airline service, but as soon as Douglas lengthened the fuselage to produce a larger 115-seat model with more attractive seat-mile operating costs, the Series 10 became almost redundant. Consequently, the majority of the early DC-9 operators switched to the bigger model, releasing the DC-9-10 onto the second-hand market within a very short time. Many of these have changed hands several times and continue to provide sterling service with smaller airlines the world over alongside younger members of the DC-9 family.

## DC-9-10: Initial Customers/Operators

| | |
|---|---:|
| Aeronaves de Mexico | 9 |
| Air Canada | 6 |
| Allegheny Airlines | 1 |
| Avensa | 2 |
| Bonanza Air Lines | 3 |
| Continental Airlines | 23 |
| Delta Air Lines | 14 |
| Eastern Air Lines | 15 |
| Hawaiian Airlines | 2 |
| KLM Royal Dutch Airlines | 6 |
| LAV-Linea Aeropostal Venezolana | 1 |
| Northeast Airlines | 1 |
| Ozark Air Lines | 6 |
| Saudia-Saudi Arabian Airlines | 3 |
| Southern Airways | 6 |
| Standard Airways | 2 |
| Swissair | 5 |
| Tracinda Investment Corporation | 1 |
| Trans-Texas Airways/Texas International | 7 |
| TWA-Trans World Airlines | 20 |
| West Coast Airlines | 4 |
| **Total:** | **137** |

*Below:*
**US Supplemental Airline, Standard Airways, operated two new DC-9-15s between November 1966 and October 1968.**
*J. M. G. Gradidge*

# 2 Accelerating Development

When Douglas had orders for only 58 aircraft at the time of the first flight, there was then no indication of the enormous success its latest commercial series was destined to achieve. From the outset, however, the DC-9 programme had been planned for substantial growth and Douglas were quick to capitalise when a requirement for a larger aircraft emerged from Eastern Air Lines, already operating the DC-9-10. Designing the DC-9 around a basically too powerful engine, necessitating the use of JT8D engines derated from their normal take-off thrust of 14,000lb (62.28kN) to 12,000lb (53.38kN) in the initial Series 10 aircraft, in combination with its MGTOW limited to 80,000lb (36,287kg) for two-man crew operations, soon proved to have been a far-sighted decision. With the subsequent relaxation of the FAA's weight restriction, Douglas were thus able to increase the DC-9's capacity by the relatively simple expedient of lengthening the airframe. During negotiations with Eastern Air Lines, an interim fuselage stretch of 9ft 6in (2.90m) was offered at first, but agreement was eventually reached to add 15ft 0in (4.57m) to the fuselage, providing five extra rows of seats, bringing the maximum passenger capacity up to 115, and increasing the underfloor hold volume by almost 50%. To keep take-off airfield performance as close as possible to that of the earlier versions in spite of a greater initial take-off weight of 98,000lb (44,453kg), the wing span was increased by 4ft 0in (1.22m) at the tip to 93ft 5in (28.47m). This was supplemented with new high-lift devices including full-span, leading-edge slats and triple-slotted flaps. Uprated 14,000lb (62.28kN) JT8D-1 or JT8D-7 turbofans were also fitted to the early models.

## The DC-9-30

After a short period with the designation Series 20, the new stretched model became the definitive Series 30, which made its maiden flight on 1 August 1966. The DC-9-30 was certified on 19 December 1966 and Eastern Air Lines, which eventually ordered 72 aircraft, took delivery of its first on 27 January 1967 and put the type into service early in February. The DC-9-30 became by far the most successful variant of the DC-9 family, with a total of 662 aircraft produced

*Below:*
**The first of four extended range DC-9-34CF convertible freighters was delivered to the Spanish airline Aviaco in April 1976.**

*Above left:*
**Alitalia has been a prolific DC-9 operator since 1967. Its fleet also includes three DC-9-32F all-cargo versions first introduced in May 1968.**

*Left:*
**Air West's DC-9-31s were painted in four different colour schemes, but the airline lasted for only two years.**

*Above:*
**On 6 October 1967, Overseas National Airways became the first airline to put the convertible DC-9-32CF into service.**

between 1966 and 1982, amounting to almost seven out of every 10 DC-9s built.

As was the case with the Series 10, the Series 30 was produced in a variety of models to suit the differing operational requirements of airlines in all parts of the world. The Series comprised all-passenger, Rapid Change (RC), Convertible Freighter (CF), and All-Freight (AF) versions. An executive transport configuration was also made available with extra fuel capacity, enabling parties of up to 15 persons to be carried non-stop over trans-Continental or trans-Ocean stages of 3,000 nautical miles (5,500km). All have the same external dimensions of 93ft 5in (28.47m) span, 119ft 4in (36.37m) length and 27ft 6in (8.38m) height, but offer a mix of powerplant and maxi-

mum gross take-off weight combinations. A maximum of 115 passengers can be accommodated at a seat pitch of 32in (81cm), five-abreast with an off-set aisle. Underfloor baggage/cargo holds have a total volume of 895cu ft (25.3cu m).

**DC-9-31** Basic model powered by two 14,000lb (62.28kN) JT8D-1 or JT8D-7 turbofans. MGTOW of 98,000 (44,453kg).
**DC-9-32** Powered by any one of four engines as higher-thrust models were developed, with a common MGTOW of 108,000lb (48,988kg). Engines are the 14,000 lb (62.28kN) thrust JT8D-7, 14,500lb (64.50kN) JT8D-9, 15,000lb (66.73kN) JT8D-11, or 15,500lb (68.95kN) JT8D-15.
**DC-9-32CF** 'Convertible Freighter' first put into service by Overseas National Airways in October 1967. It is powered by two JT8D-9 or JT8D-11 engines. MGTOW is the same as in the DC-9-32.
**DC-9-32-AF** 'All Freighter' variant first delivered to Alitalia on 13 May 1968. More usually designated DC-9-32F. Cargo capacity almost 40,000lb (18,144kg).
**DC-9-33F** All-cargo version with higher MGTOW of 114,000lb (51,710kg), first purchased by SAS and put into service in October 1969.

**DC-9-33CF** 'Convertible Freighter' also with JT8D-9 or -11 turbofans and same MGTOW of 114,000lb (51,710kg). First operated by Overseas National Airways in March 1969.

**DC-9-33RC** 'Rapid Change' model with the same engine options and maximum gross weight. First delivered to KLM on 30 April 1968.

**DC-9-34** Extended range version, powered by still higher thrust 16,000lb (71.17kN) JT8D-17 engines and extra fuel tankage in the lower hold. Heaviest model with an MGTOW of 121,000lb (54,885kg), an increase of 50% over the first DC-9-10.

**DC-9-34CF** 'Convertible Freighter' variant put into service by the Spanish domestic airline, Aviaco, during 1976.

All convertible and all freighter versions are fitted with a forward port-side loading door.

## In Military Dress

Military customers accounted for 44 DC-9-30 Series aircraft and included the United States armed forces, the Italian Defence Ministry and the Kuwait Government. The Italian Defence Ministry acquired two DC-9-32 for the Aeronautica Militare Italiana transport squadrons in January and March 1974, whilst the Kuwait Government took delivery of two convertible DC-9-32CFs in October 1976 to provide transport support for its small combat element. Three versions were built for the United States Air Force and United States Navy as follows:

## C-9A Nightingale (DC-9-32C9)

Aeromedical evacuation aircraft developed for the United States Air Force (USAF) from the DC-9-32CF. Retaining the forward cargo door, this military version also has a built-in stretcher loading ramp and carries a variety of specialist equipment. C-9As were produced under contract from the USAF System Command's Aeronautical Systems Division, Wright-Patterson Air Force Base, Ohio, all powered by 14,500lb (64.50kN) thrust JT8D-9s. The USAF received the first of 21 C-9As on 8 August 1968 and the type was assigned to the 375th Aeromedical Wing of the USAF Military Airlift Command at Scott Air Force Base, Illinois. Delivery of all 21 aircraft was completed by February 1973. Used to transport sick and injured military personnel between military hospitals in the United States, more than 40 ambulatory patients, 30-40 litter patients or a combination of the two, together with two nurses and three aeromedical technicians, can be

*Below:*
**The first USAF C-9A aeromedical airlift aircraft, pictured at Long Beach prior to delivery to the 375th Aeromedical Wing of the Military Airlift Command.** *Douglas*

accommodated in the C-9A on non-stop flights of up to 2,000 miles (3,220km) and at cruise speeds exceeding 500mph (805km/h). The interior also includes a special-care compartment with independent atmospheric and ventilation controls. Galleys and toilet facilities are provided fore and aft. Subsequently, C-9As have also served with units of USAFE (United States Air Forces Europe), PACAF (US Pacific Air Forces) and the Reserve.

## C-9B Skytrain II (DC-9-32C9)

A military logistics version of the convertible DC-9-32CF named after the R4D Skytrain, a DC-3 variant produced in large numbers for the US Navy. A contract for five aircraft, later increased to a total of 17, was signed by the Naval Air Systems Command on 24 April 1972, and the first aircraft made its initial flight in February 1973. The first two aircraft were accepted on 8 May 1973 for use by the Fleet Tactical Support Squadrons 1 (VR-1) at Naval Air Station Norfolk, Virginia, and 30 (VR-30) at NAS Alameda, California. The Skytrain II was also delivered to the US Marine Corps (USMC), and second-hand DC-9-31s were later acquired for conversion to C-9Bs and used by other squadrons.

Like the C-9A powered by JT8D-9 turbofans, the C-9B can be laid out in a standard arrangement for 90 passengers, five-abreast at 38in (97cm) pitch; for 107 passengers at 34in (86cm) pitch; in all-cargo configuration accommodating eight standard military pallets; or in a combination of both. In a typical passenger/cargo layout, three pallets are carried in the forward area, with 45 passengers in the rear section. Galley and toilet facilities are located at each end of the cabin. A smoke barrier curtain separates the cargo section from the passengers. Normal passenger access is via port and rear ventral doors, both with hydraulically-operated airstairs. These, together with an APU supplying electrical and hydraulic services, make the C-9B virtually independent of ground facilities.

An increased fuel capacity of 5,930 US gallons/4,937 Imperial gallons (22,443 litres) provided by additional tanks in the forward and rear underfloor cargo holds, gives a typical range of some 3,000 miles (4,700km). The C-9B incorporates advanced navigation and communication equipment, including Omega and inertial navigation systems.

## VC-9C (DC-9-32VC)

A VIP transport version of the DC-9-32, three of which were delivered during Spring 1975 for use by the Special Air Missions Unit of the United States Air Force at Andrews AFB, Maryland, near Washington.

## Commercial Service

The DC-9-30 met with considerable success, accounting in its civil and military guises for two out of every three DC-9s built. With operating costs only marginally higher than those of the DC-9-10, but carrying up to 25 more passengers, the Series 30 achieved remarkably low seat-mile costs, especially over short sectors. Eastern Air Lines, which had been instrumental in defining the final configuration of this larger model, was the first to put the type into service on 1 February 1967, little more than a year after the Series 10 made its debut with Delta. Eastern initially employed the -30s on its shuttle services between New York and Boston, and between New York and Washington, before extending its area of operation onto other regular routes as more and more of its 72 aircraft were delivered. In the first six months of 1967, Ansett-ANA, Trans Australia Airlines, Iberia and Swissair all introduced the DC-9-30 onto their short to medium-haul routes. Of the original airline customers for the DC-9-10, only Continental, Saudia, Standard Airways and TWA did not order the bigger version. Korean Air Lines became the first operator in the Far East when putting a single DC-9-32 onto its local routes in July 1967. The first break-through into the African market was made when East African Airways, the flag carrier of the three nations of Kenya, Uganda and Tanzania, took delivery of three DC-9-32s between December 1970 and February 1971. The wide appeal of the DC-9-30 was borne out by the spread of orders received, which came from 49 different customers from all six continents. These not only included scheduled and charter airlines of all sizes, but also corporate owners, government agencies and armed forces.

## DC-9-30: Initial Customers/Operators

| | |
|---|---|
| Aeromexico | 15 |
| Air Canada | 44 |
| Air Jamaica | 3 |
| Air West | 15 |
| Alitalia | 38 |
| Allegheny Airlines/USAir | 61 |
| ALM 3 | |
| Ansett-ANA/Ansett Airlines 12 | |
| ATI | 14 |
| Atlantis Airways | 3 |
| Austrian Airlines | 9 |
| Avensa | 1 |
| Aviaco | 16 |
| Balair | 1 |
| Bonanza Air Lines | 1 |
| BWIA International | 1 |
| Caribair | 3 |
| Delta Air Lines | 63 |

## Scandinavian Specialities: The DC-9-20 and DC-9-40

Two versions of the DC-9 were developed to meet specific requirements of Scandinavian Airlines System (SAS) for its intra-Scandinavian network. One was intended to operate in and out of smaller airfields with relatively short runways hitherto accessible only to propeller-driven airliners, the other for a short-range, high-capacity transport. The former was the Series 20, introduced after the Series 30, which combines the fuselage and capacity of the Series 10 with the long-span wing of the Series 30, complete with leading-edge slats and double-slotted flaps. This combination, when making its first flight on 18 September 1968, demonstrated its quick lift-off capability, requiring a take-off roll of less than 2,400ft (730m) before climbing steeply skyward from Long Beach Municipal Airport. The DC-9-20 was certified at an MGTOW of 100,000lb (45,359kg), although SAS limited the gross weight to 87,000lb (39,463kg). Driven by two 14,500lb (64.50kN) thrust JT8D-9s, it can carry up to 90 passengers over ranges of more than 1,800 miles (2,900km), at speeds in excess of 550mph (885km/h).

The Series 20 was acquired only by SAS, which accepted 10 DC-9-21s between December

*Below:*
Scandinavian Airlines System was the only customer for the DC-9-21, accepting 10 aircraft between December 1968 and May 1969.

1968 and May 1969. In spite of the penalty of high seat-mile costs, the airline has successfully operated this model for more than 20 years, since it first went into service on 27 January 1969.

The Series 40, first flown on 28 November 1967, before the Series 20, traded range and airfield length requirements for higher seating capacity and payload. With the fuselage stretched an additional 6ft 2in (1.88m) over the DC-9-30 to 125ft 7in (38.27m), the Series 40 can seat up to 125 passengers in a high-density configuration. Together with an increase in fuel, this brought the certificated maximum weight to 114,000lb (51,710kg). A choice of power plants included the 14,500lb (64.50kN) thrust JT8D-9, 15,000lb (66.73kN) JT8D-11, or the 15,500lb (68.95kN) JT8D-15.

SAS initially ordered 10 DC-9-41s, the first of which entered service on 12 March 1968, following certification on 27 February. The Scandinavian carrier later increased its orders to

cover a total of 49 aircraft. The last order, placed on 30 January 1973 for 16 with options on another four, incorporated special noise abatement features, which included lining certain parts of the engines and nacelles with sound-absorbing materials to obtain certification to FAR (Federal Aviation Regulations) Part 36 Noise Standards. These costly modifications incurred a penalty of increased aircraft weight with a consequent reduction in payload. Although the -40 lacked the range of the DC-9-30, with an additional 10 passengers, it still produced better seat-mile costs and proved well suited to the airline's short-haul network. SAS did have an option on a DC-9-40F, but this was not taken up.

Four SAS DC-9-41s were leased to Swissair for a year in 1974/75, and two were operated by Thai Airways International, with whom SAS was associated, between January 1970 and April 1972. The specialised nature of this model limited its appeal to other operators, and six years elapsed before Toa Domestic Airlines (now Japan Air System) became the second and only other customer for this version, when it ordered 14 DC-9-41s (later increased to 22) for its dense, high-frequency inter-island services. Deliveries commenced in March 1974 and were completed by January 1979, bringing the total of the series produced to 71 aircraft.

## The DC-9-50

In July 1973, Douglas announced the development of the Series 50 which combined the long-span, slatted wing first introduced on the Series 30, with yet another fuselage stretch, bringing the overall length to 133ft 7in (40.71m) and maximum accommodation up to 139 passengers. Taking advantage of the availability of the more powerful 16,000lb (71.17kN) thrust JT8D-17, enabled the manufacturer to increase the MGTOW to 121,000lb (54,885kg). The maximum payload range was comparable to that of the Series 30, and its extremely high fuel capacity guaranteed efficient operation of several flight sectors, without the need for refuelling. The DC-9-50, which also incorporated several engineering improvements, was first flown on 17 December 1974 and became the first version to be certified from the outset to FAR Part 36 Noise Standards.

A total of 96 DC-9-50s were built between 1975 and 1981, during which period it became the main production version. Under the model designation of DC-9-51, it entered service on 24 August 1975 with Swissair, the airline which originated the requirement for the type with an order for 12 aircraft and also sponsored the later DC-9 Super 80. The majority of DC-9-50s were ordered by previous DC-9 customers, but the order book also included two first-time DC-9 buyers, among them BWIA International, which ordered four DC-9-51s together with one DC-9-34CF in 1976, at the same time becoming the 50th DC-9 operator. The other was Ghana Airways, only the second customer in Africa, which took delivery of one DC-9-51 for use on regional routes from Accra to other West African points on 13 July 1978.

### DC-9-50: Initial Customers/Operators

| | |
|---|---:|
| Allegheny Airlines | 8 |
| Austrian Airlines | 5 |
| BWIA International | 4 |
| Eastern Air Lines | 9 |
| Finnair | 12 |
| Ghana Airways | 1 |
| Hawaiian Airlines | 10 |
| Inex Adria Aviopromet | 2 |
| LAV | 5 |
| North Central Airlines/Republic Airlines | 28 |
| Swissair | 12 |
| **Total:** | 96 |

*Left:*
**The DC-9-51 entered service with Swissair on 24 August 1975. In the background is the earlier DC-9-32.**

*Above:*
**BWIA International operated this DC-9-51 on lease from Finnair before taking delivery of its own aircraft in summer 1977.**

*Below:*
**View of the DC-9-51 flight deck.**

Production of all DC-9 variants totalled 976 aircraft, with the last, a Series 32C9 being delivered to the United States Navy on 28 October 1982.

## DC-9 Production

| | Series | No built |
|---|---|---|
| DC-9-10 | 11 | 2 |
| | 14 | 53 |
| | 15 | 58 |
| | 15MC | 5 |
| | 15RC | 19 |
| **Total:** | | 137 |
| DC-9-20 | 21 | 10 |
| **Total:** | | 10 |
| DC-9-30 | 31 | 242 |
| | 32 | 336 |
| | 32F | 3 |
| | 32CF | 6 |
| | 32C9 | 38 |
| | 32VC | 3 |
| | 33F | 3 |
| | 33CF | 5 |
| | 33RC | 14 |
| | 34 | 7 |
| | 34CF | 5 |
| **Total:** | | 662 |
| DC-9-40 | 41 | 71 |
| **Total:** | | 71 |
| DC-9-50 | 51 | 96 |
| **Total:** | | 96 |

Even before the first flight of the Series 50, Douglas Aircraft Co turned its attention to the next major development, known as the DC-9-60, to take advantage of the new re-fanned versions of the Pratt & Whitney JT8D engine. An early example of this engine, the JT8D-109, was flight-tested on a DC-9-32 starting on 9 January 1975. Advanced studies explored a number of other DC-9 derivatives, ranging from the DC-9-17R with JT8D-17R turbofans incorporating automatic power reserve, to re-fanned versions such as the DC-9-50RS (Re-fan, Stretched); DC-9-50RSS (Re-fan, Super Stretch) and the later and similar DC-9-55. All had a bigger wing, more power and a longer fuselage, which would have enabled the new aircraft to carry greater passenger loads than the DC-9-50 over the same distance as the extended-range DC-9-34. Another innovative proposal was the DC-9SC, which featured an all-new super-critical wing. Also actively under consideration was the DC-9-QSF (Quiet, Short-Field), offered to Japanese airlines seeking a replacement for their NAMC YS-11 turboprops. This was basically a DC-9-40 with a new wing

enlarged by the insertion of a 10ft (3.04m) centre section, and re-fanned JT8D-209 engines, rated at 18,000lb (80kN) thrust. With a gross weight of 114,000lb (51,710kg), similar to the DC-9-40, the DC-9-QSF was intended to carry a passenger load of 120, all year round, from 4,000ft (1,220m) runways. Similar claims to meet the requirements of the Japanese airlines were made for the proposed DC-9-22, first announced in 1977. This up-rated development of the 'hot-rod" DC-9-21 operated by SAS, featured the installation of the more powerful JT8D-15 or -17 turbofans, additional wing spoilers and an improved braking system. Both designs were shelved in favour of the more advanced concepts, which clearly and almost exclusively pointed the way to the new re-fanned JT8D-200 series of turbofans, which was given the go-ahead in March 1977. Uprated engines were rejected on grounds of noise, and

*Below:*
**The wide body look of the MD-80 series.**

*Right:*
**Fuselage construction of the MD-80 at Long Beach.**

entirely new engines because of their costs. The all-new super-critical wing was also discarded as being too expensive.

The various options considered evolved into the DC-9 Super 80, a further stretched version of the DC-9 with JT8D-209 re-fanned engines and other new features. The aircraft was launched in October 1977 following strong pressure from Swissair, even though earlier that year McDonnell Douglas had insisted on an order from a major US carrier before giving the go-ahead. Eastern Air Lines, already a DC-9 operator with a large fleet of 70-plus aircraft, did express an interest but later went over to the larger Boeing 757. Launch orders included 15 firm and five options from Swissair, eight firm and four options from Austrian Airlines, as well as a conditional commitment for four aircraft from US regional carrier, Southern Airways. The cancellation of the Southern Airways order in June 1978 came as a blow to the manufacturer, although this was soon offset when Pacific Southwest Airlines decided to adopt the type as a replacement for its Boeing 727s. Southern's decision was largely influenced by the US Air Line Pilots Association's (ALPA) insistence that the Super 80 would have to be flown by a three-man crew in US service, even though earlier DC-9s had been successfully operated by a two-man crew since 1965. Southern correctly assessed that a third crew member would have seriously jeopardised the economics

of the Super 80. This, together with strong competition from Boeing, which set an attractively low price for its appreciably larger 757 and offered generous buy-back terms on 727s to bridge the gap between the time of service entry of the Super 80 and the availability of its own new twin-jet, did not bode well for the continuance of the DC-9 line. In the event, the manufacturer's fears proved unfounded. Once ALPA's objections had been swept aside, the aircraft's excellent economic performance over short, high-density routes attracted attention from all over the world, helping to turn the DC-9 Super 80 Series, later re-designated MD-80, into the most successful of all DC-9 variants.

**Super Take-off**
Aimed at improving still further the operating economics of the DC-9, as well as meeting stringent new noise regulations and the growing demand for greater fuel efficiency, the DC-9 Super 80 made its first flight from Long Beach on 18 October 1979, some three months later than projected. Two further aircraft required for certification took to the air on 6 December 1979 and 29 February 1980 A series of strikes and a shortage of materials and skilled labour in the

southern California area badly affected the Super 80 programme, adding further to the early difficulties faced by the manufacturer.

Although its antecedents are clearly visible, in detail the Super 80 is a very different aircraft from its predecessors. Combined with extensive structural 'beefing-up', the fuselage has been stretched to a total of 147ft 10in (45.05m), to provide increased capacity by the addition of an eight-frame plug (152in/3.86m) forward of the wing and a single frame extension (19in/0.48m) in the aft fuselage. Typical mixed-class accommodation is 137 seats, with a maximum of 172 possible. The cabin was given a 'wide look' decor with large enclosed overhead baggage compartments, acoustic ceiling and fluorescent lighting. Access to the cabin is via a passenger door at the front port side with built-in electrically-operated airstairs and through a rear hydraulically-operated ventral stair which is fitted as standard. Underfloor cargo volume is 1,294cu ft (36.6cu m), more than double that of the DC-9-10. Airfield and cruise performance has been maintained, in spite of the higher gross weight of 140,000lb (63,503kg), by an increase in wing span and wing area. The Super 80 wing incorporates a completely new centre section of 10ft 6in (3.20m) and 2ft (0.61m) parallel-chord extensions to each wing tip, which increase area by 28% to 1,279sq ft (118.82sq m) and span by 14ft 6in (4.42m) to 107ft 11in (32.89m). The wing has also been fitted with a new four-position full-span leading-edge slat for enhanced performance, as well as three spoilers, the two outboard segments of which act as flight and ground spoilers, with the inboard as ground spoiler only. The enlarged wing provides space for an additional 1,520 US gallons/1,265 Imperial gallons (5,754 litres) of fuel, and room for a modified landing gear. Most of the wing control runs and the cable-powered slat system had to be re-located to fit in with the new design. Other major airframe changes include a 3ft 6in (1.06m) increase in tailplane span and a 1ft 4in increase in overall height. Other improvements in operating economics are derived from the use of the re-fanned JT8D-209 turbofans, rated at 18,500lb (82.30kN) thrust with an additional 750lb (3.34kN) of automatic power reserve (APR). This emergency thrust reserve becomes available automatically in an engine-out situation. With a bypass ratio of 1.78, compared to 1.1 in earlier engines, the re-fanned version boasts lower specific fuel consumption and reduced noise emission. Enlarged and sound-proofed nacelles keep the Super 80 well within the FAR Part 36 noise requirements, as well as enabling it to comply with the more stringent ICAO stipulations for new designs produced in the 1980s.

Operating systems include dual air cycle air-conditioning and pressurisation using engine bleed air; two separate hydraulic systems for the operation of spoilers, flaps, slats, rudder, landing gear, brakes, thrust reversers and ventral stairway; a pneumatic system for air-conditioning, pressurisation, engine starting and ice protection utilising engine bleed air and/or the APU; and an electrical system comprising three 40kVA alternators, two engine-driven, one driven by the APU. Ant-icing of wing and engine inlets and de-icing of the tailplane is achieved with engine bleed air, whilst the windscreen is de-iced electrically.

McDonnell Douglas chose completely revised avionics for the Super 80, with a digital electronics integrated flight guidance and control system developed by Sundstrand, incorporating a cathode-ray tube to display computer-generated approach information. The new flight guidance system also controls the autothrottle to provide the APR facility for the JT8D-209 engines. Other improvements include a Sperry CAT IIIA autoland, a 'dial a flap' system to permit more accurate selection of flap settings for optimum take-off performance, a larger capacity APU and an advanced digital fuel quantity gauging system.

An electronic Performance Management System (PMS) became standard on all MD-80s from April 1983. The PMS is coupled through autopilot and autothrottle systems, automatically controlling the aircraft's pitch and thrust to give optimum speed and therefore maximum fuel efficiency during climb, cruise and descent modes.

### MD-81 (DC-9-81)
Another attempt at the Japanese STOL contest had been made in 1978 with the derivative DC-9 Super 80SF, combining the advanced wing and engines of the basic Super 80 with the fuselage of the DC-9-40. The project had its attraction for both McDonnell Douglas and Toa Domestic Airlines, as most of the development costs would have been covered under the Super 80 programme. In the end, it was decided that the progressive installation of the more powerful JT8D-217 engines in the versions already projected would provide similar airfield performance and the Super 80SF was not proceeded with. The initially developed basic version, therefore, was the DC-9-81, which gained FAA certification on 26 August 1980 and entered service with Swissair on 5 October that same year, flying a Zurich-Frankfurt round trip.

### MD-82 (DC-9-82)
The DC-9-81 was soon joined by the DC-9-82 which was first announced on 16 April 1979 and made its initial flight on 8 January 1981. With the same overall dimensions and fuel capacity, the

DC-9-82 was fitted with the more powerful JT8D-217 engines, generating a thrust of 20,000lb (88.97kN) plus an 850lb (3.78kN) automatic thrust reserve. Regarded as being particularly suitable for operation from 'hot and high' airports, the increased power also permitted a better pay-load/range performance from standard airports. The -82 was certificated on 30 July 1981 and entered commercial service with Republic Airlines in August. From autumn 1982, the DC-9-82 was offered with a higher gross weight option of 149,500lb (67,812kg) and improved JT8D-217A engines, providing a further significant increase in operating range with maximum structural pay-load.

## Co-production with China
Having signed a letter of intent on 11 January 1984, McDonnell Douglas reached an agreement on 12 April 1985 with China Aero-Technology Import/Export Corporation (CATIC) and the Shanghai Aviation Industrial Corporation (SAIC) for the production of 25 MD-82s through 1991. The agreement called for the jetliners to be built by SAIC, with sub-assemblies and components shipped from Long Beach, and also led to related offset and counter-trade deals under which MD-80 parts are manufactured at factories in Shanghai and Chengdu, not only for the SAIC-assembled aircraft but also for supply to the Long Beach assembly line. SAIC had already been producing landing gear doors for the MD-80 under sub-contract since 1980. The first shipment of major aircraft components was made in January 1986, with assembly at Shanghai commencing the following April. McDonnell Douglas supplied complete major sub-assemblies for the first three aircraft only; thereafter, the Chinese industry took on an increasing share in the manu-facturing process. The first Shanghai-built MD-82 made its maiden flight on 2 July 1987 and was delivered to CAAC (Civil Aviation Administration of China) on the last day of that same month for use by the Shenyang and Shanghai bureaus on routes serving Beijing, Shanghai, Changchun, Dalian, Harbin, Hefei, Nanjing, Qingdao, Shenyang, Hangzhou, and regionally to Hong Kong and Nagasaki. The first revenue service was undertaken on 4 August 1987. All 25 have now been completed. SAIC's quality standards are recognised by the FAA through an extension of the aircraft production certificate which covers the McDonnell Douglas Long Beach plant. Airliners built in China receive Certificates of Airworthiness from the FAA.

*Above:*
**China Eastern Airlines operates several SAIC-assembled MD-82s. B2127 was photographed at Hong Kong in May 1990.** *R. Finlayson*

In April 1990, the Chinese Government approved an extension of the co-production agreement with SAIC for an additional 20 aircraft, bringing China's total orders for MD-80s to 50, of which 45 have been or will be built in the People's Republic. Five others were delivered direct from Long Beach, beginning in 1983 and are flown by China Eastern Airlines and China Northern Airlines based at Shanghai and Shenyang respectively. The new order will continue co-production activities into 1994.

Discussions are currently in progress with CATIC and Chinese airlines on the joint development and possible joint venture production to fulfil the People's Republic's requirement for a new airliner to serve its high density trunk routes. Up to 150 new airliners are stated to be needed before the end of the decade. The aircraft could be based on the MD-90 twin-jet series being developed for service entry in late 1994, and would be a logical extension of the co-production programme currently in force.

## MD-83 (DC-9-83)
Announced on 31 January 1983, the third sub-variant of similar external configuration, the DC-9-83, differed principally in having higher thrust 21,000lb (93.42kN) JT8D-219 turbofans, an increased MGTOW of 160,000lb (72,575kg), and carrying an additional 1,160 US gallons/966 Imperial gallons (4,390 litres) of fuel in cargo compartment tanks. The DC-9-83, by then redesignated MD-83, first flew on 17 December 1984 and was certificated late in 1985. It entered service with launch customers Finnair and Alaska Airlines before the end of the year.

In December 1984, McDonnell Douglas and the GPA Group based at Shannon in Ireland, formed a joint venture company named Irish Aerospace Limited, in order to acquire 24 MD-83s for subsequent operating leases to airlines. Initial leases were effected to Frontier Airlines, which took the first four aircraft starting on 29 April 1986.

The MD-83 is also available in executive versions, typically offering a range of 4,720 miles (7,600km) when equipped with auxiliary fuel tanks and configured with 20 luxury seats. To date, no executive models have been ordered.

## MD-87
Some of the work was directed at applying the advances of the Super 80 to smaller members of the DC-9 family, partly to combat the expected competition from the Boeing 737-300. These DC-9 Super XX studies centred on the 100-120 seat

*Above left:*
**Alaska Airlines was the first airline to order the extended range MD-83.**

*Left:*
**Spanair, a Spanish charter airline, operates a fleet of seven leased MD-83s configured in an all-tourist layout for 163 passengers.**

*Above:*
**The latest McDonnell Douglas twin-jet model in the Japan Air System fleet is the MD-87 introduced in 1988. Japan Air System was formerly known as TDA – Toa Domestic Airlines.**

bracket with a maximum weight of between 110,000 and 120,000lb (50,000-55,000kg). Both the JT8D-200 series and the CFM International CFM56-3 were being considered as possible powerplants. Among the perceived advantages were crew interchangeability and commonality of maintenance, training and spares with the Super 80. These studies resulted in the MD-87, the first member of the basic MD-80 family to differ in size. Announced on 3 January 1985, the MD-87`s external distinguishing feature is a fuselage shortened by 16ft 5in (5.00m), reducing maxi-

mum passenger accommodation to 139, similar to the DC-9-51, which has the same length fuselage. Executive variants are also being offered. To balance the smaller moment arm, a 10in (0.25m) extension was introduced to the fin about the tailplane, which was also modified to include improved sealing on horizontal surfaces and a low-drag tail cone. Other cruise performance enhancements were introduced in the shape of a fillet fairing between fuselage and engine pylons, a fairing on the APU and low-drag flap hinges and fairings. Douglas decided to stay with Pratt & Whitney engines, offering the MD-87 with 20,000lb (88.97kN) thrust JT8D-217B and later with the similar thrust -217C with reduced fuel consumption. Other engines, such as the JT8D-219, can be fitted to suit customer requirements. Optional auxiliary fuel tanks were made available to supplement the standard capacity of 5,840 US gallons/4,863 Imperial gallons (22,106 litres). The MD-87 was first ordered by Finnair and Austrian Airlines and made its maiden flight on 4 December 1986. Certification was granted in October 1987, and this was followed by the aircraft`s entry into service with Austrian Airlines on 17 December 1985. The first sale to a corporate customer was made in March 1987.

## MD-88

An announcement by McDonnell Douglas that it would proceed with a fifth member of the family was made on 23 January 1986, following an order for up to 80 aircraft from Delta Air Lines for the MD-88. A close relative of the MD-82, this state-of-the-art twin-jet has 20,000lb (88.97kN) JT8D-217C or 21,000lb (93.42kN) JT8D-219 engines, a maximum gross weight of 160,000lb (72,575kg) and several systems and equipment refinements as standard features. These include an electronic flight instrument system (EFIS), a flight management system (FMS) and an inertial reference system (IRS) in its advanced 'glass' cockpit. Increased use has been made of composite materials in the airframe, and the interior has been re-designed with a wider aisle and new overhead storage bins. Typical accommodation is for 142 passengers in a mixed-class arrangement.

The MD-88 model took to the air on 15 August 1987 and first entered revenue service on 5 January 1988. The initial eight aircraft delivered to Delta were re-engined and suitably modified MD-82s. Provision has been made in the design of the MD-88 for an eventual retrofit of propfan engines, but this now seems unlikely.

## Windshear

In June 1989, the FAA certified a new, technologically advanced windshear system for the MD-80 twin-jet series, which is expected to become standard on all models from 1991 and will also be available for retrofit on aircraft already in service. The new windshear system goes one step further, being able to couple the aircraft's autopilot with the windshear alert and flight director guidance functions, giving the pilot the option to select an autopilot-controlled escape manoeuvre.

## Longer Life

In September 1989, McDonnell Douglas in co-operation with the Air Transport Association (ATA)/Aerospace Industries Association (AIA) Airworthiness Assurance Task Force, announced a service programme that will ensure the continued airworthiness of its older DC-9 and MD-80 passenger jets, as well as the DC-8 and DC-10 airliners. The Task Force's recommendations have been compiled into Service Bulletins and passed to the FAA for review. Task Force members comprised airlines, manufacturers, the US Air Force, the National Aeronautics & Space Association (NASA), the Professional Aviation Mechanics Association, as well as various inter-

national regulatory bodies, including the FAA. The programme, developed after a 14-month study, calls for repair, modification, or replacement of key structural aircraft components, well before their increasing age poses any threat to safety. Of a total of more than 3,900 possible service actions considered by the Task Force, only 52 were deemed necessary for the DC-9, while early production MD-80s will need just 22 such actions. The estimated costs to operators are stated to amount to $90,000 per aircraft for the MD-80 and $490,000 for the DC-9s.

In February 1991, the FAA granted flight certification for a noise reduction kit which will bring the JT8D-powered DC-9-10 series within Stage 3 noise levels and thereby extend the useful life of the aircraft. The kit consists of an acoustically treated inlet and tailpipe, modified thrust reverser and the Pratt & Whitney advanced technology internal exhaust mixer. The internal exhaust mixer combines fan and core air in the tailipe, reducing the velocity of the hot core exhaust air and reducing low frequency jet noise. FAA certificates are also expected second quarter of 1991 for hush kits for DC-9-30 aircraft with JT8D-7 and -9 engines.

## The Pratt & Whitney JT8D Turbofan

The JT8D engine, powering all DC-9/MD-80 models, as well as Boeing 727s and early 737 versions, is the most widely used commercial engine in the world, operated by some 350 customers. Almost 12,000 examples are in service, having to date accumulated a staggering total of 400 million flight hours. The JT8D powers more than half of all commercial transport aircraft in current operation.

Pratt & Whitney began design work on its first JT8D, the JT8D-1, in April 1960. Based on the gas generation of its JT8 turbojet and the two-stage fan of the JT3D, the JT8D evolved into a high compression ratio (17:1), low-bypass ratio (1:1.1) turbofan engine with two fan stages at the front of the 13-stage, axial-flow two-spool compressor. The first experimental engine run was held on 7 April 1961, followed by the first flight test, on a Boeing 707 testbed, on 1 May 1962. FAA certification was achieved on 9 February 1963. The long commercial life of the JT8D began on 1 February 1964 on an Eastern Airlines Boeing 727. The 14,000lb (62.28kN) JT8D-1 was also the initial powerplant for the DC-9-10.

Over the succeeding years, Pratt & Whitney introduced several improved versions of the engine including the -7, -9, -11, -15, -17 and -17R and finally the 'A' series with better performance, longer life, improved reliability and lower maintenance costs. These were also accompanied by

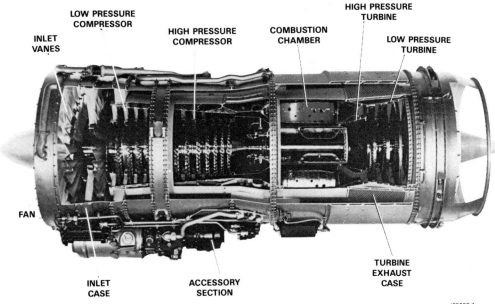

LOW PRESSURE
COMPRESSOR

INLET
VANES

HIGH PRESSURE
COMPRESSOR

COMBUSTION
CHAMBER

HIGH PRESSURE
TURBINE

LOW PRESSURE
TURBINE

FAN

INLET
CASE

ACCESSORY
SECTION

TURBINE
EXHAUST
CASE

J38020-1
880302

*Above:*
**The Pratt & Whitney JT8D is the most widely used commercial engine in the world.**

continual thrust upgrades rising ultimately to 17,400lb (77.40kN) maximum thrust in the JT8D-17R/-17AR. Design improvements were achieved through a combination of new turbine aerofoil material and the introduction of cooling schemes for high-pressure turbine blades, giving greater resistance to the higher temperatures generated by increased thrust. The -15, -17A and -17AR models introduced in the early 1980s addressed the problem of rising fuel prices by offering a 5.5% reduction in fuel burn over preceding engines. In-service reliability is said to be second to none, with an unplanned engine removal rate

## The Pratt & Whitney JT8D Turbofan Engine

| Model | Take-Off Thrust lb (kN) | Bypass Ratio | Installation | Dimensions Diameter Length | No. Compressor Stages Fan | Low | High | Turbine Stages High | Low | No. of Combustion Chambers |
|---|---|---|---|---|---|---|---|---|---|---|
| JT8D-1,-1A,-1B | 14,000 (62.28) | 1.1 | DC-9-10.-20,-30 | | | | | | | |
| JT8D-5 | 12,000 (53.38) | 1.1 | DC-9-10 | | | | | | | |
| JT8D-7,-7A,-7B | 14,000 (62.28) | 1.1 | DC-9,-10,-30 | 42 inches (1.06) 123.5 (3.14) | 2 | 4 | 7 | 1 | 3 | 9 |
| JT8D-9,-9A | 14,500 (64.50) | 1.04 | DC-9-20,-30,-40, C9 | | | | | | | |
| JT8D-11 | 15,000 (66.73) | 1.05 | DC-9-20,-30,-40 | | | | | | | |
| JT8D-15,-15A | 15,500 (68.95) | 1.03/1.04 | DC-9-30,-40,-50 | | | | | | | |
| JT8D-17,-17A | 16,000 (71.17) | 1.01/1.02 | DC-9-30,-50 | | | | | | | |
| JT8D-209 | 18,500 (82.30)[1] | 1.78 | MD-81,-82 | 49.2 (1.25) 154.2 (3.92) | 1 | 6 | 7 | 1 | 3 | 9 |
| JT8D-217, -217A,-217B | 20,000 (88.97)[2] | 1.73 | MD-81,-82,-87,-88 | | | | | | | |
| JT8D-219 | 21,000 (93.42)[3] | 1.77 | MD-83,-87,-88 | | | | | | | |

1 Additional automatic power reserve (APR) of 759lb (3.34kN), 2 APR 859lb (3.78kN), 3 APR 700lb (3.11kN)
Note: Engine models shown are those powering DC-9/MD-80 aircraft only

running at 0.10 per 1,000 hours, and in-flight shut-down rate equivalent to only one shut-down in more than 80,000 hours. With the JT8D series of engines tending to be noisier than present generation high-bypass turbofans, the manufacturer is offering `hush-kits` for retrofit to the DC-9s to bring the aircraft into compliance with the Federal Aviation Administration Stage 3 Noise Regulation.

The newest and most powerful addition to the JT8D gas turbine family is the `re-fanned` JT8D-200 series which powers all MD-80 models. The JT8D-200 traces its beginnings to NASA`s `Quiet Engine` programme which ran from 1972-1975. During that time, Pratt & Whitney developed six demonstration engines, designated the JT8D-109, which incorporated larger, single-stage fans with varying characteristics. Two of these logged about 50 hours flight testing on a modified Douglas DC-9-32. The JT8D-209 engine, rated at 18,500lb (82.30kN) take-off thrust with a reserve rating of 19,250lb (85.64kN), made its first flight aboard a McDonnell Douglas YC-15 Advanced Medium STOL Transport (AMST) prototype in March 1977. It retains the high compressor burner and high turbine sections of the earlier engines, but features an advanced low compressor, a new low turbine, new exterior casing and a single-stage increased diameter fan. The larger fan increases the bypass ratio from 1.1 to 1.78, resulting in lower fuel consumption and noise levels. An internal mixer further reduces noise by lowering peak exhaust gas velocities. The JT8D-209 entered commercial service on an MD-81, flying Swissair`s first service on 5 October 1980.

Next came the JT8D-217, certificated in November 1980, producing 20,000lb (88.97kN) take-off thrust with a reserve rating of 20,850lb (92,75kN). This is particularly suitable for aircraft operating at higher weights and in `hot and high` environments. Latest in the Series is the JT8D-219, a 21,000lb (93,42kN) thrust engine (21,700lb/96.53kN with reserve thrust) developed specifically for the higher gross weight and extended range MD-83, but now also available for the MD-87 and MD-88 series. It was certificated for commercial service in March 1985. The JT8D-219 incorporates a new high pressure turbine, a re-designed low pressure turbine with more efficient sealing of the gas path, and aerodynamically improved aerofoils. In spite of a 5% increase in normal take-off and climb thrust, the -219 is said to reduce fuel consumption by 2%.

*Below:*
**The 're-fanned' JT8D-200 series turbofan engine powers all MD-80 models.**

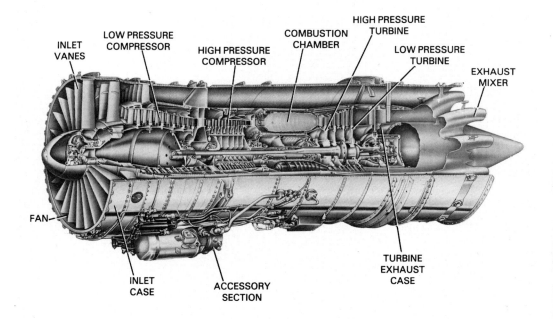

# 4 Airline Operators Past and Present

The following summary of airline operators of the DC-9/MD-80 twin-jet over the past 25 years makes impressive reading, totalling to date some 120, spread right across the world, with a predominance in Europe and the Americas. To these can be added several others who 'wet' leased the aircraft for short periods from time to time. The DC-9, and especially the smaller Series 10, also found a ready home with many corporate owners, private companies and organisations, some first time buyers, others acquiring their jets on the second-hand market. Of particular note are the Federal Aviation Administration which has been flying a DC-9-15 since 1968 and Hugh Hefner/Playboy Enterprises' jet black new DC-9-32 with the white 'bunny' on the tail, which became a familiar sight around the world in the late 1960s.

Mention must also be made of the increasing role leasing companies are playing in enabling airlines to operate the very latest aircraft, without having to expend the vast sums of money necessary today for the purchase of new equipment. In the case of the McDonnell Douglas twin-jets, this can range from $18 million for the basic MD-81 to more than $25 million for the latest MD-88. Even the early DC-9s still fetch up to $9 million for the DC-9-51 on the used aircraft market. The major leasing companies which have bought MD-80s are the GPA Group/Irish Aerospace with 30 MD-83s in service and another 34 on order, Beverly Hills-based ILFC which have ordered 18 MD-80s and 15 MD-90s plus options and Polaris Leasing of San Francisco with an order book for 15 MD-82/83s and 14 MD-88s. GPA and other smaller companies also have a sizeable fleet of DC-9s available for lease.

## Adria Airways

Adria Airways, then known as Inex Adria Aviopromet, accepted the first of two DC-9-32s on 25 April 1969 for its European charter operations out of Ljubljana. The 110-passenger jet was soon put

*Below:*
Tell-tail signs of DC-9/MD-80s at Heathrow Airport.

onto scheduled services when these were introduced, initially between Ljubljana and Belgrade in 1970. Since then, the airline has operated a total of 12 different DC-9-32/33CFs and two DC-9-51s, and in August 1978 placed an order for one MD-81 and two MD-82s, which entered service in 1981. Today, Adria's fleet comprises four 167-seat MD-82s, one 167-seat MD-81 and three 115-seat DC-9-32/33CFs. Jet services link Ljubljana, Belgrade, Sarajevo, Skopje, Maribor and Zagreb, and externally to Munich, Larnaca, Tel Aviv, Athens, Bari, Paris and London. The twin-jet airliners are also used on package tour flights and contract charters carrying migrant workers between Yugoslavia and West Germany.

## Aermediterranea
Aermediterranea, a subsidiary of Alitalia, was established in 1981 and was integrated into ATI, another subsidiary of the national carrier, in April 1985. In the intervening years, the airline served Bologna, Bergamo, Rome, Pescara, Ancona, Milan and Lamezia Terme with a fleet of DC-9-32s, which eventually numbered five aircraft. Operations with DC-9s commenced on 1 July 1981.

## Aero California
Aero California operates scheduled flights in western Mexico serving primarily the commercial and tourist centres in the Baja California and Gulf of California areas. Mainstay of a mixed fleet is the DC-9-10, first introduced on its routes in June 1982. Four DC-9-14/15s leased from GPA and one ex-Texas International DC-9-15MC are presently scheduled on a Tijuana-Los Mochis-Guadalajara route, as well as serving Mexico City, Culiacan, Colima, La Paz, Ciudad Obregon, Hermosillo, Mulege, Loreto, Guaymas and Cabo San Lucas. Plans are said to be in hand to lease a further six DC-9-15s for an expanded network.

## Aerocancun
Aerocancun Aeronautica de Cancun — is a new Mexican carrier operating inclusive tour and charter flights mainly from the United States to the tourist resort of Cancun. US points of origin include Baltimore, Chicago, Denver, Houston, New York and Los Angeles. The present fleet comprises two MD-83s obtained on lease from the GPA Group and delivered on 30 October and 22 November 1989.

## Aero Lloyd
Aero Lloyd was founded towards the end of 1980 and started flying in spring 1981, initially with three Caravelles. The first DC-9-32 flew with the Frankfurt-based airline in May 1982 and the fleet

has since been increased, taking the total to 16, including three DC-9-32, four MD-87 and nine MD-83. The first MD-83, fitted out with 167 seats, entered service in May 1986, and this was followed by 137-seat MD-87s in summer 1988. Principally a holiday charter airline, Aero Lloyd has been using its twin-jets on flights to the Mediterranean and the Canary Islands, but the aircraft are now also utilised on scheduled passenger services, linking Frankfurt, Munich, Hamburg and Düsseldorf.

## Aeromexico
In December 1989, Aeromexico accepted the first two of 10 MD-88s, the most advanced member of the MD-80 family. Eight are now in service with the final two scheduled for delivery in summer 1991. The Mexican carrier is using its MD-88s on domestic routes in Mexico and on international services to the United States, in a spacious two-class configuration carrying 20 passengers in first class and 115 in economy. The MD-88s were the first aircraft in the Aeromexico fleet to have a first class section. The Mexico City based airline, known as Aeronaves de Mexico until 1972, has an all-McDonnell Douglas jet fleet, also including six DC-9-10s, 15 DC-9-32s and eight MD-82s. The DC-9/MD-80 fleet is now approaching two and a half million landings in Aeromexico service. The first DC-9, a Series 15, was delivered on 29 May 1967.

## Airborne Express
Airborne Express, the operating name of ABX Air, is a leading small package express and freight forwarding company which was formed on 17 April 1980. Its fleet is largely composed of Douglas twins and currently includes two DC-9-15s, 26 DC-9-30s of several different variants and one ex-Japan Air System DC-9-41. A further nine DC-9-30s and 13 DC-9-41s are on order. Every night, all-cargo DC-9s converge on the airline's Wilmington, Ohio hub, where packages are sorted and transferred to flights bound for some 90 destinations spread right across the United States. Expansion into Canada and Mexico will be next on the agenda, and plans are also in hand to 'hush kit' the DC-9s.

## Air California/AirCal
Air California, formed in April 1966, put two ex-Continental DC-9-14s onto its Santa Ana-San Francisco route at the end of 1967 after overcoming strong objections to operating jets out of the small airport at Santa Ana, Orange County, surrounded by residential developments. San Jose-Oakland was the next DC-9 service to be added to the schedule as part of the process of

*Above:*
**Air Florida operated several DC-9-14/15s in the late 1970s.**

developing high-frequency intra-state services. On 6 April 1981, Air California became AirCal and seven MD-82s joined the fleet of Boeing 737s to operate expanded regional services in the Western States of California, Nevada, Oregon and Washington. MD-81 operations ceased in April 1986 when the airline was taken over and absorbed into American Airlines.

## Air Canada
Air Canada, the international airline founded on 10 April 1937 as Trans-Canada Airlines, was one of the first DC-9 operators when it took delivery of a DC-9-14 on 12 April 1966. A total of six -14s were purchased new, joined later by nine ex-Continental DC-9-15RC and 45 of the bigger DC-9-32, for use on its domestic trunk lines and regional routes to the USA and the Caribbean. 35 DC-9-32s configured for 100 passengers remain in the fleet, being used on the airline's routes within Canada serving Calgary, Charlottetown, Edmonton, Fredericton, Halifax, Moncton, Montreal, Quebec, Regina and St John, as well as to neighbouring points in the United States. The Air Canada DC-9 fleet has recorded in excess of 2 million landings.

## Air Djibouti
Air Djibouti (Red Sea Airlines), owned largely by the Djibouti Government and Air France, started operating the DC-9 in October 1986 when it acquired a single DC-9-32 on lease from JAT. It is used on international links from Djibouti City to Abu Dhabi, Addis Ababa, Aden, Cairo, Mogadishu and Sana'a. Air Djibouti was formed on 15 July 1971.

## Air Florida
Air Florida was a colourful airline which began passenger services within Floriday on 29 September 1972 and later expanded its operations to other points in the US, the Caribbean and to Europe. The airline acquired six DC-9-15F/RCs starting on 10 June 1977 to replace its Lockheed Electra turboprops. Others were leased from time to time, the twin-jet remaining in service until 1981/82. Air Florida's history was plagued by financial difficulties, which finally forced it to file for Chapter 11 bankruptcy on 3 July 1984.

## Air Jamaica
Air Jamaica was established as the national airline late in 1968 and started operations on 1 April 1969 after having taken delivery of two new DC-9-32s on 23 January and 18 February. A third joined the fleet on 28 June 1974, also bought new. The DC-9s were scheduled on the airline's important US routes serving Miami and New York from both Kingston and Montego Bay, and to various points in the Caribbean. The first two aircraft were eventually sold to USAir on 19 November 1980, while the remaining DC-9 continued to serve until November 1982.

## Air Liberté
Air Liberté operates five 169-seat MD-83s on inclusive-tour charters from Paris, Lyons, Lille, Nantes and Basle to holiday destinations in Greece, Yugoslavia, Israel, Egypt, Italy, Malta, Tunisia and other North African points. The airline

was founded in 1987 and began MD-83 operations in April 1988 with a single aircraft leased from the GPA Group. At the time of writing, two more MD-83s are on order for delivery by the 1991 summer season, bringing the fleet total to seven aircraft. Of these, two were purchased new from the manufacturer. One MD-83 is based at Monastir, flying for Air Liberté Tunisie.

## Air Malta

Air Malta, the national airline established on 1 April 1973, leased a single DC-9-32 from Austrian Airlines between 1 November 1979 and 1 April 1980. The aircraft was used on its schedules from Malta to southern Europe and points in North Africa.

## Air National

Air National, operating out of San Jose Municipal Airport, California, provided contract passenger and cargo services between 1982 and 1984. Its fleet included a total of four DC-9-15F/RC leased from Air Florida and Continental Airlines. The first aircraft was delivered on 23 September 1982, but all were returned on 15 February 1984.

## Air Panama

Air Panama International, the country's flag-carrier formed in August 1967 with the assistance of Iberia, began operations in August 1969 with a single DC-9-15, delivered on lease from Douglas on 8 July. The Douglas twin-jet flew the airline's routes from Panama City to Lima, Guayaquil, Bogota, Caracas, Mexico City and destinations in the United States. The DC-9 was returned to the manufacturer on 22 November 1972.

## AirSur

AirSur undertakes charter flights with two MD-83s, obtained on lease from the GPA Group in April and May 1987. The 165-passenger jets provide inclusive-tour services to Portugal, mainland Spain, and the Balearic and Canary Islands from points in Austria, France, Germany, Italy, Ireland, the United Kingdom, North and West Africa and others. The airline's aircraft are maintained by Swissair in Zurich. AirSur was founded in 1985 as Canafrica-Transportes Aereos and initiated charter operations in May 1986. The present title was adopted in June 1988.

## Air Tanzania

Air Tanzania was set up on 1 June 1977 following the demise of East African Airways Corporation. EAA's three DC-9-32s were taken over by Kenya Airways, but one aircraft was leased to Air Tanzania until October 1977 for its new regional routes out of Dar-es-Salaam.

## Airtours International

Airtours International is a new British airline which will start operations at the end of March 1991 with five leased MD-83s. The 167-seat aircraft will be serving with short-haul and long-haul holiday destinations from various UK airports.

## Air Vanuatu

Air Vanuatu, the national airline of this Pacific island state, was initially formed with the assistance of Ansett Airlines, who provided its first equipment in the shape of a DC-9-31. Operations started in September 1981 between Port Vila and Sydney. A replacement DC-9-31 was delivered in May 1982 and used for a short period before being replaced by Boeing aircraft.

## Air West

Air West was formed in April 1968 from the merger of Bonanza Air Lines, West Coast Airlines and Pacific Air Lines. From Bonanza and West Coast, the new airline inherited a fleet of DC-9s which comprised eight DC-9-11/14s and a single DC-9-31. The remainder of the Bonanza order for the larger twin-jet was delivered in Air West markings and the DC-9-31 fleet was built up to 16 aircraft within a short period.

Bonanza Air Lines, founded in 1945 in Phoenix, Arizona, became the first local service carrier to fly the DC-9 when it introduced two Series 11s on its main Phoenix-Las Vegas route on 1 March 1966, helping the airline to recover some lost traffic. Two DC-9-14s were added soon after, flying on local routes and to west central Mexico.

West Coast Airlines began operations in 1946 with the reliable DC-3 and 20 years later, on 29 September 1966, added the first of four DC-9-14s to its route network which had grown to encompass an area from Seattle, Washington to Portland, Oregon, Salt Lake City, parts of Idaho, San Francisco and southwestern Canada.

Air West, headquartered at San Francisco, existed for only three years, being purchased by the Hughes Air Corporation on 3 April 1970 and renamed Hughes Aircraft. Air West had incurred heavy losses, due largely to operating expensive jet equipment on routes which were far too short (one of only 11 miles/18km) to be economic.

## Alaska Airlines

Seattle-based Alaska Airlines became the first airline to order the new extended range MD-83, when it signed for nine aircraft in March 1983. Since then, the fleet has been steadily added to and now totals 27 in-service aircraft including 17 MD-83s and 10 MD-82s, with 13 more on order to be delivered from January 1991 onwards, which will build Alaska's MD-80 fleet to 40 by 1995.

Alaska Airlines planes seat 135 passengers in a two-class arrangement, including 10 first class seats. This spacious, lower density seating is featured in all of its MD-80 aircraft. The first commercial service was flown on 20 February 1985 over the Anchorage-Seattle route.

## Alisarda

Alisarda was founded 24 March 1963 with the aim of developing tourist services to Sardinia's Costa Smeralda. Now the leading private airline in Italy, Alisarda flies an all-jet fleet of six 100-seat DC-9-51s and five 175-seat MD-82s on regular scheduled and seasonal services to and from most cities in Italy and points in Switzerland, France and Germany. Another eight MD-82s are on order for delivery starting in the summer of 1992. Two DC-9-14s were used to promote the airline's first jet services in 1974. Two DC-9-32s were also leased at one time, with the MD-82s joining the fleet in 1984.

## Alitalia

Alitalia – Linee Aeree Italiane, Italy's national airline, has been a prolific DC-9 operator since it acquired the first of its DC-9-32s on 8 August 1967. Fifty-eight different aircraft have been operated since, including three all-cargo DC-9-32Fs, first introduced in May 1968. Thirty-two remain in the fleet, but are scheduled to be phased out in a structured withdrawal between now and 1995 and replaced by 25 MD-87s which are due for delivery between January 1993 and 1996. In January 1983, Alitalia ordered 30 MD-82s, later increased to a total of 53, with more on behalf of its subsidiary, ATI. The MD-82 was first delivered on 16 December 1983. A large number of options are also held for possible delivery in 1995/96. The DC-9/MD-82 fleet operates Alitalia's extensive European and domestic network taking in 13 cities in Italy and 32 in Europe. The DC-9-32s are fitted out for 102 or 107 passengers in a two-class configuration, or 123 passengers in all-economy. The bigger MD-82s can seat 155 passengers in dual class or 172 in single economy class.

## Allegheny Airlines — see USAir

## All Star Airlines

All Star Airlines obtained its operating certificate on 1 April 1983 but lasted for only just over two years, ceasing all services on 29 October 1985. In that time it provided tour flights to Atlantic City, Reno, Florida and the Caribbean, with a fleet which also included three leased DC-9-14/15Fs.

## ALM Antillean Airlines

ALM, the government-owned airline founded in 1964 as a subsidiary of KLM, started DC-9 operations when it acquired three second-hand DC-9-15s from KLM. These were later replaced with new and second-hand DC-9-32s and in October 1982 ALM added two new MD-82s, with a third leased from Continental Airlines in April 1988. The DC-9s have since left the fleet, and the three MD-82s, configured in a two-class arrangement seating 12 first class and 126 economy class passengers, are currently used on routes from Curacao to San Juan, Santo Domingo, Kingston, Port-au-Prince, Panama City, Miami and New York, and southwards to Port of Spain, Georgetown, Caracas and Medellin. Domestic flights serve all the islands in the Netherlands Antilles including Aruba, Bonaire, Curacao and St Maarten.

## Altair Airlines

Philadelphia-based Altair Airlines was an all-jet regional carrier whose fleet included three DC-9-32s leased from Air Canada from May 1982 to serve a number of metropolitan areas along America's East Coast. DC-9 operations were, however, short-lived, the airline ceasing all activities on 9 November 1982.

## American Airlines

American Airlines now owns the largest airline fleet of any single type in the world (outside the Soviet Union), currently operating 206 MD-82s and 10 MD-83s on its extensive route system right across the United States. Another 44 aircraft are on order, with 34 scheduled for delivery in 1991 and 10 in 1992. If all of its commitments, which also include 90 options, are exercised, American's MD-80 fleet will eventually number a staggering 350 aircraft. In American service, the MD-80s are configured for 12 first class and 130 economy class passengers. The first order for 20 aircraft placed in September 1982 was the result of a unique lease arrangement with McDonnell Douglas whereby the manufacturer agreed to carry not only the cost of training, but also of major maintenance. In return for a low rental, American agreed to share the profits of its 727/MD-80 fleet. The initial lease was for five years to enable the airline to transfer to an all-

*Above:*
**ALM Antillean Airlines has operated several DC-9 models, including this DC-9-32, on its routes out of Curacao.**

new 150-seater if available. Consideration is being given to acquiring the MD-90 or possibly re-engining its MD-80s.

### American International Airways
American International Airways operated a fleet of seven DC-9-31/32s on group charters and scheduled passenger flights serving Atlantic City, Boston, Chicago-Midway, Cleveland, Detroit, Philadelphia, Pittsburgh and several points in Florida. The airline, however, was short-lived. Having started charter service in September 1981, increasing financial difficulties forced the cessation of all activities on 14 September 1984. Its first DC-9 was delivered on 15 September 1981.

### Ansett Airlines (Ansett-ANA)
Although Ansett-ANA, as it was then known, was courted by Douglas as early as 1961, it was not attracted to the DC-9-10, its small capacity when fitted out in a two-class configuration being considered unsuitable for Australian operations. Instead, the airline placed a letter of intent for six of the larger DC-9-31 on 17 March 1964. The first aircraft was delivered on 17 March 1967 and regular services on its East Coast network began on 13 April. The DC-9s quickly took on an increased work-load, and began to appear on major routes throughout the system. Success led to further

orders and by the time the final contracts had been fulfilled, Ansett had a total of 12 aircraft in service. The Australian machines had internal ventral airstairs to reduce reliance on ground support, low pressure tyres for secondary routes and cockpit equipment enhancements. With an accelerating delivery programme of Boeing 737s, withdrawal of the DC-9s commenced in 1981, the last commercial service being flown on 17 June 1982 from Launceston to Melbourne. All Ansett aircraft ended up in the United States with Midway Airlines and the US Navy.

### ATI — Aero Transporti Italiani
ATI, based in Naples, was formed on 13 December 1963 and started domestic operations on 3 June 1964. A subsidiary of Alitalia, ATI utilises a large fleet of DC-9-32s and MD-82s with frequent interchanges of aircraft with the parent company. Maximum numbers of each in any one year amounted to 30 MD-82s and 26 DC-9-32s, five of the latter taken over from Aermediterranea, merged into ATI in April 1985. The airline operates Italy's largest domestic route network, together with group charter flights between Italy and other European countries and to North Africa. Major routes served by the McDonnell Douglas twin-jet airliners connect Rome with Turin, Trieste, Naples, Bari, Reggio Calabria and Cagliari, and Milan with Naples. The DC-9-32, first introduced into the fleet in May 1970, is fitted out for 123 passengers, whilst the MD-82, added on 8 April 1985, seats the maximum 172 passengers.

## Atlantis Airways

Atlantis Airways, founded as Nordseeflug in 1966, began charter operations in mid-1968 and obtained authority for trans-Atlantic flights in September that year. European IT and contract charters were undertaken with three new DC-9-32s which joined the fleet from 15 January 1970. The airline suspended activities and the DC-9s were sold in January and March 1973. Atlantis' main operating base was at Frankfurt.

## Austral

Austral Lineas Aereas is a privately-owned Argentinian airline operating a network of scheduled passenger services radiating from Buenos Aireas-Aeroparque. Flagship of the fleet since 8 January 1981, when it took delivery of its first aircraft, is the MD-80, of which four are currently in service, including two MD-81s and two MD-83s. Four more MD-83s are on order for delivery in autumn 1992. The 155-passenger jets are scheduled mainly on the airline's busiest routes from Buenos Aires to Bahia Blanca, Cordoba, Mar del Plata, Mendoza, Rosario and Tucuman. The airline also operated two DC-9-51s leased from Finnair for a short period between December 1978 and November 1980. Austral was established in June 1971 through a merger of Austral Compania Argentina de Transportes Aereos and Aerotranportes Litoral Argentino (ALA).

## Australian Airlines

Australian Airlines, until 1986 known as Trans Australia Airlines (TAA), has owned and operated a total of 12 DC-9-31s. The aircraft went into service with its first commercial flight over the Melbourne-Sydney-Brisbane route on 17 April 1967. TAA undertook a major refurbishing programme beginning in November 1981, upgrading eight aircraft with a new 'wide-body' look, new seats, decor and enclosed overhead lockers, as well as an improved dual automatic pressurisation system. Disposal of the DC-9 fleet began in 1982, but unlike that of Ansett, proceeded much more slowly, its last remaining five aircraft being sold to Australian Aircraft Sales in Autumn 1989. The airline had intended the five DC-9s to form the nucleus of a potential low-fare tourist fleet, but as a result of public reaction to ageing jets, Australian decided to pull the aircraft off its Queensland services. The DC-9s were used mainly to serve short-haul routes and included direct flights from Melbourne to Sydney, Launceston, Hobart, Canberra; Sydney to Canberra and Brisbane; Brisbane to Rockhampton and Townsville; Rockhampton-Mackay and Townsville-Cairns.

## Austrian Airlines

Austrian Airlines, formed on 30 September 1957, originally placed an order for nine DC-9-32s for delivery in 1971/72 and put the type into service on 22 June 1971 with a flight from Vienna to Frankfurt. All DC-9-32s, together with five DC-9-51s, introduced on 7 September 1975 between Vienna and Munich, have now been phased out, and the fleet currently comprises 13 MD-81s and five MD-87s. The MD-81 started services with Austrian on 26 October 1980 to Zurich, whilst the MD-87 had its first flight on 17 December 1987 from Vienna to Zagreb. Two MD-83s are on order for delivery in 1991 and 1993. Austrian's MD-80 fleet is scheduled on its network covering Europe, North Africa and the Middle East and also serves the internal routes from Vienna to Graz, Klagenfurt and Salzburg. Internal configuration is 137 seats (12 first class and 125 economy) in the MD-83 and 102 (12 first class and 90 economy) in the MD-87.

## AVENSA

AVENSA — Aerovias Venezolanas SA has been operating passenger services within Venezuela since May 1944 and now flies a large network of schedules serving such destinations as Caracas, Maracaibo, Barcelona, Maturin, Ciudad Bolivar, Porlamar, Puerto Ordaz, Barquisimeto, San Antonio and many others. International flights to Mexico and Panama are also flown. Avensa began DC-9 operations in early 1967 when it acquired two new DC-9-14s, joined by a single DC-9-32 on 27 February 1969, also purchased new from the manufacturer. In the mid-1970s the fleet was supplemented with a further three leased DC-9-14/15s, as well as six more DC-9-32s, bought from Delta Air Lines between 1976 and 1978. The three remaining DC-9-32s are currently leased to Midway Airlines.

## Aviaco

Aviaco-Aviacion y Comercio SA, founded in 1948, conducts domestic operations in Spain with 21 DC-9-30s and four MD-83s. The latter are flown on lease from the GPA Group and ILFC (two each) and serve several routes from Madrid and Barcelona to Palma, Jerez, Vigo, Asturias, Ibiza and Mahon. The MD-83, fitted out with 20 preference class and 140 tourist class seats, entered service with Aviaco on 27 March 1987 between Madrid and Jerez. Thirteen firm orders are held for the 155-passenger MD-88. Deliveries of the MD-88 are scheduled to begin in August 1991, and will be the first of this model to enter service in Europe. 110-passenger DC-9-32s and -34s have been operated since June 1974.

## Balair

Balair, Switzerland's largest charter airline, operates an all-Douglas jet fleet which presently numbers four MD-82/83s. They are used on inclusive-tour and general charter flights to intra-European and North African destinations from the Swiss gateways of Basle, Geneva and Zurich. In Balair service, the MD-80s are fitted out for 149 passengers in a two-class configuration. The first aircraft to join the fleet was a DC-9-34, delivered on 3 November 1976, and a DC-9-51 was also operated on lease from parent company Swissair. The MD-80s took over mainline short/medium-haul operations from 1982, using an MD-81 from parent company Swissair. The first of its own aircraft, an MD-82, was delivered on 1 February 1985.

## Best Airlines

Best Airlines was a scheduled airline which began services during May 1982 using a single leased Douglas DC-9-15 delivered on 6 March. Two more DC-9-14/15s were put onto its routes from Detroit to Rochester, Newark, Roanoke, Hartford/Springfield, Cleveland, Columbus, Atlanta, Raleigh/Durham, Greenboro/High Point/Winston-Salem, and Nassau in the Bahamas. All operations ceased on 20 December 1985.

## Bonanza Air Lines — see Air West

*Below:*
**Best Airlines began scheduled services from Detroit in May 1982 with a single DC-9-15.**

## British Island Airways (BIA)

British Island Airways, a London-Gatwick based airline, established on 1 April 1982, provided scheduled and charter services with a fleet which comprised four 167-seat MD-83s and eight BAC One-Elevens. The four McDonnell Douglas twins were leased from ILFC and joined the fleet in December 1987, May and December 1988 and May 1989. In addition to its IT packages to the usual holiday resorts in Europe and North Africa, BIA operated its MD-83s on scheduled passenger services to Catania and Palermo in Sicily from Gatwick, and to Malta from both Manchester and Gatwick. A general downturn in holiday traffic forced the airline out of business on 1 February 1990.

## British Midland

British Midland Airways signed a lease contract with Douglas on 18 June 1976 for up to four DC-9-10s and the first 90-seat aircraft, an ex-Avensa machine, was put into service on the London Heathrow-Teesside route in September 1976. The first two aircraft were flying under US registrations, awaiting UK certification, which was granted in 1978. The present fleet comprises six 85-seat DC-9-14/15s and eight 110-seat DC-9-32s. The British Midland DC-9s fly the airline's 'Diamond' services from London Heathrow to Amsterdam, Dublin, Liverpool, Leeds/Bradford and Teesside, between Birmingham and Brussels, and from East Midlands to Belfast, Glasgow and Paris.

*Above:*
**British Midland Airways was the first UK operator of the DC-9 when it put the Series 14 into service between London and Teesside in September 1976.**

## BWIA International

BWIA International, the national carrier of the Caribbean Islands state of Trinidad and Tobago, has a fleet of five MD-83s. The first aircraft arrived at Port of Spain on 7 May 1986, and entered service on 14 May, routeing Port of Spain-Miami-Port of Spain. The MD-83 twin-jets operate the airline's international routes to Miami, New York, Baltimore and Toronto, with inter-Caribbean stops. BWIA first became a DC-9 operator in summer 1976 when it took delivery of a leased DC-9-51 before acquiring four of its own DC-9-51s, together with a DC-9-34CF. A single ex-Frontier Airlines MD-82 was also flown for a short time between 24 June 1985 and 6 May 1986 on lease from United Airlines.

## CAAC

CAAC – Civil Aviation Administration of China, took delivery of the first two of five MD-82s direct from the manufacturer on 12 December 1983, for use by its Shanghai and Shenyang Bureaus. The first Shanghai-built MD-82 went into service on 31 July 1987 and a total of 14 have so far been completed. The MD-82s are used by both bureaus (now re-named China Eastern Airlines and China Northern Airlines) on routes serving Beijing, Shanghai, Changchun, Dalian, Harbin, Hefei, Jilin, Lianing, Heilongjiang, Nanjing, Quingdao, Shenyang, Hangzhou, and reaching as far south as Chengdu and Guangzhou. The twin-jet is also used to Hong Kong and Nagasaki.

## Canafrica-Transportes Aereos — see AirSur

## Caribair

Caribair-Caribbean Atlantic Airlines was a prominent airline founded in 1939 and based at Isla Verde, Puerto Rico. On 3 December 1967, Caribair acquired the first of three DC-9-31s to supplement its Convair twins on an extensive network of services throughout the Caribbean, including the Leeward and Windward Islands, Trinidad and Tobago, Dominica, the US Virgin Islands, and to Miami. Financial problems forced the airline to open negotiations with Eastern Air Lines in September 1970, and the takeover was finally authorised in April 1973. The DC-9s were integrated into the Eastern fleet.

## Cayman Airways

Cayman Airways, owned by the Cayman Islands Government, operated two DC-9-15Fs on lease from Air Florida, for a short period in 1978. The DC-9s were used on the airline's international routes from Georgetown (Grand Cayman) to Miami and to Kingston, Jamaica.

## Coleman Air Transport
Coleman Air Transport, a US carrier, operated charters and scheduled services mainly in the Midwest from Rockford to Milwaukee, Detroit, New York La Guardia, Cleveland, Peoria, Cedar Rapids, Indianapolis, Cincinnati, Moline and Des Moines. Among its fleet was a single DC-9-15MC operated on lease from Texas International between 31 October 1979 and early 1980. Two more DC-9s were on order but never delivered, the company ceasing operations soon after.

## Connie Kalitta Services
Connie Kalitta Services is a privately-owned carrier which commenced flying in November 1972. Among its varied activities out of Detroit's Willow Run Airport are passenger and particularly cargo charters, flown both on an ad-hoc and contract basis. Major customers are the Detroit-based car manufacturers. Among its large mixed fleet is a single DC-9-15RC, which was acquired from Republic Airlines and has been operated since July 1984.

## Continental Airlines
Continental Airlines, owned by the Texas Air Corporation, is the fourth largest US carrier, with an extensive network of scheduled passenger services covering 82 domestic and 42 international destinations. Its large fleet of Airbus, Boeing and McDonnell Douglas aircraft presently includes 67 MD-81/82/83s, 27 DC-9-31/32s and seven DC-9-14/15s. All of the DC-9s were taken into the fleet with the incorporation of Texas International in October 1982 and New York Air in February 1987, although Continental was itself an early DC-9 operator when it totally replaced its propeller fleet with four DC-9-14s and 19 convertible DC-9-15RCs starting on 4 March 1966. By April 1967, Continental was an all-jet airline expanding rapidly outside its normal area of operation. All DC-9s had gone by 1977, but in June 1983, the airline placed its first order for a single MD-82. Follow-up orders, together with some second-hand aircraft, brought the fleet up to the present mixture of MD-80s, all configured for 24 first class and 117 economy class passengers. The DC-9-10s and DC-9-30s seat 81 and 108 passengers respectively, both types laid out with eight first class accommodation.

## Cruzeiro do Sul
Cruzeiro do Sul, sister company to Varig, the Brazilian flag carrier, operated a single MD-82 on local routes between 8 December 1982 and 13 March 1983. The aircraft was leased from McDonnell Douglas.

## CTA-Compagnie de Transport Aerien
CTA, now a member of the Swissair Group, was founded in September 1978. After operating successfully with Caravelles for 10 years, the airline introduced the first of four MD-87s into commercial service on 30 April 1988 with a flight to Antalya in Turkey. The 125-passenger aircraft are used principally on charters from Zurich and Geneva to Greek destinations, the Balearics and Canary Islands, and to Naples and Palermo in Italy. Sub-charters are also flown for Swissair, accounting for some 40% of the airline's business.

## Cyprus Airways
Following suspension of all services due to the Cypriot war between July 1974 and February 1975, when its fleet was damaged and left stranded at Nicosia International Airport, Cyprus Airways had to rely on leased equipment to get it back onto its feet. This included two DC-9-15s from KLM which were operated between August 1975 and November 1976 on routes from Larnaca to points in Europe, the Middle East and North Africa. A third, also leased from KLM, joined the fleet for a month in November/December 1975.

## Cyprus Turkish Airlines — see THY-Turk Hava Yollari

## Delta Air Lines
To Delta Air Lines fell the distinction of inaugurating the world's first commercial DC-9 service when a Series 14 operated an Atlanta-Memphis-Kansas City round trip on 8 December 1965, having started route proving on 29 November. Of its launch order of 15 DC-9-14s, Delta took delivery of 14 before switching to the bigger DC-9-32 from April 1967, eventually acquiring 63 new from the manufacturer and 14 more from its takeover of Northeast Airlines in August 1972. By the end of 1973, Delta completed a multi-million dollar refit programme, installing smoke emission devices on all DC-9 and 727 engines to reduce environmental pollution.

An order for up to 80 aircraft announced in January 1986 launched the MD-88, the most advanced of the MD-80 series. The first eight aircraft were delivered as MD-82s, starting on 9 March 1987, and later converted to MD-88s. Delta's present McDonnell Douglas twin-jet fleet comprises 36 DC-9-32s, fitted out for 12 first-class and 86 economy passengers, and 70 MD-88s, accommodating 142 passengers in a

14/128 configuration. A total of 150 have been ordered including to date 107 firm and 43 options. Also on order or option are 160 of the latest MD-9-30 series. The DC-9/MD-80 twins are scheduled on Delta's vast domestic network, which serves 160 cities in 42 states across the US from its main hubs at Atlanta, Dallas, Cincinnati, Los Angeles and Salt Lake City. Delta's DC-9 fleet alone has logged four million landings.

## Dominicana
Dominican de Aviacion, the national airline of the Dominican Republic, which has been flying since 1944, commenced DC-9 operations in December 1968 when it leased a Series 15 for its route from Santo Domingo to Miami and New York, and to San Juan, Puerto Rico. The DC-9-15 was returned on 22 October 1970, but in the meantime, Dominicana had taken delivery of a brand-new DC-9-32 which arrived at Santo Domingo on 16 December 1969. Unfortunately, this was written off at Punta Cauceda Airport on 19 March 1972.

## East African Airways (EAA)
East African Airways Corporation served as the national airline of Kenya, Uganda and Tanzania until economic and political problems grounded the airline on 1 February 1977, leading to each country forming its own airline. Between 9 December 1970 and 24 February 1971, the airline took delivery of three Douglas DC-9-32s, one registered in each country. They were utilised on regional flights to such neighbouring destinations as Addis Ababa, Beira, Blantyre, Bujumbura, Kigali, Khartoum, Kinshasa, Lusaka, Mahe, Maputo, Mogadishu, Port Louis, Tananarive and others, mainly from Nairobi and Dar-es-Salaam. All three went to Kenya Airways upon its formation.

## Eastern Air Lines
Eastern Air Lines, a subsidiary of Texas Air Corporation, having suffered severe financial difficulties compounded by an air crew and engineering strike during 1989, finally ceased to exist in March 1991. Eastern had a proud history, going back to September 1927 when it was founded as Pitcairn Aviation. It became one of the earliest DC-9 operators when it took delivery of the first of 15 DC-9-14s on 26 April 1966. These were soon joined by the larger DC-9-31, introduced on its New York-Boston and New York-Washington 'air shuttle' on 1 February 1967. Eastern had placed a first order for 31 aircraft in February 1965, and subsequent orders brought the DC-9-31 fleet to 72 aircraft. Nine DC-9-51s were purchased in June 1976 and added to with second-hand acquisitions to number 25 aircraft. Unlike its major competitors, Eastern did not continue with McDonnell Douglas by ordering the MD-80 series, opting instead for the larger Boeing 757. Eastern's route network at one time served over 100 points across the United States and to Canada, the Caribbean, Central and South America, and Europe, but has now been considerably reduced. Of its large DC-9 fleet, 38 99-passenger DC-9-31s and 25 120-seat DC-9-51s remained until 1990. In Eastern service, DC-9s have accumulated some 4.5 million landings.

## Emerald Air
Emerald Air, a privately-owned airline headquartered at Austin, Texas, provides scheduled passenger flights under contract in Texas and the Midwest, together with tour and gambling charters to Atlantic City from Orlando and several points in the Caribbean. The current fleet comprises five 90-passenger DC-9-14s out of a total of six DC-9-14s operated, as well as an equal number of DC-9-15RCs, first introduced into service in 1981. Emerald Air was incorporated in 1976, started cargo flights in October 1978 and added passenger services in June 1981.

## Emery Worldwide — see Orion Air

## Eurofly
Eurofly is a Turin-based airline operating two ex-Adria Airways DC-9-51s on inclusive-tour flights to European, North African and Asian destinations since early 1990. The company was formed in September 1978, initially to fulfil the transport needs of leading Italian industrial groups, headquartered in Turin. Executive charter services were added soon after.

## Evergreen International Airlines
Oregon-based Evergreen International Airlines maintains scheduled domestic freight services and government passenger and cargo contract flights. A mixture of DC-9-32F, -32CF and -33RC aircraft totalling nine, plus two of the smaller DC-9-15MCs, have been operated since the first DC-9 appeared in Evergreen colours in 1976. Most are still in service on scheduled cargo runs between Texas and Mexico, and on United States Air Force Logair contracts. Evergreen International came into being on 28 November 1975, when Evergreen Helicopters of McMinnville, Oregon acquired the certificate of Johnson Flying Service.

## Finnair
Finnair, the national airline of Finland, has been flying Douglas aircraft since 1941, when it began

operating DC-2s. The airline's fleet currently comprises 12 122-seat DC-9-51s and five 126-seat DC-9-41s in all-economy layout, in addition to 13 MD-82s, five MD-83s with 161 economy seating and three 114-seat MD-87s. Four more MD-82/83s are on order and will be delivered from September 1991 onwards. Three options are also held which may be either MD-82s or 83s. Finnair's first DC-9, a Series 14, was delivered on 24 January 1971, and in subsequent years the airline has operated nine DC-9-14/15s, one DC-9-15MC, seven DC-9-41s and 18 DC-9-51s. It became launch customer of the MD-83 and MD-87 when it placed orders in February and December 1984 respectively, taking delivery on 19 October 1985 and 1 November 1987. DC-9/MD-80 aircraft are scheduled on all European routes, serving most capitals in Western and Eastern Europe, as well as on major domestic lines.

## Frontier Airlines

Denver-based Frontier Airlines was a major scheduled jet airline, which operated an extensive network of services covering more than 50 points in the West and Midwest regions of the United States, as well as to a number of international destinations in nearby Canada and Mexico. Its large jet fleet of more than 50 aircraft included five MD-82s, first delivered on 22 April 1982, and another five operated on lease from the GPA Group from 29 April 1986. Four MD-83s were

also on order when Frontier, founded in 1950, suspended all operations on 24 August 1986. The airline was acquired by Texas Air Corporation and merged into Continental Airlines two months later.

## Garuda Indonesia

Garuda Indonesian Airways, the government-controlled national airline founded on 31 March 1950, acquired a total of 25 new DC-9-32s over a 10-year period between October 1969 and August 1979, 18 of which remain in service. The 97-seat (20 first class and 77 economy) DC-9-32s are utilised mainly on its extensive domestic network, which links 35 of the main cities throughout the archipelago. Plans are in hand to transfer all domestic operations to its wholly-owned subsidiary, Merpati Nusantara, by 1991, including nine DC-9-32s. The remaining nine are expected to be replaced by Boeing 737s.

## Germanair

Germanair was a Frankfurt-based charter airline which began operations with DC-6B aircraft in 1965. Jet equipment was added on 28 April 1969 in the shape of a Douglas DC-9-15 which was used on inclusive-tour flights to the Mediter-

*Below:*
A Garuda Indonesian Airways DC-9-32, one of 25 bought new from the manufacturer, seen at Paya Lebar Airport, Singapore in 1979. *Douglas Green*

*Above:*
**Frankfurt-based Germanair used a single DC-9-15 for a few months in 1969.**

ranean island resorts, North Africa and the Middle East until 27 August 1969, when it was replaced by BAC One-Elevens.

## German Wings
German Wings, an ambitious Munich-based German scheduled airline, led a short-lived existence, ceasing operations after just one year. The airline began operating four brand-new MD-83s on 10 April 1989 on an internal German and European network serving Hamburg, Cologne, Frankfurt and Paris. Four more, two each leased from GPA and ILFC, were added late in 1989 and early 1990. In German Wings service, the MD-83 seated only 114 passengers in a 2 x 2 abreast seating configuration to appeal particularly to the business traveller. Four more MD-83s were on order for delivery by 1992.

## Ghana Airways
Ghana Airways Corporation was formed on 4 July 1958 to take over the operations of West African Airways Corporation, and since 14 February 1961 has been wholly government-owned. The airline's fleet includes a single DC-9-51, delivered brand-new on 13 July 1978. Fitted out for 10 first class and 122 economy class passengers, the DC-9 shares regional and domestic services with the Fokker Fellowship linking Accra

with Abidjan, Banjul, Conakry, Cotonou, Dakar, Freetown, Lome, Monrovia, Las Palmas and Takoradi. Ghana Airways is looking to replace its DC-9-51 with the later, bigger capacity MD-82.

## Great American Airways
Great American Airways made its first revenue flight on 26 September 1979 between Seattle and Reno, using a DC-9-15 configured for the maximum 90 passengers. A second similar aircraft has since been added. The airline carries out group charter and contract jet flights to Reno and Lake Tahoe area casinos from points throughout the western US and British Columbia, Canada.

## Hawaiian Air
Hawaiian Airlines, incorporated as long ago as 30 January 1929 under the name of Inter-Island Airways, began jet service with two 85-passenger DC-9-15s on 1 April 1966. The aircraft proved so popular that in September the purchase of two of the larger DC-9-31s was announced for delivery the following year, leading to a large fleet of Douglas twin-jets which included the DC-9-14, DC-9-15, DC-9-15RC, DC-9-15MC, DC-9-31, DC-9-32CF and the DC-9-33RC model. The last-named was used to open an all-cargo service to the islands from Honolulu International Airport. The first of eight new 139-passenger DC-9-51s were introduced in October 1975. Today's fleet includes the eight DC-9-51s, as well as two MD-81s, the type being added to the fleet in spring 1981. The twin-jets are utilised on high-frequency

or multiple daily inter-island flights reaching seven airports on six islands. Points served are Hilo and Kona (Hawaii), Honolulu (Oahu), Kahului (Maui), Kaunakakai (Molokai), Lanai City (Lanai) and Lihue (Kauai).

## Hughes Airwest
Hughes Airwest was a major carrier which served more than 50 cities in the Western USA, Mexico and Canada, before being acquired by Republic Airlines on 1 October 1980. It was established on 3 April 1970 when the Hughes Air Corporation bought the assets of Air West. The largest proportion of its 'Sundance' fleet was made up of DC-9s and included 29 103-passenger DC-9-30s and 10 75-seat DC-9-10s. The majority of those were taken over from Air West and the others were purchased mostly from Eastern, Continental and Hawaiian Airlines in the mid-1970s. From 1 October 1978, Hughes Airwest offered a new 'Business Coach' section featuring four-abreast seating on all DC-9s. Closed overhead storage compartments were installed, and range and payload capabilities were boosted through a programme of upgrading engines on its DC-9-30s.

## Iberia
Iberia-Lines Aereas de Espana, the national airline of Spain, currently operates 28 DC-9 twin-jets, comprising 24 105-seat DC-9-32 and four convertible DC-9-33RC models, as well as 15 MD-87s with nine more on order. A shorter member of the MD-80 family, it will feature a two-class interior seating a maximum of 109 passengers. The MD-87s will also be equipped with a 21-screen entertainment system, believed to be the first of its kind on a commercial aircraft. 5in (127mm) monitors will be installed in the over-head compartments on both sides of the aisle, serving two rows of passengers each.

The purchase of the MD-80s is part of Iberia's plan eventually to replace the DC-9s on intra-European routes, the first of which joined the fleet on 30 June 1967. A total of 35 aircraft were purchased direct from Douglas, consisting of 31 DC-9-32s and four DC-9-33RCs. The DC-9s are extensively used on Iberia's European network, as well as internally, serving major points in mainland Spain, the Balearics and the Canary Islands.

## Intercontinental Colombia
Intercontinental de Aviacion was founded in October 1965 as Aeropesca, and adopted the present title in December 1982. Two months before, the airline acquired two DC-9-15s on lease to supplement its Vickers Viscounts. Both are still in service and have been joined by a third aircraft, flying a domestic route network which includes Bogota, Florencia, Popayan, Pasto, Ipiales, Valledupar, Riohacha, Arauca, Cucuta, Cali, Leticia, Santa Marta and Medellin. The DC-9s are fitted out for 85 single-class passengers.

## IPEC Aviation
IPEC Aviation, a division of Interstate Parcel Express Company, was formed in 1976 to operate the Bass Strait freight service, linking Essendon Airport, Melbourne with Launceston, Tasmania. Services were inaugurated on 1 February 1982 with an Armstrong-Whitworth Argosy, replaced in July 1982 with an ex-Yugoslav DC-9-33CF. A second similar aircraft was added in November 1989. The DC-9s now

*Below:*
**Ipec-Aviation flies a single DC-9-33CF on all-cargo services from Melbourne.**

fly the Melbourne-Launceston route several times daily and are also used on schedules to Adelaide, Sydney and Brisbane and on cargo charter work. More DC-9s may be added to replace the three Argosies.

## Itavia

Aerolinee Itavia was a major private Italian domestic airline which served a large number of cities with an all-jet fleet comprised of Fokker F28 Fellowships and Douglas DC-9s. Cities served included Ancona, Bergamo, Bologna, Catanzaro, Cagliari, Catania, Forli, Lamezia Terme, Milan, Palermo, Pescara, Pisa, Rome, Treviso and Turin. Its first DC-9-15 arrived in Rome on 12 October 1971, being the forerunner of several leased models which included five DC-9-14/15s, one DC-9-21, four DC-9-31/32CF/33CFs and one DC-9-51, the last named being delivered on 14 June 1976. Operations were suspended in December 1980.

## Japan Air System

Japan Air System, prior to April 1988 known as Toa Domestic Airlines (TDA), was formed on 15 May 1971 from a merger of TOA Airways and Japan Domestic Airlines (JDA). At that time, the airline introduced Boeing 727s and two DC-9-31s as an interim measure preceding the purchase of a large number of DC-9-41s, which formed the backbone of the fleet throughout the 1970s. A total of 22 were acquired, first delivered on 18 March 1974. In August 1978, TDA placed its first order for five MD-81s, taking delivery from 30 January 1981 onwards. Since then follow-up orders have been placed on a regular basis to total 32 aircraft. Of these 20 are currently in service, with the remaining 12 aircraft scheduled for delivery between 1991 and 1997. The progressive introduction of the MD-81s will release the DC-9-41s, which are due to be sold to Airborne Express. The present fleet, which apart from the 128-seat DC-9-41s and 163-seat MD-81s also includes four 130-seat MD-87s introduced in 1988, provides multiple daily non-stop services to most major points in the main Japanese islands and to Okinawa in the far south, from its primary traffic hubs at Tokyo, Osaka, Sapporo, Fukuoka and Kagoshima. Japan Air System has placed an order for 10 of the new MD-90-31 twin-jet.

## JAT — Yugoslav Airlines

JAT, the state-run national airline, announced its first order for five DC-9-32 jetliners on 19 January 1970, after having provided DC-9 service on its European and Middle East routes since the previous April, using an aircraft leased on an interim basis. In the configuration ordered by JAT, the DC-9 seated 99 passengers, since changed to a two-class 107 passenger layout. A total of 16 DC-9s were eventually bought, nine of which remain in service on domestic and European routes. One DC-9-32 has been on lease to Air Djibouti since October 1986.

## Jet Alsace

Jet Alsace, founded in 1988 and based at Basle-Mulhouse Airport, has been operating a Minerve MD-83 since July 1989. This was replaced in April 1990 with an ex-British Island Airways aircraft acquired on lease from ILFC. Jet Alsace is an affiliate of Minerve SA and undertakes charters between Basle and Paris, and from Basle to the Mediterranean countries.

## Jet America

Based at Long Beach, California, Jet America Airlines appropriately operated an exclusive fleet of eight locally-built MD-82s on low-cost scheduled passenger services linking California, the Midwest and Texas. Group charters and contract flights were also undertaken. The first two aircraft were handed over on 13 November 1981, flying the first revenue service between Chicago and Long Beach three days later. The 147-passenger jets, configured with 12 first class and 135 coach class seats, were scheduled on several daily flights out of Long Beach, Ontario, Burbank and Oakland, serving Chicago, Dallas/Fort Worth, St Louis, Las Vegas, Milwaukee and Washington, until the cessation of all operations in November 1987.

## Kenya Airways

Kenya Airways took over three DC-9-32s following the collapse of the tri-national East African Airways Corporation. Founded on 22 January 1977, the airline put the twin-jets to work on its regional routes to Cairo, Harare, Khartoum, Addis Ababa, Mogadishu, Entebbe, Lusaka and the Seychelles. One aircraft was leased to Air Tanzania until October, but upon its return was disposed of with one other. Kenya Airways retained the remaining DC-9-32, fitted out for 12 first class and 85 economy class passengers, until 1989.

## KLM

KLM Royal Dutch Airlines, founded on 7 October 1919 and the world's oldest airline still operating under the same name, has been a faithful Douglas customer since 1934, when it added the DC-2 to its fleet. From then on, it has operated all DC series, taking delivery of its first of six DC-9-15s on 25 March 1966, and putting the type into service on 29 April, routeing Amsterdam-Geneva-

Nice and Amsterdam-Paris. The fleet was increased from November 1967 with the larger DC-9-30, the airline acquiring 13 DC-9-32s and five DC-9-33RCs. The DC-9s were scheduled on KLM's extensive European network, serving all the major destinations, until gradually being replaced with Boeing 737-300s, the last DC-9 leaving the fleet in 1989.

*Above:*
**Korean Air Lines introduced this DC-9-32 onto its routes in July 1967.**

## Korean Air

Korean Air Lines presently operates eight 164-passenger MD-82s, with two more on order for delivery in July and September 1994. Two options are also held. The MD-82s, which first entered service with the airline in August 1985, are scheduled on regional routes to Bangkok, Colombo, Kuala Lumpur, Singapore, Manila,

*Below:*
**Kenya Airways acquired three DC-9-32s following the collapse of East African Airways Corporation in 1977.**

Hong Kong, Taipei, Fukuoka, Nagoya, Niigata and Tokyo, as well as on the principal domestic lines linking Seoul, the capital, with the port of Pusan and the island of Cheju. Korean Air Lines first used a Douglas twin-jet when it introduced a single DC-9-32 onto its routes in July 1967. This was later sold to Hughes Airwest in February 1973. A single DC-9-15 was also leased between 1 June 1970 and 14 December 1972.

## La Tur

Lineas Aereas La Tur is a Mexican charter airline, formed in 1987 by the Mexican Pilots Association APSA and Fiesta American Hotels. Two 168-seat MD-83s, leased from the GPA Group, are used on contract charters to the Mexican tourist resorts of Acapulco, Cancun, Puerto Vallarta, Mexico City, Ixtapa and Santa Cruz, from the US East and West Coasts. Among American points of origin are New York, Washington, Minneapolis, Orlando and San Diego. MD-83 operations commenced in December 1988.

## LAV — Linea Aeropostal Venezolana

LAV, the Venezuelan government-controlled airline founded in 1930, took delivery of its first DC-9, a Series -14 on 23 October 1968, and now operates an all-McDonnell Douglas jet fleet comprising one DC-9-15, three DC-9-32s, one DC-9-34CF, eight DC-9-51s and three MD-83s, the last-named acquired in 1986. The different size models provide seating capacities from 85 in the DC-9-15 to 163 passengers in the MD-83. The airline's routes serve the regional points of Curacao, Aruba, Barbados, Georgetown, Grenada, Havana, Pointe-a-Pitre, San Juan, Santo Domingo, Port of Spain, as well as Orlando and Atlanta in the United States. Domestic lines extend from Caracas to Barcelona, Barinas, Maturin, Porlamar, Puerto Ordaz, Barquisimeto, Acarigua, Maracaibo and many others.

## Lineas Aereas Canarias (LAC)

Lineas Aereas Canarias is a Tenerife-based airline which commenced operations on 25 September 1985 with a single Vickers Viscount between Tenerife and Lanzarote. Its first MD-83 was delivered on 19 October 1987, and this has since been joined by four more, all on lease from the GPA Group. MD-83s are used on passenger and cargo charters to the Canaries from points in Germany, Italy, France, the United Kingdom, Scandinavia, Morocco and The Gambia. Interisland services are also flown.

## Martinair Holland

Martinair Holland, founded in 1958 as Martin's Air Charter, has been a DC-9 operator since 1 August 1968, when it introduced the first of three DC-9-33RCs on its European and Mediterranean

*Below:*
**A Martinair Holland MD-82, one of three introduced in 1981.**

routes. The fleet was later joined by a single DC-9-32 and three leased MD-82s, the latter introduced in 1981. At present, Martinair retains two MD-82s which are fitted out for 165 passengers, or which in cargo configuration can carry up to 12.5 tonnes of freight. Martinair's main business is inclusive-tour and general charter work throughout Europe, parts of Africa and the Far East and to North American destinations. Freight flights also form an important part of its activities.

## Midway Airlines

Chicago-based Midway Airlines began operations out of Midway Airport on 1 November 1979 with a fleet of three 63-seat ex-TWA Douglas DC-9-14s, initially linking Chicago to Cleveland, Detroit and Kansas City. By the end of the first year's operations, a total of seven DC-9s were flying with the airline. Since then, the network has been expanded considerably to serve more than 60 destinations in the United States, Canada, the US Virgin Islands and the Bahamas from its traffic hubs at Chicago and Philadelphia. Commensurate with this expansion, Midway has added to its fleet, which now consists largely of McDonnell Douglas twins including eight 120-seat MD-87s, two MD-88s, three MD-83s, four MD-82s, all three models seating 143 passen-

*Below:*
**Chicago-based Midway Airlines began operations on 1 November 1979 with a fleet of three ex-TWA DC-9-14s.**

gers, the other 98. All DC-9/MD-80 aircraft are fitted out with eight first class seats. On 30 March 1989, when the first MD-87 was delivered, Midway Airlines announced a massive $900 million order for 37 MD-80s with another 37 on option, scheduled to be delivered between 1993 and 1997. At over 11 hours, the airline boasts one of the highest daily utilisations of any DC-9/MD-80 in airline service.

## Midwest Express

Midwest Express, with headquarters at Milwaukee's General Mitchell International Airport, is a subsidiary of K-C Aviation, which bought a DC-9-14 in 1982 to use as a corporate aircraft. The company bought more DC-9s and started Midwest Express, commencing operations on 11 June 1984. The airline, flying non-stop services from Milwaukee to Dallas/Fort Worth, Atlanta, Tampa, Fort Lauderdale, Detroit, Washington DC, Philadelphia, Newark, Boston, New York La Guardia, Denver and others, caters to the business traveller, operating its eight DC-9-14/15s in a 2 x 2 configuration seating 60 in extra wide leather seats. Three of the larger DC-9-32s are fitted for 84 passengers. Shuttle flights for its parent company are also undertaken.

## Minerve

This privately-owned French charter company, created in January 1975, introduced its first MD-83 in April 1987 to develop its medium-haul

operations throughout Europe. Fitted out for 169 passengers, the six MD-83s currently in the fleet fly charters from Paris and other French cities to various European destinations, the Mediterranean Basin, West Africa and the Middle East. The MD-83s have also been used by Minerve Canada in North America. The airline has options on two more MD-83s for delivery in October and November 1994, and plans to add a further six aircraft.

## Muse Air

Muse Air Corporation was formed by Lamar Muse at Dallas, Texas, and commenced operations during July 1981 with passenger services between Dallas Love Field and Houston's Hobby Airport. Over the years, the airline built up its fleet to include six 155-seat MD-82s, two similar capacity MD-83s and 10 130-seat DC-9-51s, to serve an extended network taking in Oklahoma City, Los Angeles, San Diego, New Orleans, Orlando, Miami and Tampa, and the Texas communities of Brownsville, McAllen, San Antonio, Lubbock and Midland/Odessa. A single DC-9-33RC was also leased from the manufacturer. On 30 June 1985 the stock of Muse Air was purchased by Southwest Airlines, who renamed the company Transtar Airlines on 17 February 1986. As a result of substantial operating losses it was decided on 1 July 1987 to discontinue operations, and scheduled flights ceased in August. All aircraft were sold, including delivery positions for two more MD-82s.

## National Airlines

National Airlines, formed in 1977, leased two MD-82s from Alisarda for the winter season between 14 December 1984 and 12 May 1985. The aircraft were used on tourist flights from its base at Kennedy International Airport, New York, to various points in the Caribbean. National was once known as Overseas National Airways, having adopted the title from the previous carrier of the same name.

## New York Air

New York Air operated a colourful fleet of 14 147-seat MD-82s, introduced in September 1982, and 16 110-seat DC-9-31/32s on low-fare scheduled services mainly out of New York's La Guardia and Newark airports. High-frequency non-stop jet services, established on 19 December 1980 in direct competition with Eastern's 'Air Shuttle', linked La Guardia with Washington (National) and Boston, both also served from Newark, New Jersey. In addition, the route network also took in points in Ohio, Georgia, Florida, Louisiana, Tennessee and North and South Carolina. Like Continental Airlines, a subsidiary of Texas Air Corporation, New York Air was integrated into Continental in February 1987.

*Below:*
**New York Air operated a colourful fleet which included 16 DC-9-31/32s.**

## North African Aviation — NAA
North African Aviation, a Cairo-based general aviation company founded in 1980, operated a single leased DC-9-51 in October and November 1988 on local charter work. The aircraft made only five flights with NAA, totalling 6 hours.

## North Central Airlines
North Central Airlines, until 1952 known as Wisconsin Central Airlines, was a major regional scheduled carrier, which on 1 July 1979 combined with Southern Airways to form Republic Airlines. North Central took delivery of its first DC-9-31 on 28 July 1967, and two of the aircraft inaugurated jet service to 17 cities on 8 September 1967. The airline experienced rapid growth, due largely to providing expanded jet service to major markets, with the route network reaching almost 100 cities in the USA and neighbouring Canada. Based at Minneapolis-St Paul, the airline's strength lay in its ability to link medium-sized cities with major metropolitan areas. The DC-9-31 fleet eventually reached 30 aircraft, joined from 6 April 1976 by 28 of the newer and bigger DC-9-51s. Ten of these were delivered after North Central had become Republic Airlines.

## Northeast Airlines
Northeast Airlines was a principal US carrier, which was founded on 11 August 1933 as Boston & Maine Airways. From 1940 when the new name was adopted, the airline proceeded to build up a strong presence in the northeastern area of the United States, eventually carrying well over three million passengers annually. On 29 December 1966, Northeast took delivery of a DC-9-15 on lease from Douglas as an interim measure, while awaiting the arrival of its 14 new DC-9-31s. The first of these was accepted on 5 May 1967 and put onto its routes which served parts of New England, Hartford, Boston, New York, Philadelphia, Washington, Baltimore, Jacksonville, Tampa, Miami, Cleveland, Detroit, Bermuda, the Bahamas and Montreal. Canada. In April 1971, severe financial difficulties forced Northeast to agree to a merger with Delta Air Lines, which became official on 1 August 1972.

## Northwest Airlines
Northwest Airlines acquired a large fleet from its merger with Republic Airlines on 12 August 1986, which included 29 DC-9-14/15s, five DC-9-15RCs, 61 DC-9-31/32s, 28 DC-9-51s and eight MD-80s. A further 16 DC-9-30s were purchased later, together with 12 DC-9-41. Currently, Northwest flies the McDonnell Douglas twin-jets into a number of mid-sized markets from its three major domestic hubs in the United States. The MD-82 is particularly effective on flights to and from John Wayne Airport in Anaheim, California, where heavy noise restrictions are in operation, requiring the quietest Stage 3 aircraft. All models in Northwest service are configured in a 2-class layout, with seating ranging from 78 in the smallest DC-9-10 to 143 in the MD-82. Northwest Airlines, founded in August 1926, is now one of the world's largest airlines, operating a fleet of some 320 aircraft of various types, with another 180 on order.

## Oasis International Airlines
Oasis International Airlines commenced operations with the MD-83 on 27 May 1988 flying a Malaga-Manchester-Malaga round trip. Three aircraft are currently in service on lease from the GPA Group, and negotiations are under way with the manufacturer for a further two of the same type. In Oasis service the MD-83 is configured for 165 passengers, and flies an extensive charter network linking Madrid, Malaga and the Balearics and Canaries with points in the UK, Northern Italy, Germany, France and other European countries.

## Orion Air
Orion Air, a subsidiary of The Aviation Group, is one of the world's largest contract carriers, providing extensive cargo operations for major small package/overnight express companies such as Emery Worldwide and United Parcel Service. Its large jet fleet includes seven DC-9-15RC and one DC-9-15MC, all converted to pure freighters, which entered service on 15 February 1984. They were initially operated on behalf of Purolator Courier until that company merged into Emery Worldwide, the present contractor, on 21 September 1987.

## Overseas National Airways — ONA
ONA, a supplemental airline formed initially at Oakland, California and later based at Kennedy International, New York, was a long-time operator of Douglas aircraft, starting with the DC-4 in 1950. On 6 October 1967, the airline took delivery of a new DC-9-32CF, becoming the first to put this convertible model into service. The twin-jet fleet eventually numbered eight DC-9-32CF/33Fs, which could be seen flying passenger and cargo charter services throughout the United States and South America, until sold to Evergreen International on 29 October 1976. At one time one of the world's largest charter airlines, ONA ceased all activities on 15 September 1978.

## Ozark Air Lines

Ozark Air Lines was a US local service airline, which commenced scheduled operations on 26 September 1950 with a fleet of Douglas DC-3s over a single route linking its base of St Louis, Missouri, with Chicago, Illinois. Fifteen years later, on 21 January 1965, the airline announced its plan to acquire three DC-9-15s, and in the same year carried one million passengers for the first time over a network that served 58 cities in 16 states, mostly in the Midwest and the District of Columbia. This first order for Douglas' smallest jet was doubled six months later, and on 25 November 1965 a third order for three was placed, this time for the stretched DC-9-31, carrying 95 dual-class passengers instead of 75 as in the previously ordered models. Ozark's first jet was delivered in late May and scheduled DC-9 service was inaugurated on 8 July 1966. More orders for new and second-hand aircraft followed and the DC-9 fleet eventually reached a total of 50 aircraft, which included 36 DC-9-30s, seven DC-9-15s, three DC-9-41s and four MD-82s. Apart from its own aircraft, Ozark also operated and maintained the Playboy DC-9-32. In November 1976 Ozark embarked on a major cabin

*Below:*
**Among the large twin-jet fleet of Ozark Air Lines was the DC-9-30 series. This DC-9-32 was photographed at Kansas City International in May 1980.** *Wilfred C. Wann Jr*

conversion programme, providing all of its DC-9-30s with a 'wide-body' look. This included the fitting of enclosed overhead lockers, soft indirect fluorescent lighting, sculptured ceiling panels and re-covered passenger seats. Ozark Air Lines was absorbed by Trans World Airlines in September 1986.

## Pan Adria Airways

Pan Adria Aerotransportno Poduzece, a government-controlled Yugoslav charter airline, purchased one DC-9-32, which was delivered to Zagreb on 16 May 1973 for use on both internal and international charter and inclusive-tour flights. The aircraft was operated for just under a year, being transferred to Inex Adria in April 1974.

## Paramount Airways

Paramount Airways, based at Bristol in the United Kingdom, operated a total of four MD-83s on lease from the GPA Group between April 1987 and August 1989 when the airline was put under administration. The 165-seat aircraft were employed on inclusive tour flights from Bristol, Belfast, Cardiff and Exeter to major resorts in Europe, around the Mediterranean and to the Canary Islands. A rescue package failed because the airline was unable to secure sufficient winter contracts, and the aircraft were repossessed by the lessor. Paramount Airways was launched on

*Above:*
**When Paramount Airways, a Bristol-based charter airline, took delivery of this MD-83, it became the first operator of the type in the UK.**

8 July 1986 and commenced flying activities on 1 May 1987. It was the first British airline to operate the type.

## PSA — Pacific Southwest Airlines
PSA, a major regional airline, started operations on 6 May 1949 with a single DC-3, plying the San Diego-Burbank route. Its first DC-9, a Series 31, was delivered on 23 March 1967 and this was later joined by five more, this time 107-seat DC-9-32s. The airline grew rapidly, and in August 1978 placed an order with McDonnell Douglas for 10 MD-81s, taking delivery of the first aircraft on 18 November 1980. The fleet eventually numbered 20 MD-81s and 11 MD-82s, both configured for 150 passengers. Five more on order were cancelled. The MD-80 jet fleet accounted for almost 300 daily departures, serving numerous destinations in the Western States of California, Arizona, Nevada, New Mexico, Oregon and Washington until 9 April 1988 when the airline was absorbed by USAir.

## Purdue Airlines
Purdue Airlines, founded in 1942 as Purdue Aeronautics Corporation, was a Lafayette-based US airline operating charter services out of Purdue University Airport to points throughout the United States and to Canada. The airline acquired a new DC-9-32 on 22 July 1969 and quickly built the fleet up to four aircraft, which included the ex-Playboy machine. Continuing financial difficulties forced the airline to suspend its supplemental charter activities in May 1971 and the DC-9s were sold, with the last joining Ozark Air Lines on 11 October 1972.

## Purolator Courier — see Orion Air

## Republic Airlines
Formed on 1 July 1979 through the merger of North Central Airlines and Southern Airways, both well-established major regional airlines, Republic reached the distinction of becoming the world's eighth largest passenger carrier, with in excess of 1,000 daily departures from 100 points across the continental United States and extending into Canada, Mexico and the Cayman Islands. The largest fleet of DC-9s in the world came from both North Central and Southern, as

*Above:*
**The Republic Airlines fleet of DC-9s was joined by eight new MD-82s from August 1981.**

well as from Hughes Airwest, which was acquired on 1 October 1980. The fleet comprised 35 DC-9-10s, 61 DC-9-30s, and 35 DC-9-51s, to which were added eight new MD-82s, which joined the fleet between August 1981 and 1982. All remaining aircraft were transferred to Northwest Airlines, following its merger with Republic on 12 August 1986.

### Ross Aviation
Ross Aviation, founded in 1953, has been operating DC-9-15RC freighters since 15 August 1979, when the first of three aircraft was delivered from Air Florida. The company is engaged mainly in contract work for the US Government and primarily for the Energy Research and Development Administration (ERDA) and the Ministry of the Interior. Scheduled flights are also provided from Albuquerque, New Mexico to the nuclear research centre at Los Alamos.

### Royale Airlines
Royale Airlines, based at Shreveport, Louisiana, used a single DC-9-14 between 27 January and 14 December 1984. The aircraft was leased from Continental Airlines and used to feed Continental's Houston hub.

### SAS — Scandinavian Airlines System
SAS, the national flag carrier of Denmark, Norway and Sweden has been a prolific operator of

the McDonnell Douglas twin-jet since it first introduced into its fleet the DC-9-41 in May 1968, which was built specifically to its own requirements for an aircraft to service its short-haul intra-Scandinavian network. A total of 49 aircraft were acquired between 1968 and 1979. Another aircraft built for SAS was the 'hot and high' DC-9-21, which was first delivered on 22 March 1969. SAS also bought two DC-9-33Fs to its cargo services, and later also supplemented its fleet with DC-9-32s and DC-9-51s, thus operating every model except the small DC-9-10.

The latest order for eight more MD-80s was announced in December 1989 for use on domestic and European routes. The first four aircraft will be MD-82s, scheduled for delivery in 1991, with the remainder MD-87s. Including this latest transaction, SAS now holds 73 firm orders and 33 commitments for the MD-80 family, 51 of which (133-seat MD-81s, 156-seat single class MD-82s, 133-seat MD-83s and 110-seat MD-87s) are already in service. The SAS fleet will number 106 aircraft by 1994 if all commitments are converted to firm orders. The fleet still includes 54 DC-9s of varying series, including the DC-9-21, and -41. DC-9s and MD-80s are used on main European routes and extensively within the Scandinavian countries, serving Copenhagen, Aalborg, Aarhus, Oslo, Bergen, Bodo, Haugesund, Tromso, Trondheim, Bardufoss, Evenes, Alta, Kirkenes, Stockholm, Gothenburg, Malmo, and Lulea.

### Saudia
Saudi Arabian Airlines, the largest carrier in the Middle East, bought three new DC-9-15s, which

arrived at Jeddah between 8 February and 29 April 1967. They were employed on Saudia's local routes from Jeddah, Dhahran and Riyadh to such destinations as Bombay, Karachi, Khartoum, Amman, Baghdad, Bahrain, Beirut, Cairo, Damascus, Doha, Dubai, Kuwait, Muscat, Sana'a, Tripoli and Tunis, until being replaced by Boeing 737s. All three DC-9s were sold in June/July 1972.

## Southern Airways

Southern Airways was a major regional air carrier, which began scheduled services on 10 June 1949. In the mid-1960s it made a massive leap by going straight from the Martin 404 piston-engined airliner to jet aircraft in the shape of the Douglas DC-9-15, the first of six on order being delivered on 11 May 1967 and entering service on 15 June. Twenty more of the Series 10,

*Below:*
**Line-up of SAS DC-9-41s at Copenhagen Kastrup Airport in 1977.**

including -14 and -15RC models, were obtained second-hand over the following years. On 29 April 1969 the first DC-9-31 joined the fleet. The airline's network grew so that by the end of 1976 Southern was serving 14 states, the District of Colombia and the Cayman Islands in the West Indies. More than 95% of Southern's revenue passenger miles were generated aboard its DC-9 fleet, which served 56 out of 63 cities on the network. By the time the airline merged with North Central to form Republic Airlines on 1 July 1979, the DC-9 fleet numbered four 96-seat DC-9-31s and 20 75-seat DC-9-14/15s.

## Spanair

Spanair has a fleet of seven leased MD-83s, configured in an all-tourist layout for 163 passengers. The aircraft are employed on the airline's charter programme, which serves all popular Spanish destinations, as well as towns and cities in the United Kingdom, Norway, Sweden, Denmark, Germany, France, the Benelux countries, Switzerland, Austria, Italy and Greece. Spanair's

first flight took place on 1 June 1988 from Palma de Mallorca to Bilbao.

## Spantax

Spantax SA Transportes Aereos, once Spain's biggest charter airline, finally succumbed to financial pressures in April 1988 after 27 years in the business. In its last years it maintained a mixed jet fleet, which included several McDonnell Douglas products, including two 160-seat MD-83s leased from IAL. They were employed on inclusive-tour flights to holiday destinations in mainland Spain, the Balearics and the Canary Islands from points around Europe. Aircraft were based in Madrid, Palma de Mallorca and Las Palmas de Gran Canaria. Spantax had first used the McDonnell Douglas twin in 1974 when it introduced three DC-9-14s from 23 February. DC-9-32s were leased in April 1982 and 1983.

## Standard Airways

Standard Airways, founded in 1946 and with headquarters at Seattle in Washington State, was a US supplemental airline with an area of charter operations encompassing the continental United States, Canada, Mexico and the Caribbean. In November 1966 it added to its fleet of Boeing 707s two DC-9-15s, acquired new from the manufacturer and delivered on the 3rd and 30th of the month. The DC-9s were operated for only two years, both aircraft going to Ozark Air Lines on 1 October 1968. Standard Airways ceased operations on 24 September 1969.

## Südflug

Süddeutsche Fluggesellschaft, founded in 1962, operated charter services in the mid-1960s with Douglas DC-8s and DC-9s. Its two DC-9-32s were delivered new from Douglas on 21 May 1968 but remained in Südflug service for only five months, before the airline succumbed to financial pressures and was merged into Condor on 1 January 1969. Both aircraft went to Swissair in October 1968.

## Sunworld International Airways

Sunworld International Airways provided low-cost jet flights from Las Vegas until November 1988 when all services ceased. The airline was established on 4 June 1981 as Jetwest International, but did not start operations until 27 May 1983, by which time the new name had been adopted. Two 90-passenger DC-9-14s were delivered in May for its first services, which linked Las Vegas to Ontario and San Jose in California. The fleet was later increased by two more DC-9-14s and two DC-9-31s, to service an increased network which also took in Oklahoma City, Tucson, Reno, Spokane, Portland, Oakland, Omaha and Milwaukee.

## Swissair

Swissair was one of the first companies to operate the DC-9-10, taking delivery of five Series 15

aircraft between 20 July 1966 and 26 June 1967. These were soon supplemented and later replaced by the larger DC-9-30, the airline eventually operating 29 different aircraft including one DC-9-33F all-cargo version. During 1974/75, two DC-9-41s were leased from SAS, before Swissair expanded its twin-jet fleet further with the DC-9-51, which entered service on 24 August 1975. The Swiss national carrier originated the requirement for this higher-capacity airliner with an order for 12 aircraft, and also became the launch customer (along with Austrian Airlines) of the MD-80 series when it ordered 15 with five options in October 1977. Swissair's first MD-81 service took place on 5 October 1980, flying a Zurich-Frankfurt round trip. A total of 22 114-seat, three-class MD-81s are currently in service, with two more scheduled for delivery in December 1990 and January 1991. The airline will also lease two additional aircraft from GPA in spring 1993, bringing the MD-81 fleet to 26. MD-81s are used to serve Swissair destinations within Europe. Preliminary decisions on a successor are already being finalised, with first deliveries pencilled in for 1995. Assessment of likely aircraft is being made jointly with SAS, Finnair and Austrian Airlines, all MD-80 operators.

## TAA Trans Australia Airlines — see Australian Airlines

## Texas International Airlines
Texas International Airlines began operations on

*Above:*
**The Texas International fleet of DC-9s, including this DC-9-31, provided 95% of total seat capacity on its extensive route network.**

11 October 1947 as Trans-Texas Airways, serving eight cities in Texas with a fleet of two DC-3s acquired from American Airlines. On 30 October 1966, Trans-Texas Airways introduced the 80-seat DC-9-14 onto its routes from Dallas and Houston to Harlingen, McAllen, Monterrey, Tampico and Veracruz, and became the only airline to purchase the DC-9-15MC convertible model, taking delivery of five aircraft between September 1967 and January 1968. By February 1969 Texas International, as it had by then become, had taken delivery of two DC-9-31s, forerunners of a total fleet of 21 aircraft, of which 13 were purchased new. This 99-passenger version proved a great success on the airline's higher density routes. Other second-hand purchases included seven DC-9-14/15s, the complete DC-9 fleet offering 95% of total seat capacity on its routes in Arkansas, California, Colorado, Louisiana, Mexico, Mississippi, New Mexico, Tennessee and Texas. On 31 October 1982 Texas Air Corporation, the parent company, merged Texas International Airlines into Continental Airlines.

## Thai International
Thai Airways International, established on 24 August 1959, leased two DC-9-41s from SAS, which at that time had a 30% shareholding in the

Thai international flag-carrier. The two aircraft arrived at Bangkok in late January 1970 and operated some of the airline's 'Royal Orchid' services in southeast Asia to such destinations as Kathmandu, Calcutta, Dacca, Kuala Lumpur and others. The DC-9s were returned to SAS in October 1971 and April 1972.

### THY-Turk Hava Yollari

THY Turkish Airlines, the government-controlled airline formed in May 1933 as Devlet Hava Yollari, purchased 10 new DC-9-32s from 9 July 1968, nine of which remain in service to this day. Fitted out for 111 or 115 passengers, the DC-9s are scheduled on THY's European routes to such destinations as Amman, Athens, Frankfurt, Milan and Munich and on its extensive domestic network taking in Ankara, Antalya, Adana, Diyarbakir, Erzurum, Gaziantep, Istanbul, Izmir, Malatya, Trabzon and Van. DC-9s are also frequently leased to Kibris Turk Hava Yollari (Cyprus Turkish Airlines) for its services from Ankara, Antalya, Adana, Izmir and Istanbul to Ercan (Tymbou) airport east of Nicosia.

### Toa Domestic Airlines (TDA) — see Japan Air System

### Touraine Air Transport (TAT)

Touraine Air Transport, now known as Transport Aérien Transrégional (TAT), is France's premier regional airline, with a large domestic network criss-crossing the country, as well as some international connections. On 11 September 1981, TAT leased two DC-9-21s from SAS, principally for its jet schedules operated on behalf of Air France. Both aircraft were returned on 23 October 1982, and immediately followed by a single DC-9-14 on a short-term lease from Finnair.

### Tradewinds

Tradewinds, a subsidiary of Singapore Airlines, operates a single 130-seat MD-87 on scheduled regional services from Singapore to Kuantan (Malaysia), Hat Yai, Phuket and Pattaya (Thailand) and to Kaohsiung (Taiwan). The MD-87 was acquired new from the GPA Group in January 1989 on a two-year lease, with the option to renew the contract for another two years. It is, however, expected to be replaced with Boeing 737-300s. Tradewinds was formed in 1975, initially to undertake charter flights on behalf of the parent company.

### Transtar Airlines — see Muse Air

### Trans-Texas Airways — see Texas International Airlines

### Transwede Airways

Transwede Airways was formed early in 1985 to operate inclusive-tour charters from Sweden and Norway with a Sud-Aviation Caravelle 10B. In July 1987 the airline placed an order with McDonnell Douglas for two MD-87s, the first of which was delivered in August 1988. By then four MD-83s had also been added to the fleet on lease. At the time of writing, four more MD-83s are on order for delivery in March 1991 and 1992, with options for a further four aircraft, two each due in 1994 and 1995. The 161-seat MD-83s and 132-seat MD-87s are used on holiday flights to the Mediterranean, the Canaries, Israel and the United Kingdom. The airline's fleet achieves one of the highest daily utilisations, being in excess of 10 hours.

### TWA — Trans World Airlines

TWA initially ordered 20 DC-9-15s in July 1964 to meet demand on its short-to-medium length routes, and took delivery of its first example on 25 March 1966. The DC-9s proved extremely popular, yet unlike other major US and foreign carriers, TWA never re-ordered the later versions of the DC-9, but acquired a large fleet of several variants when it absorbed Ozark Air Lines in September 1986. These presently number seven DC-9-14/15s, 38 DC-9-31/32/33CF/34s and three DC-9-41s. In October 1982, TWA obtained 15 MD-82s from McDonnell Douglas on similar favourable lease terms as American Airlines. The fleet has since grown to 33 aircraft, four of which are MD-83s, and the airline is looking to purchase additional MD-82s. The 142-passenger jets (12 first class and 130 economy class seats), fly TWA's domestic network from a main hub at St Louis, principally in central states, to the East Coast and Florida. The first MD-82 was delivered on 18 April 1983.

### Unifly Express

Unifly Express is a privately-owned carrier founded in 1980. Its main fleet consists of two leased MD-83s, two MD-82s, and two DC-9-15Fs, the latter acquired in March and May 1988 when the airline started DC-9 operations. The aircraft are used on ad hoc and contract passenger and freight operations out of Rome's Ciampino airport to European and Mediterranean destinations and to the Canary Islands. Two more MD-82s are on order for delivery in May 1991, as well as three MD-83s scheduled to arrive in Rome in February and March 1991. The twin-jets will be transferred to the airline's Milan-based subsidiary, Alinord, for its scheduled domestic and regional services.

## USAir

USAir, until 28 October 1979 known as Allegheny Airlines, was formed in March 1937 as All-American Aviation. Today, and. several acquisitions later, the airline is one of the world's largest, serving almost 200 points in 36 US states and abroad from hubs at Charlotte, Pittsburgh, Baltimore, Philadelphia, Dayton and Syracuse. Allegheny placed the DC-9 into service on 1 September 1966, testing the market with a single DC-9-14. This was supplemented the following year with the first of what is now a fleet of 74 DC-9-31/32s, fitted out for 110 passengers. In June 1974 an order was placed for eight new DC-9-51s, which entered service between 10 October 1975 and 27 February 1976. The present fleet also includes 19 MD-81s and 12 MD-82s, obtained through the April 1988 acquisition of Pacific Southwest Airlines, and these will be joined from September 1992 onwards by 20 new MD-82s ordered in early 1989. Another 20 aircraft are on option. The MD-81/82s are configured for either 150 single-class passengers or for 143 (8/135) in dual layout. The DC-9-30s are used on short-to-medium routes, while the MD-80s fly longer semi-transcontinental routes across the United States.

## VIASA

VIASA-Venezolana Internacional de Aviacion, Venezuela's international flag carrier, utilised two MD-82s for a short time in 1983/84 on its network to Central and South America and the Caribbean. The two aircraft were delivered on 7 January 1983, but severe financial difficulties caused the cancellation of many services and a reduction in the fleet, which resulted in the disposal of both MD-82s to Jet America Airlines on 30 May 1984. From time to time, VIASA has also used LAV DC-9-51s on some of its services.

## Viva Air

Viva Air, a joint venture charter airline formed by Iberia and Lufthansa, has been operating three Iberia DC-9-32s since January 1990. They are used exclusively on Iberia's behalf, operating a number of scheduled domestic services.

## West Coast Airlines — see Air West

## ZAS Airline of Egypt

ZAS Airline of Egypt was established in June 1982 and obtained a passenger licence in September 1987. An MD-82 was acquired on lease from McDonnell Douglas in March 1988, supplemented by a 115-seat DC-9-33CF, also obtained on lease. The current fleet comprises two MD-83s, fitted out for 167 passengers in a single-class layout, and these are utilised on the airline's scheduled Cairo-Amsterdam route and on its domestic network linking Cairo with Aswan, Luxor, Abu Simbel and Hurghada. The MD-83s are also employed on IT charter work.

*Below:*
**VIASA, Venezuela's international flag carrier, operated two MD-82s for a short time in 1983/84.**

# 5 Into the 1990s - the MD-90

Conceptual thoughts to further develop its highly successful twin-jet airliner to serve the future 100-180 passenger market over short-to-medium distances, have occupied McDonnell Douglas since the mid-1980s. Engineering and design activities of what was then tentatively referred to as the MD-X, were initiated in 1985, built firmly around the new concept of Ultra-High-Bypass (UHB) engines driving highly-contoured, counter-rotating, multi-blade fans. Developing the UHB engine, also referred to as Unducted Fan (UDF), to form the basis of a new range of derivatives was undertaken in co-operation with Aeritalia, Saab-Scania and SAIC. These projects crystallised into two new versions, the 114-seat MD-91X and the 165-seat MD-92X, which were being offered to potential customer airlines from early 1988. At that time, a technical demonstrator had already been in flight testing from Edwards AFB since 18 May 1987, using the General Electric GE36 UHB engine mounted on the port side of an MD-80. Initially, the General Electric engine was tested with two 8-blade fans of 12ft (3.66m) diameter. Flight trials with an improved engine with a 10-blade fan in front and an 8-blade fan at the rear, were begun on 15 August. Studies indicated that the UHB could burn up to 35% less fuel than an advanced turbofan, and as much as 50% less than current engines. Tests with a PW-Allison 578-DX powerplant commenced in March 1989.

The company also projected an all-new propfan follow-on to the MD-80, dubbed the MD-94X. In addition to the UHB engines, this 160-180 passenger airliner featured laminar and turbulent boundary layer control, very high aspect ratio super-critical wings, flight-critical active stability augmentation, digital control systems, fly-by-wire and fly-by-light technologies and all-electric secondary power systems. An UHB retrofit

*Right:*
**MD-90-30 configuration features.**

*Below right:*
**MD-90 flight arrangement study.**

*Below:*
**A modified MD-80 commercial transport equipped with a PW-Allison 578-DX propfan ultra high-bypass (UHB) engine undertook 50 hours of airborne testing.**

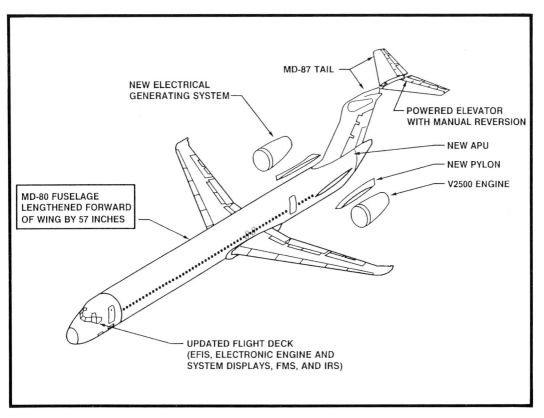

NEW ELECTRICAL
GENERATING SYSTEM

MD-87 TAIL

POWERED ELEVATOR
WITH MANUAL REVERSION

NEW APU

NEW PYLON

V2500 ENGINE

MD-80 FUSELAGE
LENGTHENED FORWARD
OF WING BY 57 INCHES

UPDATED FLIGHT DECK
(EFIS, ELECTRONIC ENGINE AND
SYSTEM DISPLAYS, FMS, AND IRS)

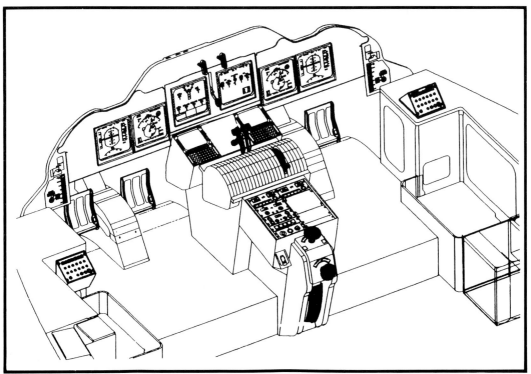

programme for the MD-80 was also actively persued, said to achieve an up to 40% reduction in fuel consumption.

At around the same time, McDonnell Douglas also presented to the airlines as an alternative the MD-90V Series, powered by IAE V2500 advanced high-bypass engines. The series comprised the similar-sized MD-91V with accommodation for 114 passengers, and the 165-seat MD-92V. A still larger third variant was added to the programme later in response to airline interest. This was the MD-93V with up to 180 seats in a two-class configuration. The design was being finely tuned towards optimum customer requirements, and it became clear that the immediate future lay with the V2500, which was a fully developed and certified engine and provided earlier availability for commercial service, a considerable advantage in a highly competitive business. The radical and operationally unproven concept of the propfan came too soon for airlines to take on board.

On 14 November 1989, after four years of stop-go and a number of transformations in size, performance and powerplant, McDonnell Douglas finally announced the programme launch of a new family of twin-jet aircraft for the 1990s and beyond. Known as the MD-90 family, it is planned as a series of three sizes of transports, each powered by the International Aero Engines V2500 powerplant, said to be the quietest and most fuel-efficient in its class. An advanced high-lift wing and electronic flight instrumentation (EFIS) display system in the cockpit, are other standard MD-90 features. All MD-90s will also have the new windshear detection system approved this year by the FAA, as well as TCAS, a traffic and collision avoidance system. Cross-section will be identical to the MD-80 Series, similarly providing five-abreast, single-aisle accommodation. Range is

2,400 miles (3,870km). The three models are to be the MD-90-30 with a 153-passenger mixed-class capacity, a larger MD-90-40 with about 180 seats, and an MD-90-10 with mixed-class seating for 114 passengers. The -20 designation is being kept in reserve for possible re-engined versions of in-service MD-80s. The MD-90-10, optimised for 'hot and high' operations over longer ranges, has the same fuselage as the MD-87, whilst the -30 is similar to the MD-81/82/83 with the fuselage lengthened forward of the wing by 57in (1.448m). The MD-90-40 has two plugs inserted, one of 190in (4.826m) forward and 95in (2.413m) aft, giving an overall length of 154ft 2in (46.99m).

At the time of the go-ahead, the manufacturer announced an order and options from Delta Air Lines for 26 and 134 MD-90s respectively. Since then and within quick succession, other orders and commitments followed from Alaska Airlines for 20 firm and 20 optional MD-90s, with deliveries scheduled to begin in December 1994, and from Japan Air System for 10 firm and 10 options. On 30 January 1990, International Lease Finance Corporation (ILFC), became the fourth customer to order the new aircraft, placing 15 firm orders and 15 options. ILFC, a Beverly Hills-based leasing organisation, is scheduled to receive its first aircraft in January 1995. In addition, there are what the manufacturer quaintly refers to as 'unannouncable' firm orders and options, bringing the total order book to more than 250.

The programmed schedule for the MD-90-30 calls for the development of a prototype. With a first flight projected for the end of 1992. Series production will start in Spring 1994, followed by certification and deliveries to airlines in the fourth quarter of that year. The MD-90-10 will be developed in concert with the MD-90-30, with the -40 expected to make its debut late in 1994 with entry into service by the end of 1995.

Discussions are in progress with European airlines to expand the MD-90 family to satisfy the unique needs of the European community and this will include specific designs in the areas of avionics, performance, passenger comfort, a new technology flight deck, and still lower levels of noise and emissions. Flight deck studies incorporated a six-across electronic display, ARINC 700 avionics, IRS (Inertial Reference System), advanced FMS (Flight Management System), centralised fault display, Category IIIB operation, modularised overhead, improved visibility windscreen and ergonomic improvements. Other potential MD-90 enhancements would be increases in operating weights, aerodynamic improvements to the wing (trailing-edge extension), and automatic cargo handling. The MD-90EC (European Community)

versions are projected with higher thrust engines of up to 28,000lb (124.6kN) in the V2500-D5. The range would also be increased by up to an additional 680 miles (1,100km).

The world demand for the MD-90s is anticipated at more than 800 units, beginning in 1994 and extending well beyond the year 2000. Both MD-80 and MD-90 single-aisle transports will be built simultaneously at the McDonnell Douglas production facility at Long Beach. The introduction and extensive use of interchangeable, standardised modules has been designed to enhance production commonality, and will allow the rapid and cost-effective incorporation of new technological advances. It is also sure to trim lead-in times to full production of the new airliner. This will also bring additional benefits to the airlines who, apart from enjoying a degree of commonality between their existing MD-80s and the MD-90, should be able to acquire these new-generation twin-jets on much more favourable terms than an all-new airliner.

## Douglas ponders improved MD-80

In order to provide a smoother transition to the new MD-90, Douglas is considering an improved version, merging some of the best elements of the MD-90 design with a new engine for the existing MD-80 airframe. In addition to the engine, which so far exists only on paper, the MD-80 Advanced would offer a new flight deck instrumentation package and new passenger compartment design. All would be available as retrofit for existing MD-80s and could be in service by July 1993, whereas the MD-90 will not be delivered to launch customers until late 1994. Development of the MD-80 Advanced depends on whether Pratt & Whitney will launch the JT8D-290, an improved version of the JT8D-217C, with lower noise signature and a targeted 25% reduction in noxious emissions.

The MD-80 Advanced would incorporate the advanced flight deck from the MD-88, including a choice of reference systems, with an inertial reference system as standard and attitude/heading optional. It would also be equipped with an electronic flight instrument system, an optional second flight management system computer, light-emitting diode dot matrix electronic engine and systems displays, a Honeywell windshear computer, and provision for an optional traffic-alert and collision avoidance system. The new interior would have a 12% increase in overhead baggage space and stowage compartment lights that come on when the door opens, as well as a new video system featuring drop-down 5in liquid crystal display (LCD) monitors above every other seat row.

## 1 TYPICAL DC-9 SERIES SPECIFICATIONS

|  | DC-9-14 | DC-9-15F | DC-9-21 | DC-9-31 | DC9-33F | DC-9-41 | DC9-51 |
|---|---|---|---|---|---|---|---|
| Wing Span ft (m) | 89 ft 5 in (27.25) | 89 ft 5 in (27.25) | 93 ft 5 in (28.47) | 93 ft 5 in (28.47) | 93 ft 5 in (28.47) | 93 ft 5 in (28.47) | 93 ft 5 in (28.47) |
| O/A Length ft (m) | 104 ft 5 in (31.82) | 104 ft 5 in (31.82) | 104 ft 5 in (31.82) | 119 ft 5 in (36.39) | 119 ft 5 in (36.39) | 125 ft 7 in (38.27) | 133 ft 7 in (40.71) |
| O/A Height ft (m) | 27 ft 6 in (8.38) | 27 ft 6 in (8.38) | 27 ft 6 in (8.38) | 27 ft 6 in (8.38) | 27 ft 6 in (8.38) | 28 ft 1 in (8.56) | 28 ft 1 in (8.56) |
| Wing Area sq ft (sq m) | 934.3 (86.6) | 934.3 (86.8) | 1,000.7 (92.97) | 1,000.7 (92.97) | 1,000.7 (92.97) | 1,000.7 (92.97) | 1,000.7 (92.97) |
| Powerplant thrust lb (kN) ea | 2x P&W JT8D-1 | -1 or -7 | -9 | -1 or -7 | -11 | -11 or -15 | -17 |
|  | 14,000 (62.28) | 14.000 (62.28) | 14,500 (64.50) | 14,000 (62.28) | 15.000 (66.73) | 15,000 (66.73) 15,500 (68.95) | 16,000 (71.17) |
| Maximum Accommodation | 90 | – | 90 | 115 | – | 125 | 139 |
| Cargo Capacity in hold cu ft (cu m) | 607 (17.2) | 2,762 (78.2) | 607 (17.2) | 895 (25.3) | 4,195 (119) | 1,021 (28.9) | 1,034 (29.3) |
| Operating WT. empty lb (kg) | 49,162 (22,300) | 53,200 (24,131) | 52,640 (23,877) | 56,855 (25,789) | 56,430 (25,596) | 59,130 (26,821) | 65,000 (29,484) |
| Maximum gross take-off weight lb (kg) | 90,700 (41,141) | 90,700 (41,141) | 100,000 (45,359) | 108,000 (48,988) | 114,000 (51,710) | 114,000 (51,710) | 121,000 (54,885) |
| Maximum structural payload lb (kg) | 24,838 (11,266) | 20,800 (9,435) | 25,360 (11,505) | 30,145 (13,674) | 13,530 (6,137) | 36,360 (16,495) | 33,825 (15,343) |
| Maximum payload range miles (km) | 995 (1,600) | 995 (1,600) | 1,150 (1,850) | 1,778 (2,863) | 1,778 (2,863) | 670 (1,080) | 805 (1,295) |
| Take-off field length at sea level ft (m) | 5,300 (1,615) | 5,300 (1,615) | 5,500 (1,675) | 5,500 (1,675) | 6,860 (2,091) | 6,860 (2,091) | 8,200 (2,500) |
| Max. Cruise speed mph (km/h) | 563 (907) | 563 (907) | 563 (907) | 563 (907) | 563 (907) | 563 (907) | 563 (907) |

*Below:*
**The first four DC-9s in the air at the same time.** *Douglas*

# DC-9-15 GENERAL DIMENSIONS

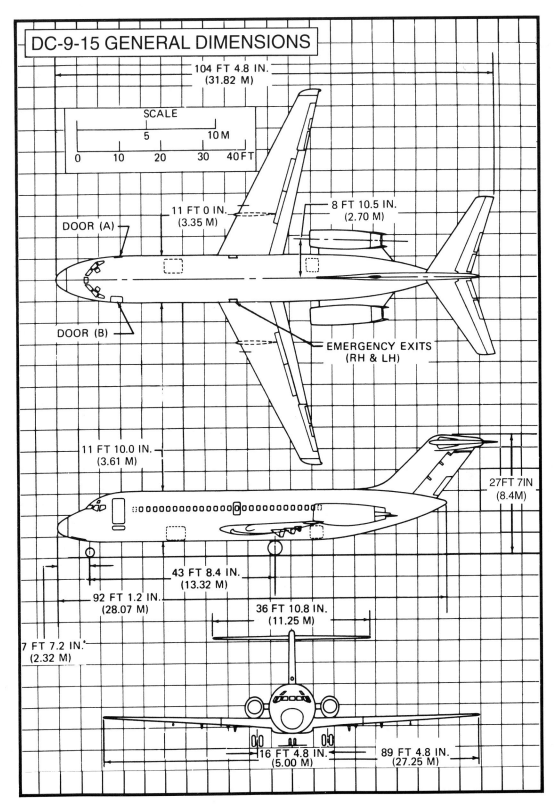

104 FT 4.8 IN.
(31.82 M)

SCALE

5          10 M

0   10   20   30   40 FT

11 FT 0 IN.
(3.35 M)

8 FT 10.5 IN.
(2.70 M)

DOOR (A)

DOOR (B)

EMERGENCY EXITS
(RH & LH)

11 FT 10.0 IN.
(3.61 M)

27FT 7IN
(8.4M)

43 FT 8.4 IN.
(13.32 M)

92 FT 1.2 IN.
(28.07 M)

36 FT 10.8 IN.
(11.25 M)

7 FT 7.2 IN.
(2.32 M)

16 FT 4.8 IN.
(5.00 M)

89 FT 4.8 IN.
(27.25 M)

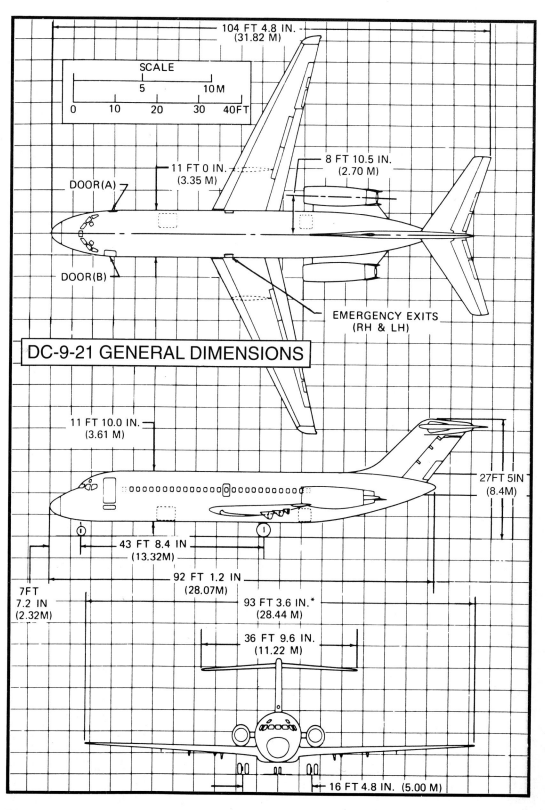

DC-9-21 GENERAL DIMENSIONS

104 FT 4.8 IN. (31.82 M)

SCALE

5    10M
0   10   20   30   40FT

11 FT 0 IN. (3.35 M)

DOOR(A)

DOOR(B)

8 FT 10.5 IN. (2.70 M)

EMERGENCY EXITS (RH & LH)

11 FT 10.0 IN. (3.61 M)

27FT 5IN (8.4M)

43 FT 8.4 IN (13.32M)

92 FT 1.2 IN (28.07M)

7FT 7.2 IN (2.32M)

93 FT 3.6 IN.* (28.44 M)

36 FT 9.6 IN. (11.22 M)

16 FT 4.8 IN. (5.00 M)

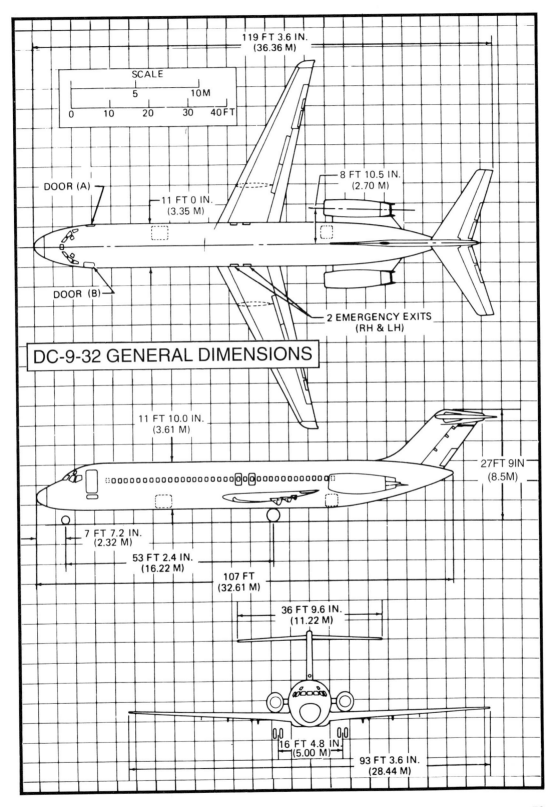

119 FT 3.6 IN.
(36.36 M)

SCALE
5        10 M
0    10    20    30    40 FT

DOOR (A)

11 FT 0 IN.
(3.35 M)

8 FT 10.5 IN.
(2.70 M)

DOOR (B)

2 EMERGENCY EXITS
(RH & LH)

DC-9-32 GENERAL DIMENSIONS

11 FT 10.0 IN.
(3.61 M)

27 FT 9 IN
(8.5 M)

7 FT 7.2 IN.
(2.32 M)

53 FT 2.4 IN.
(16.22 M)

107 FT
(32.61 M)

36 FT 9.6 IN.
(11.22 M)

16 FT 4.8 IN.
(5.00 M)

93 FT 3.6 IN.
(28.44 M)

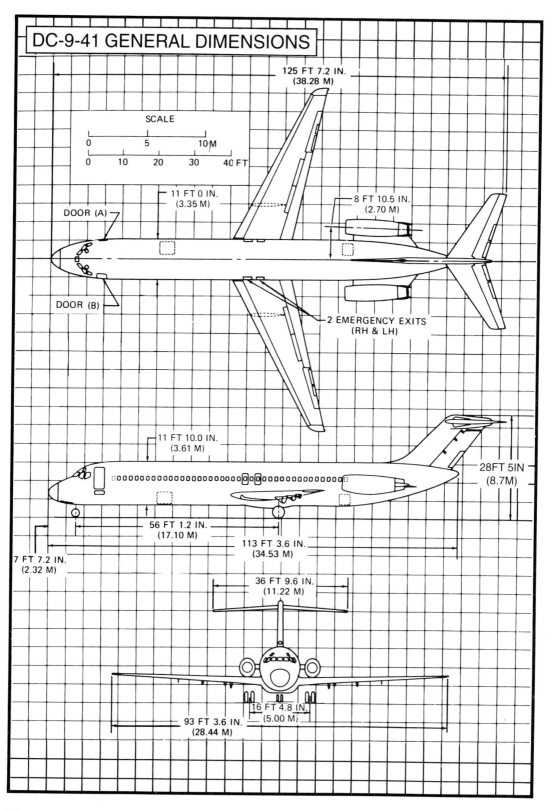

# DC-9-41 GENERAL DIMENSIONS

SCALE

| 0 | 5 | 10 M |
| 0 | 10 | 20 | 30 | 40 FT |

125 FT 7.2 IN.
(38.28 M)

11 FT 0 IN.
(3.35 M)

8 FT 10.5 IN.
(2.70 M)

DOOR (A)

DOOR (B)

2 EMERGENCY EXITS
(RH & LH)

11 FT 10.0 IN.
(3.61 M)

28FT 5IN
(8.7M)

56 FT 1.2 IN.
(17.10 M)

113 FT 3.6 IN.
(34.53 M)

7 FT 7.2 IN.
(2.32 M)

36 FT 9.6 IN.
(11.22 M)

16 FT 4.8 IN.
(5.00 M)

93 FT 3.6 IN.
(28.44 M)

74

# DC-9-51 GENERAL DIMENSIONS

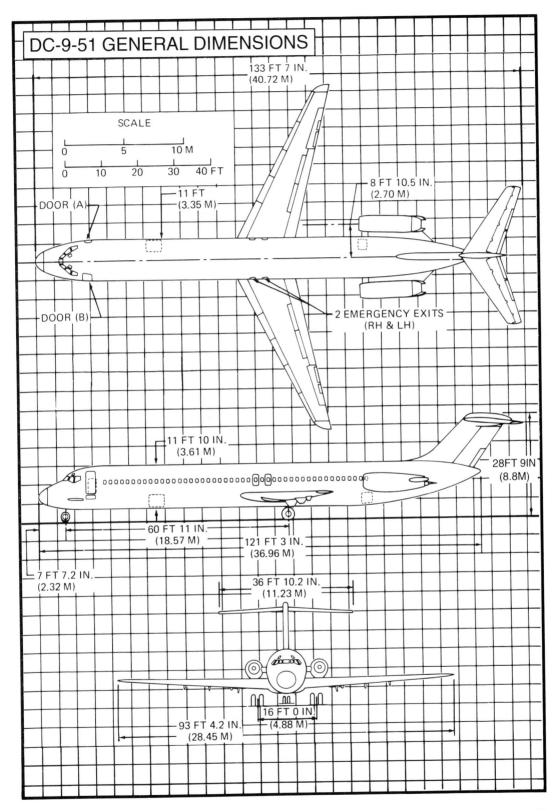

133 FT 7 IN.
(40.72 M)

SCALE

| 0 | 5 | 10 M |

| 0 | 10 | 20 | 30 | 40 FT |

8 FT 10.5 IN.
(2.70 M)

11 FT
(3.35 M)

DOOR (A)

DOOR (B)

2 EMERGENCY EXITS
(RH & LH)

11 FT 10 IN.
(3.61 M)

28FT 9IN
(8.8M)

60 FT 11 IN.
(18.57 M)

121 FT 3 IN.
(36.96 M)

7 FT 7.2 IN.
(2.32 M)

36 FT 10.2 IN.
(11.23 M)

16 FT 0 IN.
(4.88 M)

93 FT 4.2 IN.
(28.45 M)

## 2  TYPICAL MD-80 SERIES SPECIFICATIONS

|  | MD-81 | MD-82 | MD-83 | MD-87 | MD-88 |
|---|---|---|---|---|---|
| Wing Span ft m) | 107 ft 10 (32.87) | 107 ft 10 in (32.87) | 107 ft 10 in (32.81) | 107 ft 10 in (32.81) | 107 ft 10 in (32.81) |
| O/A Length ft (m) | 147 ft 11 in (45.08) | 147 ft 11 in (45.08) | 147 ft 11 in (45.08) | 130 ft 6 in (39.75) | 147 ft 7 in (45.08) |
| O/A Height ft (m) | 29 ft 7 in (9.02) | 29 ft 7 in (9.02) | 29 ft 7 in (9.02) | 30 ft 6 in (9.30) | 29 ft 7 in (9.02) |
| Wing area sq ft (sq m) | 1,209 (112.3) | 1,209 (112.3) | 1,209 (112.3) | 1,209 (112.3) | 1,209 (112.3) |
| Powerplant thrust lb (kN) ea | 2x P&W JT8D-209 | -217A/B | -219 | -217A/B | -219 |
|  | 18,500 (82.30) | 20,000 (88.97) | 21,000 (93.42) | 20,000 (88.97) | 21,000 (93.42) |
| Maximum accomodation | 172 | 172 | 172 | 139 | 172 |
| Cargo capacity in hold cu ft (cu m) | 1,243 (35.2) | 1,243 (35.2) | 1,243 (35.2) | 938 (26.6) | 1,243 (35.2) |
| Operating WT. empty lb (kg) | 78,420 (35,570) | 78,545 (35,630) | 80,230 (36,620) | 73,157 (33,253) | 80,563 (36,543) |
| Maximum gross take-off weight lb (kg) | 140,000 (63,500) | 149,50 (67,812) | 160.000 (72,580) | 140,000 (63,500) | 160,000 (72,580) |
| Maximum payload lb (kg) | 39,580 (17,953) | 41,451 (18,802) | 41,273 (18,721) | 38,843 (17,619) | 43,451 (19,709) |
| Maximum payload range miles (km) | 1,590 (2,565) | 2,140 (3,445) | 2,725 (4,387) | 2,140 (3,445) |  |
| Take-off field length at sea level ft (m) | 7,200 (2,195) | 7,460 (2,274) | 8,370 (2,551) | 6,120 (1,865) | 8,375 (2,553) |
| Max. cruise speed mph (km/h) | 575 (925) | 575 (925) | 575 (925) | 575 (925) | 575 (925) |

*Below:*
**Airtours International has acquired five MD-83s for holiday flights from the UK.**

*Right:*
**One of the first of American Airlines huge fleet of MD-80s pictured prior to delivery.** *McDonnell Douglas*

# MD-81, MD-82, MD-83, MD-88 GENERAL DIMENSIONS

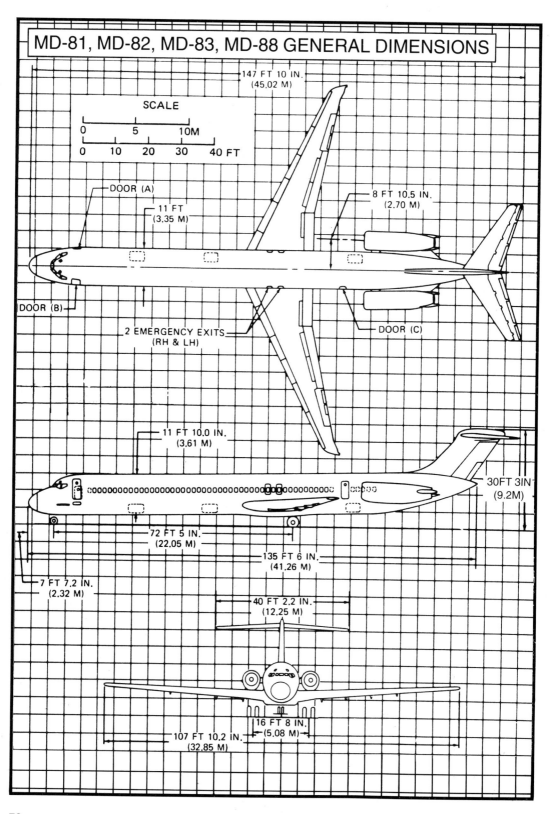

147 FT 10 IN.
(45.02 M)

SCALE

0    5    10M

0   10   20   30   40 FT

DOOR (A)

11 FT
(3.35 M)

8 FT 10.5 IN.
(2.70 M)

DOOR (B)

2 EMERGENCY EXITS
(RH & LH)

DOOR (C)

11 FT 10.0 IN.
(3.61 M)

30FT 3IN.
(9.2M)

72 FT 5 IN.
(22.05 M)

135 FT 6 IN.
(41.26 M)

7 FT 7.2 IN.
(2.32 M)

40 FT 2.2 IN.
(12.25 M)

16 FT 8 IN.
(5.08 M)

107 FT 10.2 IN.
(32.85 M)

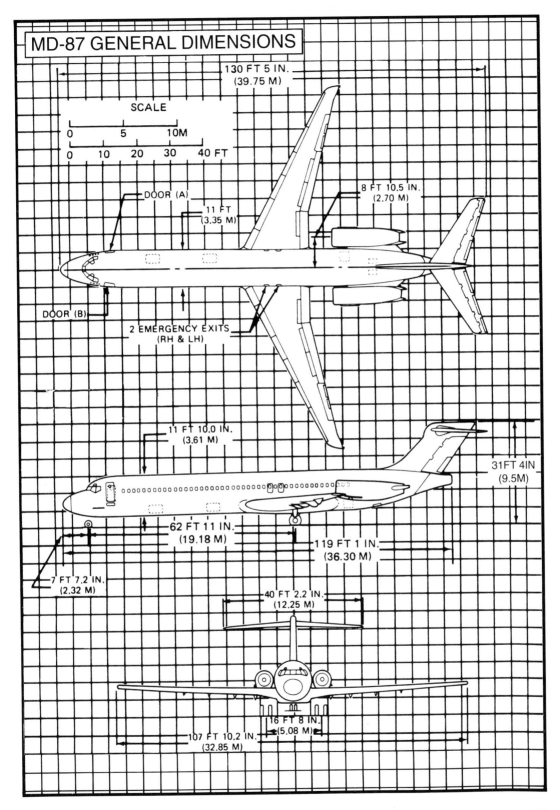

MD-87 GENERAL DIMENSIONS

130 FT 5 IN.
(39.75 M)

SCALE

| 0 | 5 | 10M |
| 0 | 10 | 20 | 30 | 40 FT |

DOOR (A)

11 FT
(3.35 M)

8 FT 10.5 IN.
(2.70 M)

DOOR (B)

2 EMERGENCY EXITS
(RH & LH)

11 FT 10.0 IN.
(3.61 M)

31FT 4IN
(9.5M)

62 FT 11 IN.
(19.18 M)

119 FT 1 IN.
(36.30 M)

7 FT 7.2 IN.
(2.32 M)

40 FT 2.2 IN.
(12.25 M)

16 FT 8 IN.
(5.08 M)

107 FT 10.2 IN.
(32.85 M)

# 3 TYPICAL MD-90 SERIES SPECIFICATIONS

| | MD-90-10 | MD-90-10EC | MD-90-30 | MD-90-30EC | MD-90-40 | MD-90-40EC |
|---|---|---|---|---|---|---|
| Wing Span ft (m) | 107 ft (32.87) | 107 ft (32.87) | 107 ft (32.87) | 107 ft (32.87) | 107 ft 10 in (32.87) | 107 ft 10 in (32.87) |
| Length ft (m) | 130 ft 5 in (39.75) | 130 ft 5 in (39.75) | 152 ft 8 in (46.53) | 152 ft 8 in (46.53) | 171 ft 8 in (52.32) | 171 ft 8 in (52.32) |
| Powerplant | 2xIAE V2500-D2 | -D2 | -D1 | -D1 | -D5 | -D5 |
| Thrust lb (Kn) | 22,000 (97.86) | 22,000 (97.86) | 25,000 (111.2) | 25,000 (111.2) | 28,000 (124.6) | 28,000 (124.6) |
| | | -D1 25,000 (111.2) | | -D5 28,000 (124.6) | | |
| Typical Mixed Accommodation | 114 | | 153 | 153 | 180 | 180 |
| Cargo capacity in hold sg ft (sq m) | 938 (26.6) | 938 (26.6) | 1,343 (38.0) | 1,343 (38.0) | 1,609 (45.6) | 1,609 (45.6) |
| Operating WT. empty lb (kg) | 81,536 (36,984) | 84,600 (38,386) | 86,882 (39,409) | 94,100 (42,700) | 95,069 (43,123) | 100,000 (45,377) |
| Max. Gross to weight lb (kg) | 139,000 (63,050) | 154,000 (69,880) | 156,000 (70,760) | 172,500 (78,275) | 163,500 (74,164) | 172,500 (78,275) |
| Range miles (km) | 2,750 (4,425) | 3,450 (5,555) | 2,750 (4,425) | 3,220 (5,185) | 1,990 (3,200) | 2,200 (3,540) |
| Take-off field length sea level ft (m) | 6,300 (1,921) | 8,800 (2,683) 6,600 (2,012) | 7,150 (2,012) | 9,700 (2,189) 8,000 (2,439) | 7,200 (2,957) | 8,000 (2,439) |
| Cruise speed mach | 0.76 | 0.76 | 0.76 | 0.76 | 0.76 | 0.76 |
| Cruising altitude ft (m) | 33,700 (10,272) | 33,200 (10,119) | 31,750 (9,677) | 31,000 (9,449) | 30,660 (9,345) | 31,000 (9,449) |

*Below:*
**Twin-jet family modules.**

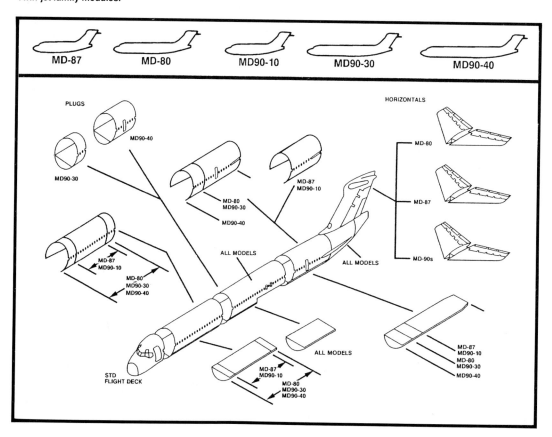

| Fuselage Number | Serial Number | Model | Registration | Operator | Delivery Date |
|---|---|---|---|---|---|
| | | | N9DC | Douglas Aircraft Co | FF25/02/65 |
| 1 | 45695 | -14 | N1301T | Trans-Texas Airways | 30/09/66 |
| 2 | 45696 | -14 | N3301L | Delta Air Lines | 19/07/66 |
| 3 | 45697 | -14 | N3302L | Delta Air Lines | 09/06/66 |
| 4 | 45711 | -14 | CF-TLB | Air Canada | 12/04/66 |
| 5 | 45698 | -14 | N3303L | Delta Air Lines | 04/12/66 |
| 6 | 45712 | -14 | CF-TLC | Air Canada | 06/01/66 |
| 7 | 45714 | -14 | N1051T | TWA Trans World Airlines | 25/03/66 |
| 8 | 45699 | -14 | N3304L | Delta Air Lines | 18/09/65 |
| 9 | 45713 | -14 | CF-TLD | Air Canada | 09/02/66 |
| 10 | 45715 | -14 | N1052T | TWA | 05/02/66 |
| 11 | 45700 | -14 | N3305L | Delta Air Lines | 26/11/65 |
| 12 | 45701 | -14 | N3306L | Delta Air Lines | 30/11/65 |
| 13 | 45716 | -14 | N1053T | TWA | 19/02/66 |
| 14 | 45728 | -11 | N945L | Bonanza Air Lines | 19/12/65 |
| 15 | 45702 | -14 | N3307L | Delta Air Lines | 11/01/66 |
| 16 | 45729 | -11 | N946L | Bonanza Air Lines | 17/01/66 |
| 17 | 45718 | -15 | PH-DNA | KLM Royal Dutch Airlines | 25/03/66 |
| 18 | 45719 | -15 | PH-DNB | KLM | 03/04/66 |
| 19 | 45725 | -14 | CF-TLE | Air Canada | 24/02/66 |
| 20 | 45717 | -15 | N901H | Hawaiian Airlines | 12/03/66 |
| 21 | 45703 | -14 | N3308L | Delta Air Lines | 16/03/66 |
| 22 | 45724 | -15 | N902H | Hawaiian Airlines | 29/03/66 |
| 23 | 45842 | -14 | N8961 | Continental Airlines | 04/03/66 |
| 24 | 45704 | -14 | N3309L | Delta Air Lines | 28/04/66 |
| 25 | 45735 | -14 | N1054T | TWA | 21/04/66 |
| 26 | 45742 | -14 | N8901E | Eastern Air Lines | 26/04/66 |
| 27 | 45720 | -15 | PH-DNC | KLM | 02/05/66 |
| 28 | 45843 | -14 | N8962 | Continental Airlines | 01/05/66 |
| 29 | 45743 | -14 | N8902E | Eastern Air Lines | 13/05/66 |
| 30 | 45772 | -15 | N970Z | Ozark Air Lines | 25/05/66 |
| 31 | 45744 | -14 | N8903E | Eastern Air Lines | 19/05/66 |
| 32 | 45745 | -14 | N8904E | Eastern Air Lines | 31/05/66 |
| 33 | 45844 | -14 | N8963 | Continental Airlines | 02/06/66 |
| 34 | 45731 | -15 | HB-IFA | Swissair | 20/07/66 |
| 35 | 47048 | -15 | N8964 | Continental Airlines | 03/07/66 |
| 36 | 45726 | -15 | CF-TLF | Air Canada | 24/06/66 |
| 37 | 45730 | -14 | N947L | Bonanza Air Lines | 01/07/66 |
| 38 | 45746 | -14 | N8905E | Eastern Air Lines | 01/07/66 |
| 39 | 45773 | -15 | N971Z | Ozark Air Lines | 10/07/66 |
| 40 | 45747 | -14 | N8906E | Eastern Air Lines | 19/07/66 |
| 41 | 45732 | -15 | HB-IFB | Swissair | 01/08/66 |
| 42 | 47049 | -14 | N6140A | Allegheny Airlines | 29/07/66 |
| 43 | 45727 | -14 | CF-TLG | Air Canada | 31/07/66 |
| 44 | 45721 | -15 | PH-DND | KLM | 17/08/66 |
| 45 | 45736 | -14 | N1055T | TWA | 26/08/66 |
| 46 | 45841 | -15 | N972Z | Ozark Air Lines | 24/08/66 |
| 47 | 45748 | -14 | N8907E | Eastern Air Lines | 29/08/66 |
| 48 | 45733 | -31 | N8916E | Eastern Air Lines | 20/10/67 |
| 49 | 45737 | -15 | N1056T | TWA | 12/09/66 |
| 50 | 45749 | -14 | N8908E | Eastern Air Lines | 11/09/66 |
| 51 | 45797 | -15 | N8953U | Northeast Airlines | 29/12/66 |
| 52 | 45794 | -14 | N9101 | West Coast Airlines | 16/09/66 |
| 53 | 45705 | -14 | N3310L | Delta Air Lines | 24/09/66 |
| 54 | 45738 | -15 | N1057T | TWA | 11/10/66 |
| 55 | 45722 | -15 | PH-DNE | KLM | 10/10/66 |
| 56 | 45739 | -15 | N1058T | TWA | 28/10/66 |
| 57 | 45770 | -14 | N8909E | Eastern Air Lines | 07/11/66 |
| 58 | 45771 | -14 | N8910E | Eastern Air Lines | 27/10/66 |
| 59 | 45798 | -15 | N490SA | Standard Airways | 03/11/66 |
| 60 | 45734 | -31 | N8917E | Eastern Air Lines | 27/03/67 |
| 61 | 45706 | -14 | N3311L | Delta Air Lines | 27/10/66 |
| 62 | 45740 | -15 | N1059T | TWA | 16/11/66 |
| 63 | 45723 | -15 | PH-DNF | KLM | 16/11/66 |
| 64 | 45785 | -15 | HB-IFC | Swissair | 30/11/66 |
| 65 | 45795 | -14 | N9102 | West Coast Airlines | 04/11/66 |
| 66 | 45741 | -15 | N1060T | TWA | 29/11/66 |
| 67 | 45825 | -14 | N8911E | Eastern Air Lines | 24/11/66 |
| 68 | 45829 | -14 | N8912E | Eastern Air Lines | 30/11/66 |
| 69 | 45799 | -15 | N491SA | Standard Airways | 30/11/66 |
| 70 | 45707 | -14 | N3312L | Delta Air Lines | 23/11/66 |
| 71 | 45775 | -15 | N1061T | TWA | 20/12/66 |
| 72 | 45776 | -15 | N1062T | TWA | 22/12/66 |
| 73 | 45833 | -31 | N8918E | Eastern Air Lines | 27/01/67 |
| 74 | 45796 | -14 | N9103 | West Coast Airlines | 15/12/66 |
| 75 | 45830 | -14 | N8913E | Eastern Air Lines | 23/12/66 |
| 76 | 45831 | -14 | N8914E | Eastern Air Lines | 29/12/66 |
| 77 | 45708 | -14 | N3313L | Delta Air Lines | 30/12/66 |
| 78 | 45709 | -14 | N3314L | Delta Air Lines | 06/01/67 |
| 79 | 45826 | -15RC | N8901 | Continental Airlines | 07/03/67 |
| 80 | 45777 | -15 | N1063T | TWA | 19/01/67 |
| 81 | 47004 | -31 | VH-CZB | Ansett - ANA | 11/04/67 |
| 82 | 45778 | -15 | N1064T | TWA | 02/02/67 |
| 83 | 47000 | -15 | HZ-AEA | Saudia - Saudi Arabian Airlines | 08/02/67 |
| 84 | 45832 | -14 | N8915E | Eastern Air Lines | 08/02/67 |
| 85 | 45834 | -31 | N8919E | Eastern Air Lines | 22/02/67 |
| 86 | 47003 | -31 | VH-CZA | Ansett - ANA | 17/03/67 |
| 87 | 47007 | -31 | VH-TJJ | TAA - Trans Australia Airlines | 18/03/67 |
| 88 | 47043 | -14 | N1302T | Trans-Texas Airways | 02/02/67 |
| 89 | 47056 | -14 | YV-C-AVM | Avensa-Aerovias Venezolanas | 28/02/67 |
| 90 | 45786 | -15 | HB-IFD | Swissair | 11/03/67 |
| 91 | 45845 | -32 | CF-TLH | Air Canada | 07/03/67 |
| 92 | 45779 | -15 | N1065T | TWA | 13/03/67 |
| 93 | 45780 | -15 | N1066T | TWA | 31/03/67 |
| 94 | 47001 | -15 | HZ-AEB | Saudia | 30/03/67 |
| 95 | 45835 | -31 | N8920E | Eastern Air Lines | 29/03/67 |
| 96 | 45836 | -31 | N8921E | Eastern Air Lines | 22/03/67 |
| 97 | 47010 | -15RC | N8902 | Continental Airlines | 11/04/67 |
| 98 | 47008 | -31 | VH-TJK | TAA | 14/04/67 |
| 99 | 47006 | -31 | N891PS | PSA - Pacific Southwest Airlines | 23/03/67 |
| 100 | 45710 | -32 | N3315L | Delta Air Lines | 09/04/67 |
| 101 | 45781 | -15 | N1067T | TWA | 11/04/67 |
| 102 | 47011 | -15RC | N8903 | Continental Airlines | 25/04/67 |
| 103 | 45837 | -31 | N8922E | Eastern Air Lines | 13/04/67 |
| 104 | 45838 | -31 | N8923E | Eastern Air Lines | 18/04/67 |
| 105 | 47002 | -15 | HZ-AEC | Saudia | 29/04/67 |
| 106 | 47025 | -32 | N3316L | Delta Air Lines | 02/05/67 |
| 107 | 47053 | -31 | N970NE | Northeast Airlines | 05/05/67 |
| 108 | 47098 | -31 | N938PR | Caribair - Caribbean Atlantic Airlines | 01/06/67 |
| 109 | 47060 | -14 | YV-C-AVR | Avensa | 10/05/67 |
| 110 | 47054 | -31 | N971NE | Northeast Airlines | 08/05/67 |
| 111 | 47063 | -15 | N91S | Southern Airways | 11/05/67 |
| 112 | 45846 | -32 | CF-TLI | Air Canada | 12/05/67 |
| 113 | 47019 | -32 | CF-TLJ | Air Canada | 21/05/67 |
| 114 | 45782 | -15 | N1068T | TWA | 30/05/67 |
| 115 | 47012 | -15RC | N8904 | Continental Airlines | 23/05/67 |
| 116 | 45839 | -31 | N8924E | Eastern Air Lines | 30/05/67 |
| 117 | 45840 | -31 | N8925E | Eastern Air Lines | 28/05/67 |
| 118 | 47050 | -31 | N970VJ | Allegheny Airlines | 02/06/67 |
| 119 | 47026 | -32 | N3317L | Delta Air Lines | 14/06/67 |
| 120 | 47064 | -15 | N92S | Southern Airways | 09/06/67 |
| 121 | 47037 | -32 | EC-BIG | Iberia | 30/06/67 |
| 122 | 47057 | -31 | N972NE | Northeast Airlines | 14/06/67 |
| 123 | 47058 | -31 | N973NE | Northeast Airlines | 16/06/67 |
| 124 | 45863 | -31 | N8926E | Eastern Air Lines | 21/06/67 |
| 125 | 47059 | -15 | XA-SOA | Aeronaves de Mexico | 29/05/67 |
| 126 | 47020 | -32 | CF-TLK | Air Canada | 30/05/67 |
| 127 | 45787 | -15 | HB-IFE | Swissair | 26/06/67 |
| 128 | 45783 | -15 | N1069T | TWA | 01/07/67 |
| 129 | 47013 | -15RC | N8905 | Continental Airlines | 26/06/67 |
| 130 | 45864 | -31 | N8927E | Eastern Air Lines | 01/07/67 |
| 131 | 47051 | -31 | N971VJ | Allegheny Airlines | 26/06/67 |
| 132 | 47027 | -32 | N3318L | Delta Air Lines | 10/07/67 |
| 133 | 47021 | -32 | CF-TLL | Air Canada | 07/07/67 |
| 134 | 47076 | -32 | EC-BIH | Iberia | 19/07/67 |
| 135 | 45827 | -32 | HL-7201 | Korean Air Lines | 19/07/67 |
| 136 | 47038 | -32 | I-DIKA | Alitalia | 08/08/67 |
| 137 | 45865 | -31 | N8928E | Eastern Air Lines | 27/07/67 |
| 138 | 45866 | -31 | N8929E | Eastern Air Lines | 29/07/67 |
| 139 | 47085 | -15 | XA-SOY | Aeronaves de Mexico | 19/07/67 |
| 140 | 45784 | -15 | N1070T | TWA | 19/08/67 |
| 141 | 47014 | -15RC | N8906 | Continental Airlines | 23/07/67 |
| 142 | 47052 | -31 | N972VJ | Allegheny Airlines | 28/07/67 |
| 143 | 47067 | -31 | N951N | North Central Airlines | 27/07/67 |
| 144 | 47022 | -32 | CF-TLM | Air Canada | 27/07/67 |
| 145 | 47028 | -32 | N3319L | Delta Air Lines | 02/08/67 |
| 146 | 47078 | -31 | N93S | Southern Airways | 28/07/67 |
| 147 | 47033 | -15 | N973Z | Ozark Air Lines | 31/07/67 |
| 148 | 47077 | -32 | EC-BII | Iberia | 14/08/67 |
| 149 | 47094 | -32 | HB-IFN | Swissair | 13/09/67 |

| Fuselage Number | Serial Number | Model | Registration | Operator | Delivery Date |
|---|---|---|---|---|---|
| 150 | 47066 | -31 | N974NE | Northeast Airlines | 14/08/67 |
| 151 | 47005 | -31 | VH-CZC | Ansett - ANA | 24/08/67 |
| 152 | 47009 | -31 | VH-TJL | TAA | 20/08/67 |
| 153 | 47100 | -15 | XA-SOC | Aeronaves de Mexico | 25/08/67 |
| 154 | 47039 | -32 | I-DIKE | Alitalia | 01/09/67 |
| 155 | 47081 | -14 | N9104 | West Coast Airlines | 23/08/67 |
| 156 | 47015 | -15RC | N8907 | Continental Airlines | 29/08/67 |
| 157 | 47029 | -32 | N3320L | Delta Air Lines | 01/09/67 |
| 158 | 47023 | -32 | CF-TLN | Air Canada | 30/08/67 |
| 159 | 47024 | -32 | CF-TLO | Air Canada | 31/08/67 |
| 160 | 47068 | -32 | CF-TLP | Air Canada | 31/08/67 |
| 161 | 47073 | -31 | N952N | North Central Airlines | 01/09/67 |
| 162 | 47034 | -15 | N974Z | Ozark Air Lines | 01/09/67 |
| 163 | 47079 | -32 | EC-BIJ | Iberia | 15/09/67 |
| 164 | 47080 | -32 | EC-BIK | Iberia | 14/09/67 |
| 165 | 47044 | -15MC | N1303T | Trans-Texas Airways | 28/09/67 |
| 166 | 47075 | -31 | N975NE | Northeast Airlines | 25/09/67 |
| 167 | 47110 | -32 | HB-IFO | Swissair | 08/10/67 |
| 168 | 47046 | -32 | I-DIKI | Alitalia | 25/09/67 |
| 169 | 47139 | -31 | N8930E | Eastern Air Lines | 04/10/67 |
| 170 | 47152 | -15RC | N8908 | Continental Airlines | 22/09/67 |
| 171 | 45788 | -32 | HB-IFF | Swissair | 21/10/67 |
| 172 | 47040 | -32CF | N931F | Overseas National Airways | 06/10/67 |
| 173 | 47016 | -15RC | N8909 | Continental Airlines | 04/10/67 |
| 174 | 47030 | -32 | N3321L | Delta Air Lines | 03/10/67 |
| 175 | 47069 | -32 | CF-TLQ | Air Canada | 30/09/67 |
| 176 | 47070 | -32 | CF-TLR | Air Canada | 30/09/67 |
| 177 | 47083 | -31 | N953N | North Central Airlines | 05/10/67 |
| 178 | 47035 | -15 | N975Z | Ozark Air Lines | 10/10/67 |
| 179 | 47084 | -32 | EC-BIL | Iberia | 11/10/67 |
| 180 | 47088 | -32 | EC-BIM | Iberia | 28/10/67 |
| 181 | 47082 | -31 | N976NE | Northeast Airlines | 19/10/67 |
| 182 | 47111 | -32 | HB-IFP | Swissair | 07/11/67 |
| 183 | 47047 | -32 | I-DIKO | Alitalia | 31/10/67 |
| 184 | 47045 | -15MC | N1304T | Trans-Texas Airways | 09/11/67 |
| 185 | 47153 | -15RC | N8910 | Continental Airlines | 18/10/67 |
| 186 | 47017 | -15RC | N8911 | Continental Airlines | 28/10/67 |
| 187 | 47031 | -32 | N3322L | Delta Air Lines | 01/11/67 |
| 188 | 47071 | -32 | CF-TLS | Air Canada | 02/11/67 |
| 189 | 47089 | -32 | EC-BIN | Iberia | 06/11/67 |
| 190 | 47090 | -32 | EC-BIO | Iberia | 07/11/67 |
| 191 | 47095 | -31 | N977NE | Northeast Airlines | 03/11/67 |
| 192 | 47096 | -31 | N978NE | Northeast Airlines | 04/11/67 |
| 193 | 47097 | -31 | N979NE | Northeast Airlines | 06/11/67 |
| 194 | 47055 | -15MC | N1305T | Trans-Texas Airways | 22/11/67 |
| 195 | 47101 | -32 | I-DIKU | Alitalia | 24/11/67 |
| 196 | 47118 | -32 | I-DIKB | Alitalia | 22/11/67 |
| 197 | 47099 | -31 | N973VJ | Allegheny Airlines | 14/11/67 |
| 198 | 47102 | -32 | PH-DNG | KLM | 21/11/67 |
| 199 | 47112 | -32 | HB-IFR | Swissair | 04/12/67 |
| 200 | 47041 | -32CF | N932F | Overseas National | 07/11/67 |
| 201 | 47154 | -15RC | N8912 | Continental Airlines | 28/11/67 |
| 202 | 47149 | -31 | N903H | Hawaiian Airlines | 22/11/67 |
| 203 | 47018 | -15RC | N8913 | Continental Airlines | 22/11/67 |
| 204 | 47032 | -32 | N3323L | Delta Air Lines | 01/12/67 |
| 205 | 47103 | -32 | N3324L | Delta Air Lines | 30/11/67 |
| 206 | 47091 | -32 | EC-BIP | Iberia | 05/12/67 |
| 207 | 47061 | -15MC | N1306T | Trans-Texas Airways | 22/12/67 |
| 208 | 47147 | -32CF | N933F | Overseas National | 14/12/67 |
| 209 | 47120 | -31 | N939PR | Caribair | 12/12/67 |
| 210 | 47128 | -32 | I-DIKC | Alitalia | 11/12/67 |
| 211 | 47130 | -31 | N974VJ | Allegheny Airlines | 08/12/67 |
| 212 | 47140 | -31 | N8931E | Eastern Air Lines | 07/12/67 |
| 213 | 47113 | -32 | HB-IFS | Swissair | 20/12/67 |
| 214 | 47131 | -32 | PH-DNH | KLM | 16/12/67 |
| 215 | 47134 | -31 | N980NE | Northeast Airlines | 15/12/67 |
| 216 | 47155 | -15RC | N8914 | Continental Airlines | 11/12/67 |
| 217 | 45789 | -32 | HB-IFG | Swissair | 23/12/67 |
| 218 | 47144 | -41 | SE-DBX | SAS - Scandinavian Airlines System | 23/05/68 |
| 219 | 47086 | -15RC | N8915 | Continental Airlines | 16/12/67 |
| 220 | 47104 | -32 | N3325L | Delta Air Lines | 19/12/67 |
| 221 | 47105 | -32 | N3326L | Delta Air Lines | 20/12/67 |
| 222 | 47092 | -32 | EC-BIQ | Iberia | 20/12/67 |
| 223 | 47062 | -15MC | N1307T | Texas International | 26/01/68 |
| 224 | 47122 | -15 | XA-SOD | Aeronaves de Mexico | 20/12/67 |
| 225 | 47129 | -32 | I-DIKD | Alitalia | 25/12/67 |
| 226 | 47146 | -31 | N975VJ | Allegheny Airlines | 28/12/67 |
| 227 | 47141 | -31 | N8932E | Eastern Air Lines | 23/12/67 |
| 228 | 47156 | -15RC | N8916 | Continental Airlines | 29/12/67 |
| 229 | 47132 | -32 | PH-DNI | KLM | 03/01/68 |

| Fuselage Number | Serial Number | Model | Registration | Operator | Delivery Date |
|---|---|---|---|---|---|
| 230 | 47133 | -32 | PH-DNK | KLM | 15/01/68 |
| 231 | 47159 | -31 | N954N | North Central Airlines | 02/01/68 |
| 232 | 47142 | -31 | N8933E | Eastern Air Lines | 30/12/67 |
| 233 | 47135 | -31 | N981NE | Northeast Airlines | 15/01/68 |
| 234 | 47087 | -15RC | N8917 | Continental Airlines | 09/01/68 |
| 235 | 47106 | -32 | N3327L | Delta Air Lines | 13/01/68 |
| 236 | 47107 | -32 | N3328L | Delta Air Lines | 12/01/68 |
| 237 | 47093 | -32 | EC-BIR | Iberia | 12/01/68 |
| 238 | 47143 | -31 | N8934E | Eastern Air Lines | 17/01/68 |
| 239 | 47144 | -31 | N8935E | Eastern Air Lines | 15/01/68 |
| 240 | 47190 | -32 | PH-DNL | KLM | 24/01/68 |
| 241 | 47160 | -31 | N955N | North Central Airlines | 16/01/68 |
| 242 | 45828 | -15RC | N8918 | Continental Airlines | 19/01/68 |
| 243 | 47136 | -31 | N982NE | Northeast Airlines | 24/01/68 |
| 244 | 47251 | -31 | N982PS | PSA | 24/01/68 |
| 245 | 47204 | -15 | N94S | Southern Airways | 09/02/68 |
| 246 | 47148 | -32CF | N934F | Overseas National | 25/01/68 |
| 247 | 41745 | -31 | N8936E | Eastern Air Lines | 30/01/68 |
| 248 | 47158 | -31 | N8937E | Eastern Air Lines | 31/01/68 |
| 249 | 47161 | -31 | N8938E | Eastern Air Lines | 02/02/68 |
| 250 | 47205 | -15 | N95S | Southern Airways | 09/02/68 |
| 251 | 47108 | -32 | N3329L | Delta Air Lines | 01/02/68 |
| 252 | 47109 | -32 | N3330L | Delta Air Lines | 06/02/68 |
| 253 | 47123 | -15 | XA-SOE | Aeronaves de Mexico | 10/02/68 |
| 254 | 47124 | -15 | XA-SOF | Aeronaves de Mexico | 08/02/68 |
| 255 | 47162 | -31 | N8939E | Eastern Air Lines | 17/02/68 |
| 256 | 47163 | -31 | N8940E | Eastern Air Lines | 15/02/68 |
| 257 | 47248 | -31 | N976Z | Ozark Air Lines | 26/02/68 |
| 258 | 47137 | -31 | N983NE | Northeast Airlines | 23/02/68 |
| 259 | 47164 | -31 | N8941E | Eastern Air Lines | 19/02/68 |
| 260 | 47165 | -31 | NH8942E | Eastern Air Lines | 22/02/68 |
| 261 | 47115 | -41 | OY-KGA | SAS-Scandinavian Airlines System | 29/02/68 |
| 262 | 47312 | -32 | EC-BIS | Iberia | 24/02/68 |
| 263 | 47172 | -32 | N3331L | Iberia | 29/02/68 |
| 264 | 75790 | -32 | HB-IFH | Swissair | 28/02/68 |
| 265 | 47166 | -31 | N8943E | Eastern Air Lines | 25/02/68 |
| 266 | 47167 | -31 | N8944E | Eastern Air Lines | 27/02/68 |
| 267 | 47181 | -31 | N8945E | Eastern Air Lines | 29/02/68 |
| 268 | 47313 | -32 | EC-BIT | Iberia | 08/03/68 |
| 269 | 47065 | -31 | VH-CZD | Ansett - ANA | 08/03/68 |
| 270 | 47072 | -31 | VH-TJM | TAA | 08/03/68 |
| 271 | 47182 | -31 | N8946E | Eastern Air Lines | 08/03/68 |
| 272 | 47183 | -31 | N8947E | Eastern Air Lines | 14/03/68 |
| 273 | 47173 | -32 | N3332L | Delta Air Lines | 18/03/68 |
| 274 | 47184 | -31 | N8948E | Eastern Air Lines | 22/03/68 |
| 275 | 47185 | -31 | N8949E | Eastern Air Lines | 16/03/68 |
| 276 | 47186 | -31 | N8950E | Eastern Air Lines | 20/03/68 |
| 277 | 47121 | -31 | N967PR | Caribair | 23/03/68 |
| 278 | 47195 | -32 | CF-TLT | Air Canada | 21/03/68 |
| 279 | 47314 | -32 | FC-RIII | Iberia | 28/03/68 |
| 280 | 47191 | -33RC | PH-DNM | KLM | 30/04/68 |
| 281 | 47241 | -32C9 | 67-22583 | USAF-United States Air Force | 13/09/68 |
| 282 | 47187 | -31 | N8951E | Eastern Air Lines | 26/03/68 |
| 283 | 45867 | -31 | N8952E | Eastern Air Lines | 28/03/68 |
| 284 | 47150 | -31 | N905H | Hawaiian Airlines | 05/04/68 |
| 285 | 47151 | -15 | N228Z | Tracinda Investment | 21/04/68 |
| 286 | 47174 | -32 | N3333L | Delta Air Lines | 07/04/68 |
| 287 | 47192 | -33RC | PH-DNN | KLM | 17/04/68 |
| 288 | 47196 | -32 | CF-TLU | Air Canada | 07/04/68 |
| 289 | 47197 | -32 | CF-TLV | Air Canada | 07/04/68 |
| 290 | 45868 | -31 | N8953E | Eastern Air Lines | 11/04/68 |
| 291 | 47188 | -31 | N8954E | Eastern Air Lines | 11/04/68 |
| 292 | 47246 | -31 | N950L | Bonaza Air Lines | 24/06/68 |
| 293 | 47207 | -31 | N984VJ | Allegheny Airlines | 17/04/68 |
| 294 | 47252 | -31 | N956N | North Central Airlines | 15/04/68 |
| 295 | 47253 | -31 | N957N | North Central Airlines | 19/04/68 |

| Fuselage Number | Serial Number | Model | Registration | Operator | Delivery Date | Fuselage Number | Serial Number | Model | Registration | Operator | Delivery Date |
|---|---|---|---|---|---|---|---|---|---|---|---|
| 296 | 47220 | -32F | I-DIKF | Alitalia | 03/05/68 | 312 | 47218 | -32 | D-ACEB | Südflug | 21/05/68 |
| 297 | 47249 | -31 | N977Z | Ozark Air Lines | 19/04/68 | 313 | 47215 | -31 | N8957E | Eastern Air Lines | 23/05/68 |
| 298 | 47175 | -32 | N3334L | Delta Air Lines | 28/04/68 | 314 | 47176 | -32 | N3335L | Delta Air Lines | 25/05/68 |
| 299 | 47222 | -32 | I-DIKJ | Alitalia | 03/05/68 | 315 | 47216 | -31 | N8958E | Eastern Air Lines | 25/05/68 |
| 300 | 47223 | -32 | I-DIKL | Alitalia | 30/04/68 | 316 | 47224 | -32 | I-DIKM | Alitalia | 25/05/68 |
| 301 | 47254 | -31 | N958N | North Central Airlines | 30/04/68 | 317 | 47225 | -32 | I-DIKN | Alitalia | 27/05/68 |
| 302 | 47198 | -32 | CF-TLM | Air Canada | 30/04/68 | 318 | 47138 | -31 | N9330 | Air West | 27/05/68 |
| 303 | 47189 | -31 | N8955E | Eastern Air Lines | 04/05/68 | 319 | 47117 | -41 | SE-DBW | SAS | 27/05/68 |
| 304 | 47242 | -32C9 | 67-22584 | USAF | 08/08/68 | 320 | 47263 | -31 | N9331 | Air West | 04/06/68 |
| 305 | 47221 | -32F | I-DIKG | Alitalia | 09/05/68 | 321 | 47199 | -32 | CF-TLX | Air Canada | 31/05/68 |
| 306 | 47214 | -31 | N8956E | Eastern Air Lines | 10/05/68 | 322 | 47157 | -31 | N8959E | Eastern Air Lines | 08/06/68 |
| 307 | 47208 | -31 | N985VJ | Allegheny Airlines | 10/05/68 | 323 | 47178 | -41 | OY-KGB | SAS | 10/06/68 |
| 308 | 47116 | -41 | LN-RLK | SAS | 14/05/68 | 324 | 47194 | -33RC | PH-DNP | KLM | 12/06/68 |
| 309 | 47250 | -31 | N978Z | Ozark Air Lines | 10/05/68 | 325 | 47219 | -32 | D-ACEC | Südflug | 13/06/68 |
| 310 | 47255 | -31 | N959N | North Central Airlines | 13/05/68 | 326 | 47256 | -31 | N960N | North Central Airlines | 17/06/68 |
| 311 | 47193 | -33RC | PH-DNO | KLM | 21/05/68 | 327 | 47209 | -31 | N986VJ | Allegheny Airlines | 14/06/68 |

| Fuselage Number | Serial Number | Model | Registration | Operator | Delivery Date |
|---|---|---|---|---|---|
| 328 | 47206 | -15 | N96S | Southern Airways | 17/06/68 |
| 329 | 47264 | -31 | N9332 | Air West | 20/06/68 |
| 330 | 47177 | -32 | N3336L | Delta Air Lines | 21/06/68 |
| 331 | 45869 | -31 | N8960E | Eastern Air Lines | 25/06/68 |
| 332 | 45870 | -31 | N8961E | Eastern Air Lines | 22/06/68 |
| 333 | 47226 | -32 | I-DIKP | Alitalia | 28/06/68 |
| 334 | 47227 | -32 | I-DIKQ | Alitalia | 29/06/68 |
| 335 | 47179 | -41 | LN-RLC | SAS | 25/06/68 |
| 336 | 45774 | -32 | TC-JAB | THY-Turk Hava Yollari | 09/07/68 |
| 337 | 47279 | -33RC | PH-DNR | KLM | 05/07/68 |
| 338 | 47200 | -32 | CF-TLY | Air Canada | 11/07/68 |
| 339 | 47265 | -32 | CF-TLZ | Air Canada | 10/07/68 |
| 340 | 47295 | -32C9 | 67-22585 | USAF | 21/08/68 |
| 341 | 47210 | -31 | N987VJ | Allegheny Airlines | 12/07/68 |
| 342 | 47247 | -31 | N9334 | Air West | 17/07/68 |
| 343 | 47291 | -33RC | PH-MAN | Martinair Holland | 21/07/68 |
| 344 | 45871 | -31 | N8962E | Eastern Air Lines | 19/07/68 |
| 345 | 45872 | -31 | N8963E | Eastern Air Lines | 26/07/68 |
| 346 | 47240 | -15RC | N8919 | Continental Airlines | 20/07/68 |
| 347 | 47273 | -32 | N3337L | Delta Air Lines | 25/07/68 |
| 348 | 47274 | -32 | N3338L | Delta Air Lines | 27/07/68 |
| 349 | 45791 | -32 | HB-IFI | Swissair | 28/07/68 |
| 350 | 45873 | -31 | N8964E | Eastern Air Lines | 02/08/68 |
| 351 | 45874 | -31 | N8965E | Eastern Air Lines | 01/08/68 |
| 352 | 47266 | -32 | CF-TMA | Air Canada | 27/07/68 |
| 353 | 47289 | -32 | CF-TMB | Air Canada | 29/07/68 |
| 354 | 47180 | -41 | SE-DBU | SAS | 27/07/68 |
| 355 | 47228 | -32 | I-DIKR | Alitalia | 09/08/68 |
| 356 | 47229 | -32 | I-DIKS | Alitalia | 08/08/68 |
| 357 | 47211 | -31 | N988VJ | Allegheny Airlines | 09/08/68 |
| 358 | 47213 | -32 | TC-JAC | THY | 13/08/68 |
| 359 | 47286 | -41 | OY-KGC | SAS | 16/08/68 |
| 360 | 47217 | -31 | N8966E | Eastern Airlines | 16/08/68 |
| 361 | 47267 | -31 | N8967E | Eastern Airlines | 17/08/68 |
| 362 | 47296 | -32C9 | 67-22586 | USAF | 24/09/68 |
| 363 | 47275 | -32 | N3339L | Delta Air Lines | 22/08/68 |
| 364 | 47287 | -41 | LN-RLJ | SAS | 24/08/68 |
| 365 | 45875 | -31 | N8968E | Eastern Air Lines | 24/08/68 |
| 366 | 45876 | -31 | N8969E | Eastern Air Lines | 28/08/68 |
| 367 | 47290 | -32 | CF-TMC | Air Canada | 29/08/68 |
| 368 | 47212 | -31 | N989VJ | Allegheny Airlines | 29/08/68 |
| 369 | 47288 | -41 | SE-DBT | SAS | 28/08/68 |
| 370 | 47268 | -31 | N8970E | Eastern Air Lines | 04/09/68 |
| 371 | 47269 | -31 | N8971E | Eastern Air Lines | 06/09/68 |
| 372 | 45792 | -32 | HB-IFK | Swissair | 11/09/68 |
| 373 | 47276 | -32 | H3340L | Delta Air Lines | 14/09/68 |
| 374 | 47270 | -31 | N8972E | Eastern Air Lines | 11/09/68 |
| 375 | 47036 | -31 | N8973E | Eastern Air Lines | 13/09/68 |
| 376 | 47074 | -31 | N8974E | Eastern Air Lines | 14/09/68 |
| 377 | 47297 | -32C9 | 68-8932 | USAF | 14/10/68 |
| 378 | 47119 | -31 | N8975E | Eastern Air Lines | 19/09/68 |
| 379 | 47277 | -32 | N5341L | Delta Air Lines | 25/09/68 |
| 380 | 47278 | -32 | N5342L | Delta Air Lines | 26/09/68 |
| 381 | 45793 | -32 | HB-IFL | Swissair | 28/09/68 |
| 382 | 47301 | -21 | LN-RLL | SAS | 22/03/69 |
| 383 | 47292 | -32 | CF-TMD | Air Canada | 28/09/68 |
| 384 | 47293 | -32 | CF-TME | Air Canada | 26/09/68 |
| 385 | 47317 | -32 | N1261L | Delta Air Lines | 09/10/68 |
| 386 | 47257 | -32 | N1262L | Delta Air Lines | 04/10/68 |
| 387 | 47258 | -32 | N1263L | Delta Air Lines | 10/10/68 |
| 388 | 47125 | -15 | XA-SOG | Aeronaves de Mexico | 07/10/68 |
| 389 | 47271 | -31 | N8976E | Eastern Air Lines | 09/10/68 |
| 390 | 47272 | -31 | N8977E | Eastern Air Lines | 09/10/68 |
| 391 | 47327 | -31 | N8978E | Eastern Air Lines | 15/10/68 |
| 392 | 47328 | -31 | N8979E | Eastern Air Lines | 17/10/68 |
| 393 | 47309 | -14 | YV-C-AAA | LAV-Linea Aeropostal Venezolana | 23/10/68 |
| 394 | 45847 | -32 | HB-IFM | Swissair | 17/10/68 |
| 395 | 47230 | -32 | I-DIKT | Alitalia | 18/10/68 |
| 396 | 47231 | -32 | I-DIKV | Alitalia | 19/10/68 |
| 397 | 47283 | -32 | I-DIKW | Alitalia | 24/10/68 |
| 398 | 47311 | -32 | I-DIKZ | Alitalia | 21/10/68 |
| 399 | 47298 | -32C9 | 68-8933 | USAF | 27/11/68 |
| 400 | 47202 | -31 | VH-CZE | Ansett - ANA | 02/11/68 |
| 401 | 47203 | -31 | VH-TJN | TAA | 31/10/68 |
| 402 | 47294 | -32 | CF-TMF | Air Canada | 04/11/68 |
| 403 | 47340 | -32 | CF-TMG | Air Canada | 07/11/68 |
| 404 | 47341 | -32 | CF-TMH | Air Canada | 07/11/68 |
| 405 | 47126 | -15 | XA-SOH | Aeronaves De Mexico | 12/11/68 |
| 406 | 47329 | -31 | N8980E | Eastern Air Lines | 09/11/68 |
| 407 | 47330 | -31 | N8981E | Eastern Air Lines | 09/11/68 |
| 408 | 47331 | -31 | N8982E | Eastern Air Lines | 15/11/68 |
| 409 | 47259 | -32 | N1264L | Delta Air Lines | 15/11/68 |
| 410 | 47260 | -32 | N1265L | Delta Air Lines | 21/11/68 |
| 411 | 47261 | -32 | N1266L | Delta Air Lines | 19/11/68 |
| 412 | 47262 | -32 | N1267L | Delta Air Lines | 23/11/68 |
| 413 | 47284 | -32 | N1268L | Delta Air Lines | 26/11/68 |
| 414 | 47285 | -32 | N1269L | Delta Air Lines | 07/12/68 |
| 415 | 47337 | -31 | N9335 | Air West | 27/11/68 |
| 416 | 47338 | -31 | N9336 | Air West | 26/11/68 |
| 417 | 47127 | -15 | XA-SOI | Aeronaves de Mexico | 27/11/68 |
| 418 | 47342 | -32 | CF-TMI | Air Canada | 27/11/68 |
| 419 | 47348 | -32 | CF-TMJ | Air Canada | 18/12/68 |
| 420 | 47349 | -32 | CF-TMK | Air Canada | 07/12/68 |
| 421 | 47299 | -32C9 | 68-8934 | USAF | 18/12/68 |
| 422 | 47302 | -21 | OY-KGD | SAS | 11/12/68 |
| 423 | 47168 | -32 | PH-DNS | KLM | 14/12/68 |
| 424 | 47169 | -32 | PH-DNT | KLM | 16/12/68 |
| 425 | 47170 | -32 | PH-DNV | KLM | 19/12/68 |
| 426 | 47318 | -32 | N1270L | Delta Air Lines | 14/12/68 |
| 427 | 47281 | -32 | HB-IFT | Swissair | 19/12/68 |
| 428 | 47232 | -32 | I-DIKY | Alitalia | 18/12/68 |
| 429 | 47233 | -32 | I-DIBC | Alitalia | 19/12/68 |
| 430 | 47399 | -31 | N8983E | Eastern Air Lines | 24/01/69 |
| 431 | 47350 | -32 | CF-TML | Air Canada | 29/12/68 |
| 432 | 47303 | -21 | SE-DBS | SAS | 06/01/69 |
| 433 | 47315 | -31 | N1308T | Texas International | 10/01/69 |
| 434 | 47319 | -32 | N1271L | Delta Air Lines | 06/02/69 |
| 435 | 47234 | -32 | I-DIBD | Alitalia | 04/01/69 |
| 436 | 47235 | -32 | I-DIBJ | Alitalia | 09/01/69 |
| 437 | 47339 | -32 | I-DIBN | Alitalia | 11/01/69 |
| 438 | 47300 | -32C9 | 68-8935 | USAF | 06/02/69 |
| 439 | 47316 | -31 | N1309T | Texas International | 23/01/69 |
| 440 | 47304 | -21 | LN-RLM | SAS | 29/01/69 |
| 441 | 47305 | -21 | OY-KGE | SAS | 22/01/69 |
| 442 | 47351 | -32 | 6Y-JGA | Air Jamaica | 23/01/69 |
| 443 | 47400 | -31 | N8984E | Eastern Air Lines | 30/01/69 |
| 444 | 47401 | -31 | N8985E | Eastern Air Lines | 21/03/69 |
| 445 | 47363 | -33RC | PH-MAO | Martinair Holland | 09/02/69 |
| 446 | 47282 | -32 | HB-IFU | Swissair | 31/01/69 |
| 447 | 47392 | -32 | N393PA | Purdue Airlines | 03/02/69 |
| 448 | 47243 | -32 | YV-C-AVD | Avensa | 27/02/69 |
| 449 | 47130 | -31 | N991VJ | Allegheny Airlines | 05/02/69 |
| 450 | 47236 | -32 | I-DIBQ | Alitalia | 04/02/69 |
| 451 | 47237 | -32 | I-DIBO | Alitalia | 06/02/69 |
| 452 | 47355 | -32F | I-DIBK | Alitalia | 12/02/69 |
| 453 | 47352 | -32 | 6Y-JGB | Air Jamaica | 18/02/69 |
| 454 | 47320 | -32 | N1272L | Delta Air Lines | 19/02/69 |
| 455 | 47321 | -32 | N1273L | Delta Air Lines | 28/02/69 |
| 456 | 47322 | -32 | N1274L | Delta Air Lines | 26/02/69 |
| 457 | 47404 | -33CF | N935F | Overseas National | 07/03/69 |
| 458 | 47394 | -32 | N950PB | Playboy Enterprises | 24/02/69 |
| 459 | 47201 | -32 | PH-DNM | KLM | 22/02/69 |
| 460 | 47343 | -31 | N979Z | Ozark Air Lines | 25/02/69 |
| 461 | 47332 | -31 | N993VJ | Allegheny Airlines | 27/02/69 |
| 462 | 47306 | -21 | SE-DBR | SAS | 27/02/69 |
| 463 | 47307 | -21 | LN-RLO | SAS | 06/03/69 |
| 464 | 47346 | -31 | N9337 | Air West | 06/03/69 |
| 465 | 47238 | -32 | I-DIZA | Alitalia | 14/03/69 |
| 466 | 47239 | -32 | YU-AHJ | Inex Adria Aviopromet | 25/04/69 |
| 467 | 47408 | -33CF | N936F | Overseas National | 14/03/69 |
| 468 | 47323 | -32 | N1275L | Delta Air Lines | 03/04/69 |
| 469 | 47324 | -32 | N1276L | Delta Air Lines | 16/04/69 |
| 470 | 47356 | -32 | N1277L | Delta Air Lines | 18/04/69 |
| 471 | 47353 | -32 | CF-TMO | Air Canada | 26/03/69 |
| 472 | 47308 | -31 | N980Z | Ozark Air Lines | 27/03/69 |
| 473 | 47171 | -31 | N906H | Hawaiian Airlines | 28/03/69 |
| 474 | 47308 | -21 | OY-KGF | SAS | 31/03/69 |
| 475 | 47360 | -21 | SE-DBP | SAS | 12/04/69 |
| 476 | 47357 | -32 | N1278L | Delta Air Lines | 08/05/69 |
| 477 | 47358 | -32 | N1279L | Delta Air Lines | 08/05/69 |
| 478 | 47347 | -31 | N9338 | Air West | 10/04/69 |
| 479 | 47382 | -31 | N9339 | Air West | 11/04/69 |
| 480 | 47410 | -33RC | PH-MAR | Martinair Holland | 19/04/69 |
| 481 | 47333 | -31 | N994VJ | Allegheny Airlines | 11/04/69 |
| 482 | 47402 | -31 | N8986E | Eastern Air Lines | 08/05/69 |
| 483 | 47354 | -32 | CF-TMP | Air Canada | 17/04/69 |
| 484 | 47364 | -32 | EC-BPF | Iberia | 17/04/69 |
| 485 | 47345 | -31 | N981Z | Ozark Air Lines | 21/04/69 |
| 486 | 47042 | -31 | N89S | Southern Airways | 29/04/69 |
| 487 | 47405 | -31 | N961N | North Central Airlines | 09/05/69 |
| 488 | 47361 | -21 | SE-DBO | SAS | 01/05/69 |

| Fuselage Number | Serial Number | Model | Registration | Operator | Delivery Date | Fuselage Number | Serial Number | Model | Registration | Operator | Delivery Date |
|---|---|---|---|---|---|---|---|---|---|---|---|
| 489 | 47389 | -31 | N9340 | Air West | 25/04/69 | 570 | 47418 | -31 | VH-TJP | TAA | 05/02/70 |
| 490 | 47390 | -31 | N9341 | Air West | 13/05/69 | 571 | 47501 | -31 | VH-CZG | Ansett Airlines | 13/02/70 |
| 491 | 47391 | -31 | N9342 | Air West | 13/05/69 | 572 | 47426 | -32 | N1286L | Delta Air Lines | 19/02/70 |
| 492 | 47362 | -31 | N907H | Hawaiian Airlines | 09/05/69 | 573 | 47427 | -32 | N1287L | Delta Air Lines | 25/02/70 |
| 493 | 47334 | -31 | N995VJ | Allegheny Airlines | 12/05/69 | 574 | 47502 | -32 | I-DIZE | Alitalia | 20/02/70 |
| 494 | 47335 | -31 | N996VJ | Allegheny Airlines | 14/05/69 | 575 | 47464 | -41 | SE-DAN | SAS | 03/09/70 |
| 495 | 47359 | -32 | N1280L | Delta Air Lines | 23/05/69 | 576 | 47422 | -32 | CF-TMQ | Air Canada | 28/02/70 |
| 496 | 47377 | -32 | N1281L | Delta Air Lines | 27/05/69 | 577 | 47443 | -32 | N1288L | Delta Air Lines | 10/04/70 |
| 497 | 47409 | -33CF | N937F | Overseas National | 22/05/69 | 578 | 47444 | -32 | N1289L | Delta Air Lines | 09/04/70 |
| 498 | 47244 | -31 | N90S | Southern Airways | 23/05/69 | 579 | 47455 | -32 | EC-BQY | Iberia | 18/03/70 |
| 499 | 47406 | -31 | N962N | North Central Airlines | 23/05/69 | 580 | 47456 | -32 | EC-BQZ | Iberia | 26/03/70 |
| 500 | 47336 | -31 | N997VJ | Allegheny Airlines | 27/05/69 | 581 | 47423 | -32 | CF-TMR | Air Canada | 09/04/70 |
| 501 | 47439 | -31 | N9343 | Air West | 04/06/69 | 582 | 47424 | -32 | CF-TMS | Air Canada | 08/04/70 |
| 502 | 47440 | -31 | N9344 | Air West | 04/06/69 | 583 | 47517 | -31 | N908H | Hawaiian Airlines | 28/04/70 |
| 503 | 47441 | -31 | N9345 | Air West | 04/06/69 | 584 | 47465 | -33CF | HB-IDN | Swissair | 17/04/70 |
| 504 | 47365 | -32 | EC-BPG | Iberia | 07/06/69 | 585 | 47445 | -32 | N1290L | Delta Air Lines | 06/05/70 |
| 505 | 47368 | -32 | EC-BPH | Iberia | 07/06/69 | 586 | 47505 | -31 | N960VJ | Allegheny Airlines | 11/06/71 |
| 506 | 47371 | -31 | N978VJ | Allegheny Airlines | 12/06/69 | 587 | 47503 | -32 | YU-AHR | Inex Adria | 27/04/70 |
| 507 | 47403 | -31 | N8987E | Eastern Air Lines | 11/07/69 | 588 | 47506 | -31 | N961VJ | Allegheny Airlines | 18/11/70 |
| 508 | 47378 | -32 | N1282L | Delta Air Lines | 02/07/69 | 589 | 47425 | -32 | YU-AHL | JAT-Yugoslav Airlines | 08/05/70 |
| 509 | 47379 | -32 | N1283L | Delta Air Lines | 10/07/69 | 590 | 47469 | -32 | YU-AHM | JAT | 13/05/70 |
| 510 | 47245 | -31 | N97S | Southern Airways | 20/06/69 | 591 | 47470 | -32 | YU-AHN | JAT | 15/05/70 |
| 511 | 47415 | -31 | N963N | North Central Airlines | 15/09/69 | 592 | 47482 | -32 | YU-AHT | JAT | 02/07/71 |
| 512 | 47416 | -31 | N964N | North Central Airlines | 31/07/70 | 593 | 47523 | -32 | HB-IDP | Swissair | 20/11/70 |
| 513 | 47372 | -31 | N979VJ | Allegheny Airlines | 01/07/69 | 594 | 47507 | -31 | N962VJ | Allegheny Airlines | 22/11/70 |
| 514 | 47380 | -32 | N1284L | Delta Air Lines | 08/08/69 | 595 | 47508 | -31 | N963VJ | Allegheny Airlines | 14/06/71 |
| 515 | 47325 | -31 | VH-CZF | Ansett Airlines | 10/07/69 | 596 | 47472 | -32 | YU-AHO | JAT | 08/06/70 |
| 516 | 47326 | -31 | VH-TJO | TAA | 11/07/69 | 597 | 47280 | -31 | N1334U | Southern Airways | 29/06/71 |
| 517 | 47376 | -32 | N394PA | Purdue Aviation | 22/07/69 | 598 | 47473 | -32 | YU-AHP | JAT | 18/06/70 |
| 518 | 47417 | -31 | N965N | North Central Airlines | 31/07/70 | 599 | 47491 | -31 | N985Z | Ozark Air Lines | 25/06/70 |
| 519 | 47381 | -32 | N1285L | Delta Air Lines | 03/09/69 | 600 | 47474 | -32 | I-ATIX | ATI | 04/12/70 |
| 520 | 47431 | -32 | I-ATIA | ATI-Aero Trasporti Italiani | 24/07/69 | 601 | 47494 | -41 | OY-KGI | SAS | 15/09/70 |
| 521 | 47413 | -33F | SE-DBN | SAS | 31/07/69 | 602 | 47419 | -31 | VH-TJQ | TAA | 17/08/70 |
| 522 | 47373 | -31 | N964VJ | Allegheny Airlines | 09/09/69 | 603 | 47526 | -31 | VH-CZH | Ansett Airlines | 28/08/70 |
| 523 | 47374 | -31 | N965VJ | Allegheny Airlines | 09/09/69 | 604 | 47497 | -41 | LN-RLB | SAS | 01/10/70 |
| 524 | 47442 | -32 | TC-JAG | THY | 24/08/69 | 605 | 47479 | -32 | HB-IFZ | Swissair | 18/09/70 |
| 525 | 47432 | -32 | I-DIZI | Alitalia | 28/08/69 | 606 | 47522 | -32 | EC-BYD | Iberia | 11/06/71 |
| 526 | 47433 | -32 | I-DIZU | Alitalia | 15/08/69 | 607 | 47480 | -32 | HB-IDO | Swissair | 08/10/70 |
| 527 | 47488 | -32 | TC-JAD | THY | 27/08/69 | 608 | 47393 | -31 | N1335U | Southern Airways | 29/06/71 |
| 528 | 47489 | -32 | TC-JAE | THY | 27/08/69 | 609 | 47430 | -32 | 5H-MOI | East African Airways | 09/12/70 |
| 529 | 47369 | -31 | N1798U | Hawaiian Airlines | 31/10/69 | 610 | 47535 | -32 | HB-IDR | Swissair | 22/12/70 |
| 530 | 47366 | -32C9 | 68-10958 | USAF | 30/09/69 | 611 | 47468 | -32 | 5Y-ALR | East African Airways | 19/02/71 |
| 531 | 47375 | -31 | N967VJ | Allegheny Airlines | 16/09/69 | 612 | 47478 | -32 | 5X-UVY | East African Airways | 24/02/71 |
| 532 | 47429 | -31 | N968VJ | Allegheny Airlines | 16/09/69 | 613 | 47477 | -32 | I-ATIK | ATI | 26/02/71 |
| 533 | 47411 | -31 | N983Z | Ozark Air Lines | 08/12/69 | 614 | 47518 | -32 | I-DIZO | Alitalia | 16/02/71 |
| 534 | 47412 | -31 | N984Z | Ozark Air Lines | 11/12/69 | 615 | 47519 | -32 | I-DIZF | Alitalia | 18/02/71 |
| 535 | 47450 | -32 | D-ADIT | Atlantis Airways | 23/02/70 | 616 | 47481 | -32 | PK-GNC | Garuda | 04/02/71 |
| 536 | 47414 | -33F | LN-RLW | SAS | 03/10/69 | 617 | 47528 | -31 | VH-TJR | TAA | 05/02/71 |
| 537 | 47434 | -32 | I-DIZB | Alitalia | 26/09/69 | 618 | 47527 | -31 | VH-CZI | Ansett Airlines | 17/02/71 |
| 538 | 47383 | -32 | HB-IFV | Swissair | 15/10/69 | 619 | 47514 | -32 | PH-MAX | Martinair Holland | 24/02/71 |
| 539 | 47367 | -32C9 | 68-10959 | USAF | 07/11/69 | 620 | 47457 | -32 | D-ADIU | Atlantis Airways | 01/04/71 |
| 540 | 47435 | -32 | I-DIZC | Alitalia | 15/10/69 | 621 | 47466 | -32 | N1291L | Delta Air Lines | 14/04/71 |
| 541 | 47436 | -32 | N873UM | ATI | 08/10/69 | 622 | 47547 | -31 | VH-CZJ | Ansett Airlines | 29/03/71 |
| 542 | 47385 | -32 | PK-GNA | Garuda Indonesian Airways | 15/10/69 | 623 | 47550 | -31 | VH-TJS | TAA | 01/04/71 |
| 543 | 47384 | -33F | HB-IFW | Swissair | 22/10/69 | 624 | 47530 | -33CF | YU-AHW | Inex Adria | 22/04/71 |
| 544 | 47437 | -32 | N872UM | ATI | 27/10/69 | 625 | 47529 | -32 | N1292L | Delta Air Lines | 12/05/71 |
| 545 | 47438 | -32 | I-ATIU | ATI | 07/11/69 | 626 | 47532 | -32 | YU-AHU | JAT | 07/05/71 |
| 546 | 47500 | -32 | HI-177 | Dominicana | 16/12/69 | 627 | 47460 | -32 | YU-AHV | JAT | 14/05/71 |
| 547 | 47451 | -32 | TC-JAF | THY | 07/08/70 | 628 | 47486 | -32 | N1293L | Delta Air Lines | 11/06/71 |
| 548 | 47448 | -32C9 | 68-10960 | USAF | 01/12/69 | 629 | 47521 | -32 | OE-LDA | Austrian Airlines | 10/06/71 |
| 549 | 47459 | -32 | D-ADIS | Atlantis Airways | 15/01/70 | 630 | 47516 | -32 | N1294L | Delta Air Lines | 24/06/71 |
| 550 | 47386 | -32 | PK-GNB | Garuda | 15/11/69 | 631 | 47525 | -32 | N1295L | Delta Air Lines | 08/07/71 |
| 551 | 47370 | -31 | N1799U | Hawaiian Airlines | 30/09/71 | 632 | 47524 | -32 | OE-LDB | Austrian Airlines | 09/07/71 |
| 552 | 47449 | -32C9 | 68-10961 | USAF | 31/12/69 | 633 | 47548 | -31 | VH-CZK | Ansett Airlines | 19/07/71 |
| 553 | 47487 | -31 | N1310T | Texas International | 19/11/69 | 634 | 47551 | -31 | VH-TJT | TAA | 27/07/71 |
| 554 | 47404 | -31 | N1332U | Hawaiian Airlines | 05/11/71 | 635 | 47520 | -32 | OE-LDC | Austrian Airlines | 10/08/71 |
| 555 | 47395 | -41 | OY-KGG | SAS | 25/11/69 | 636 | 47397 | -32 | TC-JAK | THY | 18/08/71 |
| 556 | 47420 | -31 | N966VJ | Allegheny Airlines | 05/12/69 | 637 | 47539 | -32 | OE-LDD | Austrian Airlines | 26/08/71 |
| 557 | 47396 | -41 | LN-RLR | SAS | 21/12/69 | 638 | 47531 | -32 | OE-LDE | Austrian Airlines | 09/09/71 |
| 558 | 47421 | -31 | N969VJ | Allegheny Airlines | 30/03/70 | 639 | 47549 | -31 | VH-CZL | Ansett Airlines | 17/11/71 |
| 559 | 47492 | -41 | SE-DAK | SAS | 09/01/70 | 640 | 47552 | -31 | VE-TJU | TAA | 14/10/71 |
| 560 | 47490 | -31 | N1311T | Texas International | 17/12/69 | 641 | 47533 | -32 | I-ATIW | ATI | 02/12/71 |
| 561 | 47446 | -32 | EC-BQT | Iberia | 24/12/69 | 642 | 47553 | -32 | I-ATIH | ATI | 09/12/71 |
| 562 | 47493 | -41 | OY-KGH | SAS | 16/01/70 | 643 | 47509 | -41 | SE-DAO | SAS | 02/12/71 |
| 563 | 47447 | -32 | EC-BQU | Iberia | 08/01/70 | 644 | 47534 | -32 | TC-JAL | THY | 09/11/71 |
| 564 | 47462 | -33RC | PH-DNY | KLM | 17/01/70 | 645 | 47510 | -41 | OY-KGK | SAS | 09/12/71 |
| 565 | 47453 | -32 | EC-BQV | Iberia | 09/01/70 | 646 | 47458 | -32 | OE-LDF | Austrian Airlines | 02/12/71 |
| 566 | 47498 | -41 | SE-DAL | SAS | 29/01/70 | 647 | 47467 | -32C9 | 71-874 | USAF | 17/12/71 |
| 567 | 47454 | -32 | EC-BQX | Iberia | 24/01/70 | 648 | 47484 | -32 | OE-LDG | Austrian Airlines | 20/12/71 |
| 568 | 47499 | -41 | SE-DAM | SAS | 18/02/70 | 649 | 47463 | -32 | PK-GND | Garuda | 05/01/72 |
| 569 | 47476 | -33RC | PH-DNZ | KLM | 06/02/70 | 650 | 47471 | -32C9 | 71-875 | USAF | 10/02/72 |

| Fuselage Number | Serial Number | Model | Registration | Operator | Delivery Date |
|---|---|---|---|---|---|
| 651 | 47504 | -32 | EC-BYE | Iberia | 04/02/72 |
| 652 | 47542 | -32 | EC-BYF | Iberia | 21/02/72 |
| 653 | 47475 | -32C9 | 71-876 | USAF | 03/03/72 |
| 654 | 47543 | -32 | EC-BYG | Iberia | 29/02/72 |
| 655 | 47546 | -32 | CF-TMT | Air Canada | 21/03/72 |
| 656 | 47495 | -32C9 | 71-877 | USAF | 31/03/72 |
| 657 | 47556 | -32 | EC-BYH | Iberia | 10/04/72 |
| 658 | 47554 | -32 | CF-TMU | Air Canada | 20/04/72 |
| 659 | 47536 | -32C9 | 71-878 | USAF | 05/05/72 |
| 660 | 47452 | -32 | EC-BYI | Iberia | 10/05/72 |
| 661 | 47557 | -32 | CF-TMV | Air Canada | 17/05/72 |
| 662 | 47537 | -32C9 | 71-879 | USAF | 24/05/72 |
| 663 | 47461 | -32 | EC-BYJ | Iberia | 09/06/72 |
| 664 | 47560 | -32 | CF-TMW | Air Canada | 14/06/72 |
| 665 | 47538 | -32C9 | 71-880 | USAF | 30/06/72 |
| 666 | 47485 | -32 | CF-TMX | Air Canada | 06/07/72 |
| 667 | 47555 | -32 | OE-LDH | Austrian Airlines | 17/07/72 |
| 668 | 47540 | -32C9 | 71-881 | USAF | 27/07/72 |
| 669 | 47428 | -33RC | EC-BYK | Iberia | 08/08/72 |
| 670 | 47541 | -32C9 | 71-882 | USAF | 18/08/72 |
| 671 | 47545 | -33RC | EC-BYL | Iberia | 29/08/72 |
| 672 | 47559 | -32 | OE-LDI | Austrian Airlines | 30/08/72 |
| 673 | 47496 | -33RC | EC-BYM | Iberia | 19/09/72 |
| 674 | 47561 | -32 | PK-GNE | Garuda | 21/09/72 |
| 675 | 47565 | -33RC | EC-BYN | Iberia | 07/10/72 |
| 676 | 47544 | -32 | I-ATIJ | ATI | 18/10/72 |
| 677 | 47511 | -41 | LN-RLU | SAS | 01/12/72 |
| 678 | 47512 | -41 | SE-DAP | SAS | 05/12/72 |
| 679 | 47513 | -41 | LN-RLX | SAS | 15/12/72 |
| 680 | 47575 | -32 | I-ATIY | ATI | 13/12/72 |
| 681 | 47564 | -31 | N950VJ | Allegheny Airlines | 06/02/73 |
| 682 | 47576 | -31 | N951VJ | Allegheny Airlines | 22/01/73 |
| 683 | 47569 | -32 | PK-GNF | Garuda | 16/01/73 |
| 684 | 47570 | -32 | YU-AJF | Pan Adria Airways | 16/05/73 |
| 685 | 47562 | -32 | YU-AJH | JAT | 12/02/73 |
| 686 | 47577 | -32C9 | 159113 | USN-United States Navy | 08/05/73 |
| 687 | 47563 | -32 | YU-AJI | JAT | 28/02/73 |
| 688 | 47567 | -32 | YU-AJJ | JAT | 19/03/73 |
| 689 | 47568 | -32 | YU-AJK | JAT | 06/04/73 |
| 690 | 47574 | -31 | N952VJ | Allegheny Airlines | 17/04/73 |
| 691 | 47566 | -31 | N949N | North Central Airlines | 10/04/73 |
| 692 | 47581 | -32C9 | 159117 | USN | 08/05/73 |
| 693 | 47579 | -32 | YU-AJN | Inex Adria | 10/05/73 |
| 694 | 47573 | -32 | N967N | North Central Airlines | 15/05/73 |
| 695 | 47571 | -32 | YU-AJL | JAT | 21/05/73 |
| 696 | 47584 | -32C9 | 159114 | USN | 13/06/73 |
| 697 | 47583 | -31 | N953VJ | Allegheny Airlines | 20/06/73 |
| 698 | 47585 | -32C9 | 159118 | USN | 03/07/73 |
| 699 | 47588 | -31 | N956VJ | Allegheny Airlines | 07/02/74 |
| 700 | 47587 | -32C9 | 159115 | USN | 26/07/73 |
| 701 | 47582 | -32 | YU-AJM | JAT | 31/07/73 |
| 702 | 47578 | -32C9 | 159119 | USN | 17/08/73 |
| 703 | 47590 | -31 | N954VJ | Allegheny Airlines | 24/08/73 |
| 704 | 47580 | -32C9 | 159116 | USN | 14/09/73 |
| 705 | 47593 | -31 | N955VJ | Allegheny Airlines | 25/09/73 |
| 706 | 47591 | -32 | I-ATIQ | ATI | 28/09/73 |
| 707 | 47586 | -32C9 | 159120 | USN | 30/10/73 |
| 708 | 47572 | -31 | N940N | North Central Airlines | 25/10/73 |
| 709 | 47595 | -32 | SM012 | Italian Defence Ministry | 19/01/74 |
| 710 | 47600 | -32 | SM013 | Italian Defence Ministry | 18/03/74 |
| 711 | 47589 | -31 | N986Z | Ozark Air Lines | 04/12/73 |
| 712 | 47592 | -32 | CF-TMY | Air Canada | 02/01/74 |
| 713 | 47597 | -41 | OY-KGL | SAS | 27/02/74 |
| 714 | 47596 | -41 | SE-DAR | SAS | 14/01/74 |
| 715 | 47601 | -32 | PK-GNG | Garuda | 23/01/74 |
| 716 | 47599 | -41 | LN-RLA | SAS | 29/01/74 |
| 717 | 47594 | -32 | XA-DEJ | Aeromexico | 11/02/74 |
| 718 | 47602 | -32 | XA-DEK | Aeromexico | 19/02/74 |
| 719 | 47598 | -32 | CF-TMZ | Air Canada | 23/02/74 |
| 720 | 47603 | -41 | JA8423 | TDA-Toa Domestic Airlines | 18/03/74 |
| 721 | 47607 | -32 | XA-DEL | Aeromexico | 21/03/74 |
| 722 | 47604 | -41 | JA8424 | TDA | 25/03/74 |
| 723 | 47609 | -32 | XA-DEM | Aeromexico | 21/03/74 |
| 724 | 47605 | -41 | JA8425 | TDA | 10/04/74 |
| 725 | 47610 | -41 | SE-DAS | SAS | 18/04/74 |
| 726 | 47611 | -32 | CF-TMM | Air Canada | 25/04/74 |
| 727 | 47606 | -41 | JA8426 | TDA | 07/05/74 |
| 728 | 47623 | -41 | LN-RLS | SAS | 14/05/74 |
| 729 | 47621 | -32 | XA-DEN | Aeromexico | 22/05/74 |
| 730 | 47638 | -31 | N3504T | Texas International | 10/06/74 |
| 731 | 47637 | -32 | EC-CGN | Aviaco-Aviacion y Comercio | 04/06/74 |
| 732 | 47608 | -41 | JA8427 | TDA | 13/06/74 |
| 733 | 47624 | -41 | OY-KGM | SAS | 18/06/74 |
| 734 | 47640 | -32 | EC-CGO | Aviaco | 02/07/74 |
| 735 | 47639 | -32 | 6Y-JIJ | Air Jamaica | 28/06/74 |
| 736 | 47612 | -41 | JA8428 | TDA | 11/07/74 |
| 737 | 47625 | -41 | SE-DAT | SAS | 18/07/74 |
| 738 | 47626 | -41 | LN-RLT | SAS | 25/07/74 |
| 739 | 47627 | -41 | SE-DAU | SAS | 05/08/74 |
| 740 | 47628 | -41 | OY-KGN | SAS | 07/08/74 |
| 741 | 47649 | -32 | YU-AJR | Inex Adria | 28/02/75 |
| 742 | 47613 | -41 | JA8429 | TDA | 13/09/74 |
| 743 | 47631 | -41 | SE-DAX | SAS | 28/08/74 |
| 744 | 47629 | -41 | SE-DAW | SAS | 05/09/74 |
| 745 | 47630 | -41 | LN-RLN | SAS | 12/09/74 |
| 746 | 47641 | -32 | I-ATJA | ATI | 19/09/74 |
| 747 | 47614 | -41 | JA8430 | TDA | 17/10/74 |
| 748 | 47632 | -41 | OY-KGO | SAS | 03/10/74 |
| 749 | 47642 | -32 | EC-CGP | Aviaco | 11/10/74 |
| 750 | 47643 | -32 | EC-CGQ | Aviaco | 18/10/74 |
| 751 | 47615 | -41 | JA8432 | TDA | 08/11/74 |
| 752 | 47633 | -41 | SE-DBM | SAS | 04/11/74 |
| 753 | 47622 | -32 | XA-DEO | Aeromexico | 15/11/74 |
| 754 | 47635 | -32 | PK-GNH | Garuda | 14/11/74 |
| 755 | 47646 | -41 | OY-KGP | SAS | 22/11/74 |
| 756 | 47634 | -41 | LN-RLZ | SAS | 18/12/74 |
| 757 | 47654 | -51 | HB-ISK | Swissair | 19/11/75 |
| 758 | 47636 | -32 | PK-GNI | Garuda | 19/12/74 |
| 759 | 47616 | -41 | JA8433 | TDA | 20/12/74 |
| 760 | 47653 | -32 | I-ATJB | ATI | 09/01/75 |
| 761 | 47648 | -32 | PJ-SNA | ALM-Antillean Airlines | 16/01/75 |
| 762 | 47617 | -41 | JA8434 | TDA | 14/02/75 |
| 763 | 47655 | -51 | HB-ISL | Swissair | 12/09/75 |
| 764 | 47618 | -41 | JA8435 | TDA | 25/02/75 |
| 765 | 47668 | -32VC | 73-1681 | USAF | 21/02/75 |
| 766 | 47667 | -32 | I-ATJC | ATI | 19/02/75 |
| 767 | 47644 | -32 | EC-CGR | Aviaco | 27/02/75 |
| 768 | 47619 | -41 | JA8436 | TDA | 20/03/75 |
| 769 | 47670 | -32VC | 73-1682 | USAF | 11/03/75 |
| 770 | 47645 | -32 | EC-CGS | Aviaco | 20/03/75 |
| 771 | 47650 | -32 | XA-DEI | Aeromexico | 27/05/75 |
| 772 | 47666 | -32 | PJ-SNB | ALM | 11/04/75 |
| 773 | 47647 | -31 | N943N | North Central Airlines | 13/05/75 |
| 774 | 47671 | -32VC | 73-1683 | USAF | 02/05/75 |
| 775 | 47664 | -31 | N945N | North Central Airlines | 20/05/75 |
| 776 | 47669 | -32 | PJ-SNC | ALM | 13/06/75 |
| 777 | 47620 | -41 | JA8437 | TDA | 28/07/75 |
| 778 | 47672 | -32 | PK-GNJ | Garuda | 26/06/75 |
| 779 | 47673 | -32 | PK-GNK | Garuda | 07/07/75 |
| 780 | 47651 | -51 | OE-LDK | Austrian Airlines | 25/08/75 |
| 781 | 47680 | -32 | PK-GNL | Garuda | 22/07/75 |
| 782 | 47675 | -32 | EC-CLD | Aviaco | 25/07/75 |
| 783 | 47656 | -51 | HB-ISM | Swissair | 14/08/75 |
| 784 | 47681 | -32C9 | 160048 | USN | 18/08/75 |
| 785 | 47676 | -51 | N609HA | Hawaiian Airlines | 10/09/75 |
| 786 | 47684 | -32C9 | 160046 | USN | 02/09/75 |
| 787 | 47657 | -51 | HB-ISN | Swissair | 11/09/75 |
| 788 | 47682 | -51 | N920VJ | Allegheny Airlines | 10/10/75 |
| 789 | 47678 | -32 | EC-CLE | Aviaco | 26/09/75 |
| 790 | 47658 | -51 | HB-ISO | Swissair | 29/09/75 |
| 791 | 47677 | -51 | N619HA | Hawaiian Airlines | 07/10/75 |
| 792 | 47683 | -51 | N921VJ | Allegheny Airlines | 13/11/75 |
| 793 | 47674 | -32 | TC-JBK | THY | 22/10/75 |
| 794 | 47685 | -51 | N922VJ | Allegheny Airlines | 21/11/75 |
| 795 | 47687 | -32C9 | 160047 | USN | 07/11/75 |
| 796 | 47665 | -51 | N923VJ | Allegheny Airlines | 16/12/75 |
| 797 | 47679 | -51 | N629HA | Hawaiian Airlines | 20/11/75 |
| 798 | 47652 | -51 | OE-LDL | Austrian Airlines | 12/12/75 |
| 799 | 47688 | -51 | N924VJ | Allegheny Airlines | 27/02/76 |
| 800 | 47686 | -51 | N925VJ | Allegheny Airlines | 27/02/76 |
| 801 | 47699 | -32C9 | 160050 | USN | 19/12/75 |
| 802 | 47689 | -51 | N639HA | Hawaiian Airlines | 19/12/75 |
| 803 | 47692 | -51 | N926VJ | Allegheny Airlines | 12/03/76 |
| 804 | 47693 | -51 | N927VJ | Allegheny Airlines | 27/02/76 |
| 805 | 47694 | -51 | OH-LYN | Finnair | 23/01/76 |
| 806 | 47695 | -51 | OH-LYO | Finnair | 30/01/76 |
| 807 | 47659 | -51 | HB-ISP | Swissair | 12/02/76 |
| 808 | 47696 | -51 | OH-LYP | Finnair | 20/02/76 |
| 809 | 47698 | -32C9 | 160049 | USN | 26/02/76 |
| 810 | 47660 | -51 | HB-ISR | Swissair | 27/02/76 |
| 811 | 47700 | -32C9 | 160051 | USN | 18/03/76 |
| 812 | 47661 | -51 | HB-ISS | Swissair | 10/03/76 |

| Fuselage Number | Serial Number | Model | Registration | Operator | Delivery Date | Fuselage Number | Serial Number | Model | Registration | Operator | Delivery Date |
|---|---|---|---|---|---|---|---|---|---|---|---|
| 813 | 47708 | -51 | N760NC | North Central Airlines | 06/04/76 | 857 | 47742 | -51 | 9Y-TFG | BWIA International | 21/06/77 |
| 814 | 47709 | -51 | N761NC | North Central Airlines | 12/04/76 | 858 | 47728 | -51 | N409EA | Eastern Air Lines | 13/07/77 |
| 815 | 47712 | -51 | N649HA | Hawaiian Airlines | 02/04/76 | 859 | 47743 | -51 | 9Y-TFH | BWIA International | 29/07/77 |
| 816 | 47697 | -51 | YU-AJP | Inex Adria | 12/05/76 | 860 | 47731 | -51 | N410EA | Eastern Air Lines | 16/08/77 |
| 817 | 47702 | -34CF | EC-CTR | Aviaco | 30/04/76 | 861 | 47732 | -51 | N411EA | Eastern Air Lines | 31/08/77 |
| 818 | 47710 | -51 | N762NC | North Central Airlines | 23/04/76 | 862 | 47733 | -51 | N412EA | Eastern Air Lines | 22/09/77 |
| 819 | 47704 | -34CF | EC-CTS | Aviaco | 10/05/76 | 863 | 47745 | -51 | N413EA | Eastern Air Lines | 05/10/77 |
| 820 | 47713 | -51 | N659HA | Hawaiian Airlines | 03/05/76 | 864 | 47746 | -51 | N414EA | Eastern Air Lines | 21/10/77 |
| 821 | 47706 | -34CF | EC-CTT | Aviaco | 21/05/76 | 865 | 47749 | -51 | N415EA | Eastern Air Lines | 03/11/77 |
| 822 | 47701 | -32 | PK-GNM | Garuda | 24/05/76 | 866 | 47751 | -51 | N416EA | Eastern Air Lines | 14/11/77 |
| 823 | 47707 | -34CF | EC-CTU | Aviaco | 13/07/76 | 867 | 47753 | -51 | N417EA | Eastern Air Lines | 21/11/77 |
| 824 | 47714 | -51 | N669HA | Hawaiian Airlines | 08/06/76 | 868 | 47734 | -32 | N920L | Ozark Air Lines | 23/11/77 |
| 825 | 47715 | -51 | N679HA | Hawaiian Airlines | 16/06/76 | 869 | 47735 | -51 | OE-LDN | Austrian Airlines | 03/12/77 |
| 826 | 47722 | -32 | PK-GNN | Garuda | 03/08/76 | 870 | 47750 | -41 | SE-DDR | SAS | 16/12/77 |
| 827 | 47736 | -51 | OH-LYR | Finnair | 15/09/76 | 871 | 47759 | -41 | JA8439 | TDA | 16/12/77 |
| 828 | 47730 | -32 | PK-GNO | Garuda | 13/08/76 | 872 | 47752 | -34CF | 9Y-TFI | BWIA International | 13/01/78 |
| 829 | 47737 | -51 | OH-LYS | Finnair | 23/07/76 | 873 | 47756 | -51 | OE-LDO | Austrian Airlines | 31/01/78 |
| 830 | 47738 | -51 | OH-LYT | Finnair | 04/10/76 | 874 | 47760 | -41 | JA8440 | TDA | 08/02/78 |
| 831 | 47725 | -41 | OY-KGR | SAS | 29/07/76 | 875 | 47761 | -41 | JA8441 | TDA | 06/03/78 |
| 832 | 47716 | -51 | N763NC | North Central Airlines | 16/09/76 | 876 | 47762 | -41 | JA8442 | TDA | 28/04/78 |
| 833 | 47717 | -51 | N764NC | North Central Airlines | 21/12/76 | 877 | 47757 | -51 | N769NC | North Central Airlines | 10/05/78 |
| 834 | 47718 | -51 | N765NC | North Central Airlines | 24/11/76 | 878 | 47755 | -51 | 9G-ACM | Ghana Airways | 13/07/78 |
| 835 | 47740 | -32 | PK-GNP | Garuda | 01/11/76 | 879 | 47763 | -51 | N699HA | Hawaiian Airlines | 11/07/78 |
| 836 | 47741 | -32 | PK-GNQ | Garuda | 16/12/76 | 880 | 47758 | -51 | N770NC | North Central Airlines | 28/07/78 |
| 837 | 47744 | -32 | PK-GNR | Garuda | 16/12/76 | 881 | 47769 | -51 | N771NC | North Central Airlines | 11/08/78 |
| 838 | 47723 | -32 | TC-JBL | THY | 30/09/76 | 882 | 47764 | -51 | N709HA | Hawaiian Airlines | 25/08/78 |
| 839 | 47747 | -41 | SE-DDP | SAS | 23/11/76 | 883 | 47771 | -51 | OH-LYU | Finnair | 01/09/78 |
| 840 | 47691 | -32CF | KAF320 | Kuwait Government | 15/10/76 | 884 | 47774 | -51 | N772NC | North Central Airlines | 08/09/78 |
| 841 | 47703 | -51 | YV-22C | LAV | 16/10/76 | 885 | 47767 | -41 | JA8448 | TDA | 20/09/78 |
| 842 | 47705 | -51 | YV-20C | LAV | 19/10/76 | 886 | 47766 | -41 | OY-KGS | SAS | 13/10/78 |
| 843 | 47690 | -32CF | KAF321 | Kuwait Government | 30/10/76 | 887 | 47768 | -41 | JA8449 | TDA | 07/10/78 |
| 844 | 47711 | -34 | HB-IDT | Balair | 03/11/76 | 888 | 47775 | -51 | N773NC | North Central Airlines | 26/10/78 |
| 845 | 47719 | -51 | YV-21C | LAV | 12/11/76 | 889 | 47776 | -51 | N774NC | North Central Airlines | 14/11/78 |
| 846 | 47720 | -31 | YV-23C | LAV | 18/11/76 | 890 | 47772 | -51 | OH-LYV | Finnair | 07/12/78 |
| 847 | 47721 | -31 | YV-25C | LAV | 10/12/76 | 891 | 47773 | -51 | N8714Q | Finnair | 14/12/78 |
| 848 | 47727 | -31 | YV-24C | LAV | 17/12/76 | 892 | 47770 | -51 | YV-32C | LAV | 22/11/78 |
| 849 | 47726 | -51 | OE-LDM | Austrian Airlines | 18/12/76 | 893 | 47782 | -51 | YV-33C | LAV | 20/12/78 |
| 850 | 47662 | -51 | HB-IST | Swissair | 04/02/77 | 894 | 47780 | -41 | JA8450 | TDA | 09/01/79 |
| 851 | 47663 | -51 | HB-ISU | Swissair | 16/02/77 | 895 | 47781 | -41 | JA8451 | TDA | 31/01/79 |
| 852 | 47739 | -51 | N766NC | North Central Airlines | 25/03/77 | 896 | 47777 | -41 | SE-DDS | SAS | 30/01/79 |
| 853 | 47724 | -51 | N767NC | North Central Airlines | 15/04/77 | 897 | 47778 | -41 | LN-RLP | SAS | 07/02/79 |
| 854 | 47729 | -51 | N768NC | North Central Airlines | 27/05/77 | 898 | 47779 | -41 | SE-DDT | SAS | 07/03/79 |
| 855 | 47748 | -41 | LN-RLH | SAS | 01/11/77 | 899 | 47783 | -51 | HB-ISV | Swissair | 07/03/79 |
| 856 | 47754 | -51 | YU-AJU | Inex Adria | 19/05/77 | 900 | 47765 | -32 | N3506T | Texas International | 14/03/79 |
| | | | | | | 901 | 47788 | -32 | N3507T | Texas International | 14/03/79 |
| | | | | | | 902 | 47784 | -51 | HB-ISW | Swissair | 02/05/79 |
| | | | | | | 903 | 47796 | -51 | 9Y-TGC | BWIA International | 18/04/79 |
| | | | | | | 904 | 47785 | -51 | N775NC | North Central Airlines | 20/04/79 |
| | | | | | | 905 | 47786 | -51 | N776NC | North Central Airlines | 27/04/79 |

*Below:*
**Minneapolis-based North Central Airlines started taking delivery of 28 DC-9-51s from 6 April 1976.**

| Fuselage Number | Serial Number | Model | Registration | Operator | Delivery Date |
|---|---|---|---|---|---|
| 906 | 47789 | -32 | PK-GNS | Garuda | 11/05/79 |
| 907 | 47790 | -32 | PK-GNT | Garuda | 16/05/79 |
| 908 | 47791 | -32 | PK-GNU | Garuda | 25/05/79 |
| 910 | 47792 | -32 | PK-GNV | Garuda | 13/06/79 |
| 911 | 47793 | -32 | PK-GNW | Garuda | 20/06/79 |
| 912 | 47787 | -51 | N777NC | North Central Airlines | 22/06/79 |
| 913 | 47797 | -32 | N3508T | Texas International | 03/07/79 |
| 914 | 47798 | -32 | N3509T | Texas International | 12/07/79 |
| 915 | 47794 | -32 | PK-GNX | Garuda | 28/07/79 |
| 916 | 47795 | -32 | PK-GNY | Garuda | 06/08/79 |
| 918 | 47799 | -32 | N3510T | Texas International | 21/08/79 |
| 919 | 48114 | -31 | N934VJ | Allegheny Airlines | 28/08/79 |
| 920 | 48115 | -31 | N935VJ | Allegheny Airlines | 11/09/79 |
| 921 | 48116 | -31 | N936VJ | Allegheny Airlines | 19/09/79 |
| 922 | 48117 | -31 | N937VJ | Allegheny Airlines | 28/09/79 |
| 923 | 48111 | -32 | N3512T | Texas International | 09/10/79 |
| 925 | 48103 | -34 | EC-DGB | Aviaco | 31/10/79 |
| 926 | 48112 | -32 | N3513T | Texas International | 02/11/79 |
| 927 | 48100 | -32 | N778NC | Republic Airlines | 02/11/79 |
| 928 | 48104 | -34 | EC-DGC | Aviaco | 19/11/79 |
| 929 | 48105 | -34 | EC-DGD | Aviaco | 30/11/79 |
| 930 | 48113 | -32 | N3514T | Texas International | 06/12/79 |
| 931 | 48101 | -51 | N779NC | Republic Airlines | 07/12/79 |
| 932 | 48102 | -51 | N780NC | Republic Airlines | 14/12/79 |
| 933 | 48106 | -34 | EC-DGE | Aviaco | 27/12/79 |
| 934 | 48123 | -34 | N927L | Ozark Air Lines | 28/12/79 |
| 935 | 48121 | -51 | N781NC | Republic Airlines | 28/12/79 |
| 936 | 48107 | -51 | N782NC | Republic Airlines | 24/01/80 |
| 937 | 48108 | -51 | N783NC | Republic Airlines | 30/01/80 |
| 939 | 48109 | -51 | N784NC | Republic Airlines | 20/02/80 |
| 940 | 48131 | -31 | N928VJ | USAir | 20/02/80 |
| 942 | 48118 | -31 | N929VJ | USAir | 03/03/80 |
| 943 | 48119 | -31 | N938VJ | USAir | 12/03/80 |
| 945 | 48110 | -51 | N785NC | Republic Airlines | 01/04/80 |
| 947 | 48125 | -32 | XA-AMA | Aeromexico | 04/04/80 |
| 949 | 48120 | -31 | N939VJ | USAir | 25/04/80 |
| 951 | 48126 | -32 | XA-AMB | Aeromexico | 30/04/80 |
| 954 | 48124 | -34 | N928L | Ozark Air Lines | 10/06/80 |
| 956 | 48132 | -32 | PH-DOA | KLM | 10/06/80 |
| 959 | 48133 | -32 | PH-DOB | KLM | 21/07/80 |
| 961 | 48127 | -32 | XA-AMC | Aeromexico | 25/07/80 |
| 964 | 48128 | -32 | XA-AMD | Aeromexico | 20/08/80 |
| 968 | 48129 | -32 | XA-AME | Aeromexico | 11/10/80 |
| 972 | 48122 | -51 | 9Y-TGP | BWIA International | 27/01/81 |
| 976 | 48130 | -32 | XA-AMF | Aeromexico | 05/12/80 |
| 980 | 48134 | -51 | OH-LYX | Finnair | 24/01/81 |
| 982 | 48137 | -32C9 | 161266 | USN | 17/03/81 |
| 984 | 48148 | -51 | N786NC | Republic Airlines | 31/12/80 |
| 987 | 48135 | -51 | OH-LYY | Finnair | 23/03/81 |
| 990 | 48149 | -51 | N787NC | Republic Airlines | 17/04/81 |
| 993 | 48136 | -51 | OH-LYZ | Finnair | 22/04/81 |
| 1014 | 48150 | -32 | N1003P | Aeromexico | 08/10/81 |
| 1017 | 48151 | -32 | N1003U | Aeromexico | 24/11/81 |
| 1021 | 48138 | -31 | N918VJ | USAir | 14/10/81 |
| 1024 | 48139 | -31 | N919VJ | USAir | 21/10/81 |
| 1027 | 48140 | -31 | N920VJ | USAir | 17/11/81 |
| 1030 | 48141 | -31 | N921VJ | USAir | 01/12/81 |
| 1033 | 48142 | -31 | N922VJ | USAir | 08/12/81 |
| 1036 | 48143 | -31 | N923VJ | USAir | 14/12/81 |
| 1039 | 48144 | -31 | N924VJ | USAir | 18/12/81 |
| 1042 | 48145 | -31 | N925VJ | USAir | 22/12/81 |
| 1044 | 48146 | -31 | N926VJ | USAir | 14/01/82 |
| 1046 | 48154 | -31 | N927VJ | USAir | 25/01/82 |
| 1048 | 48147 | -31 | N976VJ | USAir | 08/02/82 |
| 1050 | 48155 | -31 | N977VJ | USAir | 16/02/82 |
| 1052 | 48156 | -31 | N980VJ | USAir | 11/03/82 |
| 1054 | 48157 | -31 | N981VJ | USAir | 18/03/82 |
| 1056 | 48158 | -31 | N982VJ | USAir | 25/03/82 |
| 1058 | 48159 | -31 | N983VJ | USAir | 06/04/82 |
| 1081 | 48165 | -32C9 | 161529 | USN | 30/09/82 |
| 1084 | 48166 | -32C9 | 161530 | USN | 28/10/82 |

*Below:*

**USAir currently operates a fleet of 74 DC-9-31/32s and eight DC-9-51s, one of which is pictured here.**

| Fuselage Number | Serial Number | Model | Registration | Operator | Delivery Date |
|---|---|---|---|---|---|
| 909 | 48000 | -81 | N980DC | Douglas Aircraft Co | 18/10/79 |
| 917 | 48001 | -81 | N1002G | Douglas Aircraft Co | 06/12/79 |
| 924 | 48015 | -81 | OE-LDP | Douglas Aircraft Co | 29/02/80 |
| | | | | Austrian Airlines | 16/05/81 |
| 938 | 48002 | -81 | HB-INC | Swissair | 13/09/80 |
| 941 | 48016 | -81 | OE-LDR | Austrian Airlines | 03/10/80 |
| 944 | 48003 | -81 | HB-IND | Swissair | 26/10/80 |
| 946 | 48034 | -81 | N924PS | PSA-Pacific Southwest Airlines | 14/11/80 |
| 948 | 48024 | -81 | N10022 | Austral Lineas Aereas | 08/01/81 |
| 950 | 48004 | -81 | HB-INE | Swissair | 21/11/80 |
| 952 | 48025 | -81 | N10027 | Austral | 08/01/81 |
| 953. | 48029 | -81 | JA8458 | TDA-Toa Domestic Airlines | 30/01/81 |
| 955 | 48035 | -81 | N925PS | PSA | 31/03/81 |
| 957 | 48005 | -81 | HB-INF | Swissair | 28/01/81 |
| 958 | 48017 | -81 | OE-LDS | Austrian Airlines | 16/01/81 |
| 960 | 48026 | -81 | N10028 | Musa Air Corporation | 29/06/81 |
| 962 | 48030 | -81 | JA8459 | TDA | 05/03/81 |
| 963 | 48036 | -81 | N926PS | PSA | 09/03/81 |
| 965 | 48037 | -81 | N927PS | PSA | 08/01/81 |
| 966 | 48006 | -81 | HB-ING | Swissair | 03/04/81 |
| 967 | 48044 | -81 | N809HA | Hawaiian Airlines | 24/04/81 |
| 969 | 48031 | -81 | JA8460 | TDA | 17/04/81 |
| 970 | 48045 | -81 | N819HA | Hawaiian Airlines | 04/05/81 |
| 971 | 48007 | -81 | HB-INH | Swissair | 08/05/81 |
| 973 | 48027 | -81 | N475AC | Air California | 15/05/81 |
| 974 | 48052 | -81 | N928PS | PSA | 15/05/81 |
| 975 | 48051 | -81 | N829HA | Hawaiian Airlines | 10/06/81 |
| 977 | 48046 | -81 | YU-AJZ | Inex Adria Aviopromet | 10/06/81 |
| 978 | 48032 | -81 | JA8461 | TDA | 05/06/81 |
| 979 | 48028 | -81 | N476AC | Air California | 15/06/81 |
| 981 | 48008 | -81 | HB-INI | Swissair | 02/07/81 |
| 983 | 48049 | -81 | N10029 | Muse Air | 02/07/81 |
| 985 | 48009 | -81 | HB-INK | Swissair | 20/06/81 |
| 986 | 48053 | -81 | N929PS | PSA | 10/07/81 |
| 988 | 48033 | -81 | JA8462 | TDA | 29/07/81 |
| 989 | 48050 | -81 | N1003G | Austral | 08/08/81 |
| 991 | 48058 | -81 | N8839HA | Hawaiian Airlines | 20/07/81 |
| 992 | 48010 | -81 | HB-INL | Swissair | 24/07/81 |
| 994 | 48011 | -81 | HB-INM | Swissair | 05/08/81 |
| 995 | 48018 | -81 | OE-LDT | Austrian Airlines | 25/07/81 |
| 996 | 48054 | -82 | N301RC | Republic Airlines | 05/08/81 |
| 997 | 48012 | -81 | HB-INN | Swissair | 29/08/81 |
| 998 | 48047 | -82 | YU-ANA | Inex Adria | 11/08/81 |
| 999 | 48070 | -81 | JA8468 | TDA | 09/11/81 |
| 1000 | 48013 | -81 | HB-INO | Swissair | 04/09/81 |
| 1001 | 48019 | -81 | OE-LDU | Austrian Airlines | 05/09/81 |
| 1002 | 48038 | -81 | N930PS | PSA | 10/09/81 |
| 1003 | 48039 | -81 | N931PS | PSA | 10/09/81 |
| 1004 | 48071 | -81 | JA8469 | TDA | 18/12/81 |
| 1005 | 48048 | -82 | YU-ANB | Inex Adria | 19/09/81 |
| 1006 | 48040 | -81 | N932PS | PSA | 10/09/81 |
| 1007 | 48055 | -82 | N302RC | Republic Airlines | 05/09/81 |
| 1008 | 48041 | -81 | N933PS | PSA | 28/09/81 |
| 1009 | 48042 | -81 | N934PS | PSA | 28/09/81 |
| 1010 | 48043 | -81 | N935PS | PSA | 08/10/81 |
| 1011 | 48072 | -81 | JA8470 | TDA | 25/02/82 |
| 1012 | 48056 | -82 | N930MC | Muse Air | 07/05/82 |
| 1013 | 48014 | -81 | HB-INP | Swissair | 30/10/81 |
| 1015 | 48062 | -82 | N477AC | Air California | 15/10/81 |
| 1016 | 48079 | -82 | N779JA | Jet America Airlines | 13/11/81 |
| 1018 | 48073 | -81 | N849HA | Hawaiian Airlines | 25/11/81 |
| 1019 | 48066 | -82 | N479AC | Air California | 09/11/81 |
| 1020 | 48063 | -82 | N478AC | Air California | 21/10/81 |
| 1022 | 48080 | -82 | N778JA | Jet America Airlines | 13/11/81 |
| 1023 | 48057 | -82 | N931MC | Muse Air | 07/05/82 |
| 1025 | 49100 | -81 | HB-INA | Swissair | 12/12/81 |
| 1026 | 48074 | -81 | N859HA | Hawaiian Airlines | 11/12/81 |
| 1028 | 48067 | -82 | N1003X | Aeromexico | 14/12/81 |
| 1029 | 48086 | -82 | N307RC | Republic Airlines | 21/12/81 |
| 1031 | 48068 | -82 | N1003Y | Aeromexico | 22/12/81 |
| 1032 | 48069 | -82 | N1003Z | Aeromexico | 27/12/81 |
| 1034 | 48092 | -81 | N936PS | PSA | 17/12/81 |
| 1035 | 48087 | -82 | YU-ANC | Inex Adria | 02/04/82 |
| 1037 | 48088 | -82 | N309RC | Republic Airlines | 02/12/82 |
| 1038 | 48089 | -82 | N311RC | Republic Airlines | 02/12/82 |
| 1040 | 48090 | -82 | N312RC | Republic Airlines | 08/12/82 |
| 1041 | 48091 | -82 | N1004G | Republic Airlines | 26/04/83 |
| 1043 | 48083 | -82 | N10033 | Aeromexico | 26/02/82 |
| 1045 | 48020 | -81 | OE-LDV | Austrian Airlines | 12/02/82 |
| 1047 | 48059 | -81 | OE-LDW | Austrian Airlines | 20/02/82 |
| 1049 | 48093 | -81 | N937PS | PSA | 22/03/82 |
| 1051 | 49101 | -81 | HB-INB | Swissair | 17/03/82 |
| 1053 | 48094 | -81 | N938PS | PSA | 07/04/82 |
| 1055 | 48095 | -81 | N940PS | PSA | 23/04/82 |
| 1057 | 48096 | -82 | N941PS | PSA | 20/05/82 |
| 1059 | 48097 | -82 | N942PS | PSA | 20/05/82 |
| 1060 | 48098 | -82 | N943PS | PSA | 27/05/82 |
| 1061 | 49116 | -82 | N9801F | Frontier Airlines | 22/04/82 |
| 1062 | 49110 | -82 | N1004L | Republic Airlines | 26/08/83 |
| 1063 | 49117 | -82 | N9802F | Frontier Airlines | 04/05/82 |
| 1064 | 49111 | -82 | N781JA | Jet America Airlines | 09/12/83 |
| 1065 | 49118 | -82 | N9803F | Frontier Airlines | 13/05/82 |
| 1066 | 49114 | -82 | N9804F | Frontier Airlines | 03/12/82 |
| 1067 | 48099 | -81 | N939PS | PSA | 17/06/82 |
| 1068 | 49112 | -82 | N480AC | Air California | 28/05/82 |
| 1069 | 49113 | -82 | N481AC | Air California | 22/06/82 |
| 1070 | 49119 | -82 | N944PS | PSA | 15/07/82 |
| 1071 | 49120 | -81 | N932MC | Muse Air | 28/09/82 |
| 1072 | 49121 | -81 | N933MC | Muse Air | 28/09/82 |
| 1073 | 49122 | -81 | N934MC | Muse Air | 14/12/82 |
| 1074 | 49125 | -81 | N935MC | Muse Air | 29/11/82 |
| 1075 | 49123 | -82 | PJ-SEF | ALM-Antillean Airlines | 04/10/82 |
| 1076 | 49102 | -82 | N9805F | Frontier Airlines | 24/11/82 |
| 1077 | 49124 | -82 | PJ-SEG | ALM | 04/10/82 |
| 1078 | 48021 | -81 | OE-LDX | Austrian Airlines | 28/02/83 |
| 1079 | 48022 | -82 | PH-MCD | Martinair Holland | 28/03/83 |
| 1080 | 49126 | -82 | N780JA | Jet America Airlines | 11/03/83 |
| 1082 | 49127 | -82 | N801NY | New York Air | 02/09/83 |
| 1083 | 49103 | -82 | YV158C | VIASA-Venezolana Internacional de Aviacion | 30/12/82 |
| 1085 | 49104 | -82 | YV159C | VIASA | 30/12/82 |
| 1086 | 49149 | -82 | N505MD | Douglas Aircraft Co | |
| | | | PP-CJM | Cruzeiro do Sul | 08/12/82 |
| 1087 | 49150 | -82 | OH-LMN | Finnair | 11/03/83 |
| 1088 | 49151 | -82 | OH-LMO | Finnair | 25/03/83 |
| 1089 | 49152 | -82 | OH-LMP | Finnair | 29/04/83 |
| 1090 | 49138 | -82 | N945PS | PSA | 18/04/83 |
| 1091 | 49139 | -82 | N946PS | PSA | 12/05/83 |
| 1092 | 49140 | -82 | B2101 | CAAC-Civil Aviation Administration of China | 12/12/83 |
| 1093 | 49141 | -82 | B2102 | CAAC | 12/12/83 |
| 1094 | 49142 | -82 | N947PS | PSA | 17/10/83 |
| 1095 | 49143 | -82 | N948PS | PSA | 17/12/82 |
| 1096 | 49144 | -82 | PH-MBZ | Martinair Holland | 15/02/83 |
| 1097 | 49145 | -82 | N203AA | American Airlines | 12/05/83 |
| 1098 | 49166 | -82 | N901TW | TWA - Trans World Airlines | 18/04/83 |
| 1099 | 49167 | -82 | N216AA | American Airlines | 10/05/83 |
| 1100 | 49168 | -82 | N218AA | American Airlines | 04/05/83 |
| 1101 | 49153 | -82 | N902TW | TWA | 27/04/83 |
| 1102 | 49154 | -82 | N903TW | TWA | 12/05/83 |
| 1103 | 49155 | -82 | N205AA | American Airlines | 06/06/83 |
| 1104 | 49156 | -82 | N904TW | TWA | 24/05/83 |
| 1105 | 49157 | -82 | N905TW | TWA | 27/05/83 |
| 1106 | 49158 | -82 | N207AA | American Airlines | 07/06/83 |
| 1107 | 49159 | -82 | N208AA | American Airlines | 27/06/83 |
| 1108 | 49160 | -82 | N906TW | TWA | 23/06/83 |
| 1109 | 49161 | -82 | N210AA | American Airlines | 28/06/83 |
| 1110 | 49162 | -82 | N214AA | American Airlines | 29/07/83 |
| 1111 | 49163 | -82 | N215AA | American Airlines | 01/08/83 |
| 1112 | 49171 | -82 | N219AA | American Airlines | 02/08/83 |
| 1113 | 49172 | -82 | N221AA | American Airlines | 17/08/83 |
| 1114 | 49173 | -82 | N223AA | American Airlines | 02/09/83 |
| 1115 | 49174 | -82 | N224AA | American Airlines | 29/08/83 |
| 1116 | 49175 | -82 | N225AA | American Airlines | 08/09/83 |
| 1117 | 49165 | -82 | N907TW | TWA | 02/09/83 |
| 1118 | 49169 | -82 | N908TW | TWA | 22/09/83 |
| 1119 | 49170 | -82 | N909TW | TWA | 13/10/83 |
| 1120 | 49176 | -82 | N226AA | American Airlines | 26/10/83 |
| 1121 | 49177 | -82 | N227AA | American Airlines | 28/10/83 |
| 1122 | 49178 | -82 | N228AA | American Airlines | 01/11/83 |
| 1123 | 49179 | -82 | N232AA | American Airlines | 03/11/83 |
| 1124 | 49180 | -82 | N233AA | American Airlines | 30/11/83 |
| 1125 | 49181 | -82 | N234AA | American Airlines | 06/12/83 |
| 1126 | 49192 | -82 | I-DAWA | Alitalia | 16/12/83 |
| 1127 | 49193 | -82 | I-DAWE | Alitalia | 16/12/83 |

*Above:*
**Frontier Airlines' first MD-82, delivered in April 1982.**

| Fuselage Number | Serial Number | Model | Registration | Operator | Delivery Date |
|---|---|---|---|---|---|
| 1128 | 49182 | -82 | N911TW | TWA | 09/12/83 |
| 1129 | 49183 | -82 | N912TW | TWA | 20/12/83 |
| 1130 | 49194 | -82 | I-DAWI | Alitalia | 24/02/84 |
| 1131 | 49184 | -82 | N913TW | TWA | 23/03/84 |
| 1132 | 49185 | -82 | N914TW | TWA | 13/04/84 |
| 1133 | 49186 | -82 | N915TW | TWA | 19/04/84 |
| 1134 | 49187 | -82 | N916TW | TWA | 25/04/84 |
| 1135 | 49115 | -81 | OE-LDY | Austrian Airlines | 04/05/84 |
| 1136 | 49195 | -82 | I-DAWO | Alitalia | 11/05/84 |
| 1137 | 49196 | -82 | I-DAWU | Alitalia | 20/05/84 |
| 1138 | 49197 | -82 | I-DAWB | Alitalia | 27/05/84 |
| 1139 | 49222 | -82 | N802NY | New York Air | 25/06/84 |
| 1140 | 49229 | -82 | N803NY | New York Air | 21/06/84 |
| 1141 | 49230 | -82 | N950U | American Airlines | 19/06/84 |
| 1142 | 49198 | -82 | I-DAWC | Alitalia | 26/06/84 |
| 1143 | 49199 | -82 | I-DAWD | Alitalia | 30/06/84 |
| 1144 | 49237 | -82 | N949PS | PSA | 30/06/84 |
| 1145 | 49245 | -82 | N951U | American Airlines | 26/06/84 |
| 1146 | 49246 | -82 | N804NY | New York Air | 06/08/84 |
| 1147 | 49200 | -82 | I-DAWF | Alitalia | 24/07/84 |
| 1148 | 49201 | -82 | I-DAWG | Alitalia | 30/07/84 |
| 1149 | 49249 | -82 | N805NY | New York Air | 14/08/84 |
| 1150 | 49260 | 82 | N806NY | New York Air | 22/08/84 |
| 1151 | 49247 | -82 | HB-IKK | Alisarda | 20/09/84 |
| 1152 | 49248 | -82 | HB-IKL | Alisarda | 27/09/84 |
| 1153 | 49261 | -82 | N807NY | New York Air | 05/09/84 |
| 1154 | 49251 | -82 | N236AA | American Airlines | 06/09/84 |
| 1155 | 49253 | -82 | N237AA | American Airlines | 14/09/84 |
| 1156 | 49254 | -82 | N241AA | American Airlines | 11/09/84 |
| 1157 | 49255 | -82 | N242AA | American Airlines | 17/09/84 |
| 1158 | 49256 | -82 | N244AA | American Airlines | 21/09/84 |
| 1159 | 49262 | -82 | N808NY | New York Air | 15/11/84 |
| 1160 | 49257 | -82 | N245AA | American Airlines | 02/10/84 |
| 1161 | 49258 | -82 | N246AA | American Airlines | 09/10/84 |
| 1162 | 49259 | -82 | N248AA | American Airlines | 15/10/84 |
| 1163 | 49263 | -82 | N809NY | New York Air | 15/11/84 |
| 1164 | 49269 | -82 | N249AA | American Airlines | 26/10/84 |
| 1165 | 49270 | -82 | N251AA | American Airlines | 31/10/84 |
| 1166 | 49271 | -82 | N274AA | American Airlines | 07/11/84 |
| 1167 | 49272 | -82 | N275AA | American Airlines | 13/11/84 |
| 1168 | 49273 | -82 | N276AA | American Airlines | 20/11/84 |
| 1169 | 49252 | -82 | OH-LMS | Finnair | 19/10/85 |
| 1170 | 49202 | -82 | I-DAWH | Alitalia | 30/11/84 |
| 1171 | 49264 | -82 | N810NY | New York Air | 20/12/84 |
| 1172 | 49188 | -82 | XA-AMO | Aeromexico | 17/12/84 |
| 1173 | 49189 | -82 | XA-AMP | Aeromexico | 20/12/84 |
| 1174 | 49203 | -82 | I-DAWJ | ATI-Aero Transporti Italiani | 18/12/84 |

| Fuselage Number | Serial Number | Model | Registration | Operator | Delivery Date |
|---|---|---|---|---|---|
| 1175 | 49286 | -82 | N253AA | American Airlines | 04/01/85 |
| 1176 | 49287 | -82 | N255AA | American Airlines | 15/01/85 |
| 1177 | 49231 | -82 | N930AS | Alaska Airlines | 29/03/85 |
| 1178 | 49232 | -82 | N931AS | Alaska Airlines | 20/02/85 |
| 1179 | 49204 | -82 | I-DAWL | Alitalia | 19/02/85 |
| 1180 | 49190 | -82 | XA-AMQ | Aeromexico | 19/02/85 |
| 1181 | 49277 | -82 | HB-INR | Balair | 01/02/85 |
| 1182 | 49164 | -81 | OE-LDZ | Austrian Airlines | 15/02/85 |
| 1183 | 49278 | -81 | OE-LMA | Austrian Airlines | 27/02/85 |
| 1184 | 49205 | -82 | I-DAWM | Alitalia | 27/02/85 |
| 1185 | 49265 | -82 | N811NY | New York Air | 29/03/85 |
| 1186 | 49250 | -82 | N812NY | New York Air | 04/04/85 |
| 1187 | 49288 | -82 | N258AA | American Airlines | 08/03/85 |
| 1188 | 49206 | -82 | I-DAWP | Alitalia | 15/03/85 |
| 1189 | 49207 | -82 | I-DAWQ | Alitalia | 20/03/85 |
| 1190 | 49208 | -82 | I-DAWR | Alitalia | 25/03/85 |
| 1191 | 49209 | -82 | I-DAWS | Alitalia | 02/04/85 |
| 1192 | 49210 | -82 | I-DAWT | ATI | 08/04/85 |
| 1193 | 49289 | -82 | N259AA | American Airlines | 08/04/85 |
| 1194 | 49280 | -81 | JA8496 | TDA | 09/04/85 |
| 1195 | 49290 | -82 | N262AA | American Airlines | 19/04/85 |
| 1196 | 49366 | -82 | N917TW | TWA | 23/04/85 |
| 1197 | 49367 | -82 | N918TW | TWA | 25/04/85 |
| 1198 | 49368 | -82 | N919TW | TWA | 02/05/85 |
| 1199 | 49369 | -82 | N920TW | TWA | 08/05/85 |
| 1200 | 49281 | -81 | JA8497 | TDA | 20/05/85 |
| 1201 | 49373 | -82 | HL7272 | Korean Air Lines | 10/08/85 |
| 1202 | 49211 | -82 | I-DAWV | ATI | 24/05/85 |
| 1203 | 49233 | -02 | N932AS | Alaska Airlines | 14/06/85 |
| 1204 | 49234 | -82 | N933AS | Alaska Airlines | 28/06/85 |
| 1205 | 49379 | -82 | YU-ANG | Inex Adria | 08/06/85 |
| 1206 | 49370 | -82 | N816NY | New York Air | 25/06/85 |
| 1207 | 49371 | -82 | N817NY | New York Air | 28/06/85 |
| 1208 | 49374 | -82 | HL7273 | Korean Air Lines | 21/08/85 |
| 1209 | 49284 | -83 | OH-LMR | Finnair | 26/06/85 |
| 1210 | 49291 | -82 | N266AA | American Airlines | 02/07/85 |
| 1211 | 49292 | -82 | N269AA | American Airlines | 10/07/85 |
| 1212 | 49293 | -82 | N271AA | American Airlines | 16/07/85 |
| 1213 | 49294 | -82 | N278AA | American Airlines | 17/07/85 |
| 1214 | 49295 | -82 | N279AA | American Airlines | 25/07/85 |
| 1215 | 49296 | -82 | N283AA | American Airlines | 29/07/85 |
| 1216 | 49297 | -82 | N285AA | American Airlines | 03/08/85 |
| 1217 | 49298 | -82 | N286AA | American Airlines | 06/08/85 |
| 1218 | 49299 | -82 | N287AA | American Airlines | 13/08/85 |
| 1219 | 49300 | -82 | N288AA | American Airlines | 16/08/85 |
| 1220 | 49301 | -82 | N289AA | American Airlines | 22/08/85 |
| 1221 | 49302 | -82 | N290AA | American Airlines | 27/08/85 |
| 1222 | 49303 | -82 | N291AA | American Airlines | 03/09/85 |
| 1223 | 49304 | -82 | N292AA | American Airlines | 06/09/85 |
| 1224 | 49355 | -82 | B2103 | CAAC | 07/10/85 |
| 1225 | 49380 | -81 | OY-KGT | SAS-Scandinavian Airlines System | 10/10/85 |

| Fuselage Number | Serial Number | Model | Registration | Operator | Delivery Date |
|---|---|---|---|---|---|
| 1226 | 49305 | -82 | N293AA | American Airlines | 23/09/85 |
| 1227 | 49306 | -82 | N294AA | American Airlines | 25/09/85 |
| 1228 | 49307 | -82 | N295AA | American Airlines | 02/10/85 |
| 1229 | 49308 | -82 | N296AA | American Airlines | 07/10/85 |
| 1230 | 49279 | -81 | OE-LMB | Austrian Airlines | 20/10/85 |
| 1231 | 49381 | -81 | OY-KGZ | SAS | 20/10/85 |
| 1232 | 49382 | -81 | LN-RLE | SAS | 26/10/85 |
| 1233 | 49212 | -82 | I-DAWW | ATI | 04/11/85 |
| 1234 | 49235 | -83 | N934AS | Alaska Airlines | 16/11/85 |
| 1235 | 49236 | -83 | N935AS | Alaska Airlines | 10/12/85 |
| 1236 | 49383 | -82 | LN-RLF | SAS | 17/11/85 |
| 1237 | 49384 | -82 | SE-DFS | SAS | 02/12/85 |
| 1238 | 49266 | -82 | N952U | Ozark Air Lines | 27/11/85 |
| 1239 | 49267 | -82 | N953U | Ozark Air Lines | 04/12/85 |
| 1240 | 49425 | -82 | B2104 | CAAC | 28/11/85 |
| 1241 | 49428 | -82 | B2105 | CAAC | 26/12/85 |
| 1242 | 49429 | -82 | N951PS | PSA | 25/04/86 |
| 1243 | 49213 | -82 | I-DAWY | ATI | 18/12/85 |
| 1244 | 49385 | -82 | SE-DFT | SAS | 20/12/85 |
| 1245 | 49214 | -82 | I-DAWZ | ATI | 18/12/85 |
| 1246 | 49309 | -82 | N297AA | American Airlines | 10/01/86 |
| 1247 | 49310 | -82 | N298AA | American Airlines | 13/01/86 |
| 1248 | 49311 | -82 | N400AA | American Airlines | 17/01/86 |
| 1249 | 49312 | -82 | N70401 | American Airlines | 24/01/86 |
| 1250 | 49356 | -81 | HB-INS | Swissair | 25/01/86 |
| 1251 | 49357 | -81 | HB-INT | Swissair | 14/02/86 |
| 1252 | 49372 | -81 | OE-LMC | Austrian Airlines | 28/02/86 |
| 1253 | 49215 | -82 | I-DAVA | ATI | 18/02/86 |
| 1254 | 49420 | -81 | OY-KGY | SAS | 18/02/86 |
| 1255 | 49313 | -82 | N402AA | American Airlines | 28/02/86 |
| 1256 | 49314 | -82 | N403AA | American Airlines | 24/02/86 |
| 1257 | 49315 | -82 | N70404 | American Airlines | 04/03/86 |
| 1258 | 49316 | -82 | N405AA | American Airlines | 07/03/86 |
| 1259 | 49317 | -82 | N406AA | American Airlines | 11/03/86 |
| 1260 | 49415 | -82 | B2106 | SAIC 1/CAAC | 31/07/87 |
| 1261 | 49402 | -83 | D-ALLD | Aero Lloyd | 25/03/86 |
| 1262 | 49216 | -82 | I-DAVB | Alitalia | 20/03/86 |
| 1263 | 49421 | -82 | SE-DFU | SAS | 21/03/86 |
| 1264 | 49422 | -81 | SE-DFV | SAS | 26/03/86 |
| 1265 | 49318 | -82 | N407AA | American Airlines | 04/04/86 |
| 1266 | 49319 | -82 | N408AA | American Airlines | 09/04/86 |
| 1267 | 49320 | -82 | N409AA | American Airlines | 11/04/86 |
| 1268 | 49217 | -82 | I-DAVC | ATI | 29/04/86 |
| 1269 | 49390 | -83 | 9Y-THN | BWIA International | 25/04/86 |
| 1270 | 49391 | -82 | EI-BTA | Frontier Airlines | 29/04/86 |
| 1271 | 49416 | -82 | HL7275 | Korean Air Lines | 14/05/86 |
| 1272 | 49392 | -82 | EI-BTB | Frontier Airlines | 01/05/86 |
| 1273 | 49321 | -82 | N410AA | American Airlines | 09/05/86 |
| 1274 | 49218 | -82 | I-DAVD | ATI | 21/05/86 |
| 1275 | 49363 | -83 | N936AS | Alaska Airlines | 29/05/86 |
| 1276 | 49364 | -83 | N937AS | Alaska Airlines | 28/05/86 |
| 1277 | 49365 | -83 | N938AS | Alaska Airlines | 03/06/86 |
| 1278 | 49417 | -82 | HL7276 | Korean Air Lines | 01/06/86 |
| 1279 | 49393 | -82 | EI-BTC | Frontier Airlines | 02/06/86 |
| 1280 | 49322 | -82 | N411AA | American Airlines | 06/06/86 |
| 1281 | 49323 | -82 | N412AA | American Airlines | 24/06/86 |
| 1282 | 49282 | -81 | JA8498 | TDA | 20/06/86 |
| 1283 | 49423 | -82 | LN-RLG | SAS | 27/06/86 |
| 1284 | 49424 | -82 | SE-DFX | SAS | 20/06/86 |
| 1285 | 49394 | -82 | EI-BTD | Frontier Airlines | 25/06/86 |
| 1286 | 49395 | -83 | YV-36C | LAV-Linea Aeropostal Venezolana | 30/06/86 |
| 1287 | 49386 | -82 | N784JA | Jet America Airlines | 02/12/86 |
| 1288 | 49387 | -82 | N785JA | Jet America Airlines | 02/12/86 |
| 1289 | 49324 | -82 | N413AA | American Airlines | 14/07/86 |
| 1290 | 49325 | -82 | N33414 | American Airlines | 18/07/86 |
| 1291 | 49443 | -82 | N952PS | PSA | 28/07/86 |
| 1292 | 49501 | -82 | B2107 | SAIC 2/CAAC | 17/12/87 |
| 1293 | 49478 | -82 | N818NY | New York Air | 08/08/86 |
| 1294 | 49358 | -81 | HB-INU | Swissair | 28/07/86 |
| 1295 | 49326 | -82 | N415AA | American Airlines | 05/08/86 |
| 1296 | 49327 | -82 | N416AA | American Airlines | 08/08/86 |
| 1297 | 49479 | -82 | N819NY | New York Air | 15/08/86 |
| 1298 | 49480 | -82 | N820NY | New York Air | 29/08/86 |
| 1299 | 49283 | -81 | JA8499 | TDA | 13/09/86 |
| 1300 | 49502 | -82 | B2108 | SAIC 3/CAAC | 13/04/88 |
| 1301 | 49328 | -82 | N417AA | American Airlines | 22/08/86 |
| 1302 | 49329 | -82 | N418AA | American Airlines | 28/08/86 |
| 1303 | 49436 | -82 | OY-KHC | SAS | 08/09/86 |
| 1304 | 49440 | -82 | YU-ANO | Adria Airways | 10/09/86 |
| 1305 | 49396 | -83 | SE-DHB | Transwede Airways | 24/09/86 |
| 1306 | 49331 | -82 | N419AA | American Airlines | 12/09/86 |
| 1307 | 49332 | -82 | N420AA | American Airlines | 19/09/86 |
| 1308 | 49481 | -82 | N72821 | Continental Airlines | 30/09/86 |
| 1309 | 49482 | -82 | N72822 | Continental Airlines | 03/10/86 |
| 1310 | 49219 | -82 | I-DAVF | ATI | 09/10/86 |
| 1311 | 49333 | -82 | N77421 | American Airlines | 07/10/86 |
| 1312 | 49334 | -82 | N422AA | American Airlines | 10/10/86 |
| 1313 | 49448 | -83 | 9Y-THQ | BWIA International | 17/10/86 |
| 1314 | 49483 | -82 | N76823 | Continental Airlines | 22/10/86 |
| 1315 | 49484 | -82 | N72824 | Continental Airlines | 04/11/86 |
| 1316 | 49485 | -82 | N72825 | Continental Airlines | 14/11/86 |
| 1317 | 49486 | -82 | N69826 | Continental Airlines | 25/11/86 |
| 1318 | 49439 | -82 | N18835 | Continental Airlines | 19/12/86 |
| 1319 | 49220 | -82 | I-DAVG | ATI | 19/11/86 |
| 1320 | 49335 | -82 | N423AA | American Airlines | 03/11/86 |
| 1321 | 49336 | -82 | N424AA | American Airlines | 05/11/86 |
| 1322 | 49441 | -82 | N35836 | Continental Airlines | 08/12/86 |
| 1323 | 49444 | -82 | N936MC | Transtar Airlines | 12/12/86 |
| 1324 | 49450 | -82 | N937MC | Transtar Airlines | 12/12/86 |
| 1325 | 49337 | -82 | N70425 | American Airlines | 25/11/86 |
| 1326 | 49388 | -87 | N87MD | Douglas Aircraft Co | 04/12/86 |
| 1327 | 49338 | -82 | N426AA | American Airlines | 26/11/86 |
| 1328 | 49339 | -82 | N427AA | American Airlines | 05/12/86 |
| 1329 | 49340 | -82 | N428AA | American Airlines | 08/12/86 |
| 1330 | 49221 | -82 | I-DAVH | ATI | 30/12/86 |
| 1331 | 49397 | -83 | SE-DHC | Transwede Airways | 16/02/87 |
| 1332 | 49398 | -83 | G-PATA | Paramount Airways | 24/04/87 |
| 1333 | 49389 | -87 | SE-DHG | Douglas Aircraft Co | 13/01/87 |
|  |  |  |  | Transwede Airways | 04/08/88 |
| 1334 | 49430 | -82 | I-DAVI | Alitalia | 30/12/86 |
| 1335 | 49487 | -82 | N77827 | Continental Airlines | 30/12/86 |
| 1336 | 49341 | -82 | N429AA | American Airlines | 23/12/86 |
| 1337 | 49342 | -82 | N430AA | American Airlines | 06/01/87 |
| 1338 | 49532 | -82 | N901DL | Delta Air Lines | 09/03/87 |
| 1339 | 49343 | -82 | N431AA | American Airlines | 26/05/87 |
| 1340 | 49525 | -83 | N938MC | Transtar Airlines | 25/03/87 |
| 1341 | 49533 | -82 | N902DL | Delta Air Lines | 12/03/87 |
| 1342 | 49526 | -83 | N939MC | Transtar Airlines | 12/03/87 |
| 1343 | 49399 | -83 | F-GGMA | Minerve | 18/03/87 |
| 1344 | 49534 | -82 | N903DL | Delta Air Lines | 18/03/87 |
| 1345 | 49437 | -82 | LN-RLR | SAS | 06/03/87 |
| 1346 | 49503 | -82 | B2109 | SAIC 4/China Eastern | 16/07/88 |
| 1347 | 49535 | -82 | N904DL | Delta Air Lines | 28/03/87 |
| 1348 | 49536 | -82 | N905DL | Delta Air Lines | 01/04/87 |
| 1349 | 49359 | -81 | HB-INV | Swissair | 18/03/87 |
| 1350 | 49488 | -82 | N71828 | Continental Airlines | 02/04/87 |
| 1351 | 49489 | -82 | N72829 | Continental Airlines | 10/04/87 |
| 1352 | 49490 | -82 | N72830 | Continental Airlines | 10/04/87 |
| 1353 | 49438 | -81 | SE-DFY | SAS | 10/04/87 |
| 1354 | 49449 | -83 | D-ALLE | Aero Lloyd | 28/03/87 |
| 1355 | 49537 | -82 | N906DL | Delta Air Lines | 24/04/87 |
| 1356 | 49400 | -83 | G-PATB | Paramount Airways | 24/07/87 |
| 1357 | 49401 | -83 | EC-ECN | Canafrica Transportes Aereos | 29/04/87 |
| 1358 | 49442 | -83 | EC-ECO | Canafrica | 28/04/87 |
| 1359 | 49461 | -81 | JA8260 | TDA | 16/05/87 |
| 1360 | 49491 | -82 | N14831 | Continental Airlines | 05/05/87 |
| 1361 | 49492 | -82 | N35832 | Continental Airlines | 15/05/87 |
| 1362 | 49531 | -82 | I-SMEG | Alisarda | 21/05/87 |
| 1363 | 49504 | -82 | B2120 | SAIC 5/China Eastern | 01/11/88 |
| 1364 | 49493 | -82 | N18833 | Continental Airlines | 19/05/87 |
| 1365 | 49538 | -82 | N907DL | Delta Air Lines | 21/05/87 |
| 1366 | 49539 | -82 | N908DL | Delta Air Lines | 24/05/87 |
| 1367 | 49567 | -83 | YV-38C | LAV | 20/05/87 |
| 1368 | 49494 | -82 | N10834 | Continental Airlines | 29/05/87 |
| 1369 | 49580 | -82 | N14840 | Continental Airlines | 05/06/87 |
| 1370 | 49344 | -83 | N562AA | American Airlines | 03/06/87 |
| 1371 | 49345 | -83 | N563AA | American Airlines | 05/06/87 |
| 1372 | 49346 | -83 | N564AA | American Airlines | 08/06/87 |
| 1373 | 49347 | -83 | N565AA | American Airlines | 11/06/87 |
| 1374 | 49348 | -83 | N566AA | American Airlines | 15/06/87 |
| 1375 | 49349 | -83 | N568AA | American Airlines | 16/06/87 |
| 1376 | 49350 | -82 | N432AA | American Airlines | 16/06/87 |
| 1377 | 49431 | -82 | I-DAVJ | Alitalia | 23/06/87 |
| 1378 | 49432 | -82 | I-DAVK | Alitalia | 23/06/87 |
| 1379 | 49554 | -81 | LN-RMA | SAS | 07/07/87 |
| 1380 | 49568 | -83 | 9Y-THR | BWIA International | 29/06/87 |
| 1381 | 49505 | -82 | B2121 | SAIC 6/China Northern | 15/12/88 |
| 1382 | 49527 | -83 | N931TW | TWA | 10/07/87 |
| 1383 | 49528 | -83 | N9302B | TWA | 16/07/87 |
| 1384 | 49581 | -82 | N15841 | Continental Airlines | 21/07/87 |

| Fuselage Number | Serial Number | Model | Registration | Operator | Delivery Date |
|---|---|---|---|---|---|
| 1385 | 49351 | -83 | N569AA | American Airlines | 13/07/87 |
| 1386 | 49352 | -83 | N570AA | American Airlines | 16/07/87 |
| 1387 | 49353 | -83 | N571AA | American Airlines | 20/07/87 |
| 1388 | 49451 | -82 | N433AA | American Airlines | 22/07/87 |
| 1389 | 49452 | -82 | N434AA | American Airlines | 24/07/87 |
| 1390 | 49453 | -82 | N435AA | American Airlines | 29/07/87 |
| 1391 | 49454 | -82 | N436AA | American Airlines | 31/07/87 |
| 1392 | 49455 | -82 | N437AA | American Airlines | 05/08/87 |
| 1393 | 49456 | -82 | N438AA | American Airlines | 07/08/87 |
| 1394 | 49418 | -82 | HL7282 | Korean Air Lines | 18/08/87 |
| 1395 | 49540 | -88 | N909DL | Douglas Aircraft Co | 20/08/87 |
|  |  |  |  | Delta Air Lines | 29/12/87 |
| 1396 | 49529 | -83 | N9303K | TWA | 03/09/87 |
| 1397 | 49530 | -83 | N9304C | TWA | 09/09/87 |
| 1398 | 49457 | -82 | N439AA | American Airlines | 25/08/87 |
| 1399 | 49426 | -82 | N954U | TWA | 04/12/87 |
| 1400 | 49506 | -82 | B2122 | SAIC 7/China Northern | 06/03/89 |
| 1401 | 49427 | -82 | N955U | TWA | 04/12/87 |
| 1402 | 49555 | -82 | OY-KHD | SAS | 04/09/87 |
| 1403 | 49419 | -82 | HL7283 | Korean Air Lines | 09/09/87 |
| 1404 | 49403 | -87 | OH-LMA | Finnair | 01/11/87 |
| 1405 | 49569 | -82 | HB-INW | Balair | 18/09/87 |
| 1406 | 49458 | -83 | N572AA | American Airlines | 18/09/87 |
| 1407 | 49459 | -82 | N440AA | American Airlines | 21/09/87 |
| 1408 | 49460 | -82 | N441AA | American Airlines | 23/09/87 |
| 1409 | 49468 | -82 | N442AA | American Airlines | 28/09/87 |
| 1410 | 49469 | -82 | N443AA | American Airlines | 30/09/87 |
| 1411 | 49582 | -82 | N57837 | Continental Airlines | 07/10/87 |
| 1412 | 49411 | -87 | OE-LMK | Austrian Airlines | 27/11/87 |
| 1413 | 49574 | -83 | EC-EFU | LAC-Lineas Aereas Canarias | 19/10/87 |
| 1414 | 49575 | -83 | EC-EFJ | Spantax Lineas Aereas | 29/10/87 |
| 1415 | 49556 | -83 | SE-DFP | SAS | 23/12/87 |
| 1416 | 49541 | -88 | N910DL | Delta Air Lines | 19/12/87 |
| 1417 | 49470 | -82 | N73444 | American Airlines | 26/10/87 |
| 1418 | 49471 | -82 | N445AA | American Airlines | 28/10/87 |
| 1419 | 49634 | -82 | N34838 | Continental Airlines | 24/11/87 |
| 1420 | 49635 | -82 | N14839 | Continental Airlines | 24/11/87 |
| 1421 | 49642 | -83 | SE-DHF | Transwede Airways | 21/02/88 |
| 1422 | 49576 | -83 | EC-EFK | Spantax | 23/11/87 |
| 1423 | 49643 | -83 | G-BNSA | BIA-British Island Airways | 31/12/87 |
| 1424 | 49412 | -87 | OE-LML | Austrian Airlines | 23/12/87 |
| 1425 | 49507 | -82 | B2123 | SAIC 8/China Eastern | 31/05/89 |
| 1426 | 49472 | -82 | N446AA | American Airlines | 20/11/87 |
| 1427 | 49473 | -82 | N447AA | American Airlines | 24/11/87 |
| 1428 | 49433 | -82 | I-DAVL | ATI | 21/01/88 |
| 1429 | 49662 | -83 | G-PATC | Paramount Airways | 25/02/88 |
| 1430 | 49404 | -87 | OH-LMB | Finnair | 08/01/88 |
| 1431 | 49474 | -82 | N448AA | American Airlines | 11/12/87 |
| 1432 | 49475 | -82 | N449AA | American Airlines | 16/12/87 |
| 1433 | 49542 | -88 | N911DL | Delta Air Lines | 29/12/87 |
| 1434 | 49543 | -88 | N912DL | Delta Air Lines | 30/12/87 |
| 1435 | 49602 | -83 | D-ALLF | Aero Lloyd | 21/12/87 |
| 1436 | 49557 | -83 | LN-RMB | SAS | 11/02/88 |
| 1437 | 49663 | -83 | G-PATD | Paramount Airways | 29/04/88 |
| 1438 | 49659 | -83 | YV-39C | LAV | 27/02/88 |
| 1439 | 49476 | -82 | N450AA | American Airlines | 03/02/88 |
| 1440 | 49570 | -81 | HB-INX | Swissair | 25/02/88 |
| 1441 | 49477 | -82 | N451AA | American Airlines | 02/02/88 |
| 1442 | 49603 | -81 | SE-DIA | SAS | 26/04/88 |
| 1443 | 49544 | -88 | N913DL | Delta Air Lines | 21/02/88 |
| 1444 | 49545 | -88 | N914DL | Delta Air Lines | 25/02/88 |
| 1445 | 49660 | -82 | EI-BTX | Unifly Express | 10/03/88 |
| 1446 | 49434 | -82 | I-DAVM | Alitalia | 01/03/88 |
| 1447 | 49546 | -88 | N915DL | Delta Air Lines | 07/03/88 |
| 1448 | 49591 | -88 | N916DL | Delta Air Lines | 31/03/88 |
| 1449 | 49508 | -82 | B2124 | SAIC 9/China Northern | 31/08/89 |
| 1450 | 49553 | -82 | N452AA | American Airlines | 26/02/88 |
| 1451 | 49558 | -82 | N453AA | American Airlines | 02/03/88 |
| 1452 | 49661 | -82 | SU-DAK | ZAS Airline of Egypt | 10/03/88 |
| 1453 | 49670 | -87 | D-ALLG | Aero Lloyd | 15/03/88 |
| 1454 | 49577 | -83 | EC-EHT | Spanair | 25/03/88 |
| 1455 | 49578 | -83 | SE-DHD | Transwede Airways | 16/03/88 |
| 1456 | 49604 | -82 | OY-KHE | SAS | 21/04/88 |
| 1457 | 49585 | -87 | HB-IUA | CTA-Compagnie de Transport Aerien | 04/04/88 |
| 1458 | 49571 | -81 | EB-INY | Swissair | 26/03/88 |
| 1459 | 49657 | -83 | N939AS | Alaska Airlines | 08/04/88 |
| 1460 | 49559 | -82 | N454AA | American Airlines | 31/03/88 |
| 1461 | 49658 | -83 | G-BNSB | BIA | 12/05/88 |
| 1462 | 49560 | -82 | N455AA | American Airlines | 06/04/88 |
| 1463 | 49671 | -87 | D-ALLH | Aero Lloyd | 15/04/88 |
| 1464 | 49617 | -83 | F-GGMB | Minerve | 29/04/88 |
| 1465 | 49579 | -83 | EC-EIG | Spanair | 25/04/88 |
| 1466 | 49667 | -82 | EI-BTY | Unifly Express | 15/05/88 |
| 1467 | 49668 | -82 | EC-EIK | Oasis International Airlines | 26/05/88 |
| 1468 | 49572 | -81 | HB-INZ | Swissair | 07/05/88 |
| 1469 | 49573 | -88 | N917DL | Delta Air Lines | 25/05/88 |
| 1470 | 49583 | -88 | N918DL | Delta Air Lines | 14/05/88 |
| 1471 | 49584 | -88 | N919DL | Delta Air Lines | 19/05/88 |
| 1472 | 49586 | -87 | HB-IUB | CTA | 14/05/88 |
| 1473 | 49644 | -88 | N920DL | Delta Air Lines | 06/06/88 |
| 1474 | 49561 | -82 | N456AA | American Airlines | 24/05/88 |
| 1475 | 49562 | -82 | N457AA | American Airlines | 20/05/88 |
| 1476 | 49464 | -87 | JA8279 | Japan Air System | 02/06/88 |
| 1477 | 49462 | -81 | JA8261 | Japan Air System | 13/06/88 |
| 1478 | 49701 | -82 | N14846 | TWA | 17/06/88 |
| 1479 | 49702 | -82 | N14847 | TWA | 17/06/88 |
| 1480 | 49645 | -88 | N921DL | Delta Air Lines | 08/06/88 |
| 1481 | 49646 | -88 | N922DL | Delta Air Lines | 15/06/88 |
| 1482 | 49509 | -82 | B2125 | SAIC 10/China Eastern | 08/11/89 |
| 1483 | 49619 | -83 | EI-BTU | Unifly Express | 30/06/88 |
| 1484 | 49620 | -83 | EI-BTV | Unifly Express | 01/07/88 |
| 1485 | 49563 | -82 | N458AA | American Airlines | 17/06/88 |
| 1486 | 49564 | -82 | N459AA | American Airlines | 21/06/88 |
| 1487 | 49707 | -83 | F-GFZB | Air Liberté | 26/07/88 |
| 1488 | 49463 | -81 | JA8262 | Japan Air System | 21/07/88 |

*Below:*
**Austrian Airlines was the launch customer of the MD-87.**

| Fuselage Number | Serial Number | Model | Registration | Operator | Delivery Date |
|---|---|---|---|---|---|
| 1489 | 49703 | -82 | N958U | TWA | 06/07/88 |
| 1490 | 49704 | -82 | N959U | TWA | 06/07/88 |
| 1491 | 49705 | -88 | N923DL | Delta Air Lines | 15/07/88 |
| 1492 | 49711 | -88 | N924DL | Delta Air Lines | 27/07/88 |
| 1493 | 49669 | -82 | I-SMEV | Alisarda | 19/07/88 |
| 1494 | 49672 | -83 | EC-EJQ | Spanair | 27/07/88 |
| 1495 | 49621 | -83 | EC-EJU | Spanair | 29/07/88 |
| 1496 | 49565 | -82 | N460AA | American Airlines | 26/07/88 |
| 1497 | 49566 | -82 | N461AA | American Airlines | 02/08/88 |
| 1498 | 49622 | -83 | EC-EJZ | LAC-Lineas Aereas Canarias | 16/08/88 |
| 1499 | 49623 | -83 | SE-DHN | Transwede Airways | 19/08/88 |
| 1500 | 49712 | -88 | N925DL | Delta Air Lines | 16/08/88 |
| 1501 | 49605 | -87 | SE-DIB | SAS | 26/10/88 |
| 1502 | 49624 | -83 | EC-EKM | Oasis International | 24/08/88 |
| 1503 | 49625 | -83 | OH-LMG | Finnair | 26/08/88 |
| 1504 | 49435 | -82 | I-DAVN | ATI | 05/10/88 |
| 1505 | 49592 | -82 | N462AA | American Airlines | 30/08/88 |
| 1506 | 49593 | -82 | N463AA | American Airlines | 31/08/88 |
| 1507 | 49594 | -82 | N464AA | American Airlines | 12/09/88 |
| 1508 | 49673 | -87 | | Douglas Aircraft Co | 07/09/88 |
| 1509 | 49595 | -82 | N465AA | American Airlines | 14/09/88 |
| 1510 | 49596 | -82 | N466AA | American Airlines | 19/09/88 |
| 1511 | 49597 | -82 | N467AA | American Airlines | 22/09/88 |
| 1512 | 49607 | -87 | SE-DIC | SAS | 30/09/88 |
| 1513 | 49598 | -82 | N468AA | American Airlines | 28/09/88 |
| 1514 | 49510 | -82 | B2126 | SAIC 11/China Northern | 12/89 |
| 1515 | 49599 | -82 | N469AA | American Airlines | 27/09/88 |
| 1516 | 49600 | -82 | N470AA | American Airlines | 04/10/88 |
| 1517 | 49609 | -87 | OY-KHF | SAS | 07/10/88 |
| 1518 | 49601 | -82 | N471AA | American Airlines | 07/10/88 |
| 1519 | 49613 | -81 | OY-KHG | SAS | 14/10/88 |
| 1520 | 49647 | -82 | N472AA | American Airlines | 12/10/88 |
| 1521 | 49648 | -82 | N473AA | American Airlines | 17/10/88 |
| 1522 | 49611 | -82 | LN-RMG | SAS | 05/11/88 |
| 1523 | 49713 | -88 | N926DL | Delta Air Lines | 28/10/88 |
| 1524 | 49714 | -88 | N927DL | Delta Air Lines | 01/11/88 |
| 1525 | 49405 | -87 | OH-LMC | Finnair | 24/10/88 |
| 1526 | 49649 | -82 | N474AA | American Airlines | 25/10/88 |
| 1527 | 49650 | -82 | N475AA | American Airlines | 02/11/88 |
| 1528 | 49651 | -82 | N476AA | American Airlines | 28/10/88 |
| 1529 | 49652 | -82 | N477AA | American Airlines | 07/11/88 |
| 1530 | 49715 | -88 | N928DL | Delta Air Lines | 10/11/88 |
| 1531 | 49716 | -88 | N929DL | Delta Air Lines | 17/11/88 |
| 1532 | 49717 | -88 | N930DL | Delta Air Lines | 18/11/88 |
| 1533 | 49718 | -88 | N931DL | Delta Air Lines | 08/12/88 |
| 1534 | 49653 | -82 | N478AA | American Airlines | 22/11/88 |
| 1535 | 49654 | -82 | N479AA | American Airlines | 28/11/88 |
| 1536 | 49655 | -82 | N480AA | American Airlines | 30/11/88 |
| 1537 | 49511 | -82 | B2127 | SAIC 12/China Eastern | 12/89 |
| 1538 | 49626 | -83 | EC-EMG | LAC-Lineas Aereas Canarias | 09/12/88 |
| 1539 | 49822 | -83 | F-GHEB | Air Liberte | 20/12/88 |
| 1540 | 49823 | -83 | G-BPSC | BIA | 23/12/88 |
| 1541 | 49587 | -87 | HB-IUC | CTA | 16/12/88 |
| 1542 | 49709 | -83 | F-GGMC | Minerve | 05/12/88 |
| 1543 | 49615 | -82 | SE-DID | SAS | 08/12/88 |
| 1544 | 49549 | -82 | I-DAVP | ATI | 19/12/88 |
| 1545 | 49656 | -82 | N481AA | American Airlines | 12/12/88 |
| 1546 | 49675 | -82 | N482AA | American Airlines | 16/12/88 |
| 1547 | 49710 | -83 | XA-TOR | Lineas Aereas La Tur | 15/12/88 |
| 1548 | 49512 | -82 | B2128 | SAIC 13/China Northern | 12/89 |
| 1549 | 49724 | -87 | N801ML | Midway Airlines | 29/03/89 |
| 1550 | 49676 | -82 | N483AA | American Airlines | 20/12/88 |
| 1551 | 49677 | -82 | N484AA | American Airlines | 21/12/88 |
| 1552 | 49725 | -87 | N802ML | Midway Airlines | 30/03/89 |
| 1553 | 49728 | -82 | SE-DIE | SAS | 24/02/89 |
| 1554 | 49824 | -83 | 9Y-THU | BWIA International | 23/12/88 |
| 1555 | 49678 | -82 | N485AA | American Airlines | 13/01/89 |
| 1556 | 49614 | -87 | OY-KHI | SAS | 03/03/89 |
| 1557 | 49679 | -82 | N486AA | American Airlines | 20/01/89 |
| 1558 | 49680 | -82 | N487AA | American Airlines | 25/01/89 |
| 1559 | 49769 | -83 | D-ALLK | Aero Lloyd | 01/02/89 |
| 1560 | 49681 | -82 | N488AA | American Airlines | 30/01/89 |
| 1561 | 49708 | -83 | XA-TUR | Lineas Aereas La Tur | 28/02/89 |
| 1562 | 49682 | -82 | N489AA | American Airlines | 08/02/89 |
| 1563 | 49683 | -82 | N490AA | American Airlines | 06/02/89 |
| 1564 | 49684 | -82 | N491AA | American Airlines | 22/02/89 |
| 1565 | 49730 | -82 | N492AA | American Airlines | 15/02/89 |
| 1566 | 49731 | -82 | N493AA | American Airlines | 13/02/89 |
| 1567 | 49732 | -82 | N494AA | American Airlines | 21/02/89 |
| 1568 | 49513 | -82 | B2129 | SAIC 14/China Eastern | 12/89 |
| 1569 | 49606 | -87 | SE-DIF | SAS | 02/03/89 |
| 1570 | 49719 | -88 | N932DL | Delta Air Lines | 24/03/89 |
| 1571 | 49720 | -88 | N933DL | Delta Air Lines | 11/03/89 |
| 1572 | 49608 | -87 | SE-DIH | SAS | 31/03/89 |
| 1573 | 49845 | -83 | D-AGWA | German Wings | 27/03/89 |
| 1574 | 49721 | -88 | N934DL | Delta Air Lines | 15/03/89 |
| 1575 | 49722 | -88 | N935DL | Delta Air Lines | 25/03/89 |
| 1576 | 49723 | -88 | N936DL | Delta Air Lines | 28/04/89 |
| 1577 | 49825 | -83 | N940AS | Alaska Airlines | 31/03/89 |
| 1578 | 49826 | -83 | G-BPSD | BIA | 26/04/89 |
| 1579 | 49844 | -81 | HB-ISX | Swissair | 31/03/89 |
| 1580 | 49627 | -83 | EC-EOZ | Spanair | 25/04/89 |
| 1581 | 49846 | -83 | D-AGWB | German Wings | 30/03/89 |
| 1582 | 49628 | -83 | EC-EOM | Oasis International | 25/04/89 |
| 1583 | 49629 | -83 | EC-EOY | Oasis International | 15/05/89 |
| 1584 | 49550 | -82 | I-DAVR | ATI | 24/04/89 |
| 1585 | 49847 | -83 | D-AGWC | German Wings | 10/05/89 |
| 1586 | 49551 | -82 | I-DAVS | ATI | 01/05/89 |
| 1587 | 49767 | -87 | D-ALLI | Aero Lloyd | 05/05/89 |
| 1588 | 49810 | -88 | N937DL | Delta Air Lines | 20/05/89 |
| 1589 | 49514 | -82 | B | SAIC 15/China Northern | 12/89 |
| 1590 | 49811 | -88 | N938DL | Delta Air Lines | 26/05/89 |
| 1591 | 49630 | -83 | EC-216 | Spanair | 01/06/89 |
| 1592 | 49848 | -83 | D-AGWD | German Wings | 22/05/89 |
| 1593 | 49812 | -88 | N939DL | Delta Air Lines | 26/05/89 |
| 1594 | 49877 | -83 | OH-LMT | Finnair | 28/05/89 |
| 1595 | 49768 | -87 | D-ALLJ | Aero Lloyd | 07/06/89 |
| 1596 | 49631 | -83 | EC-EPM | Oasis International | 14/06/89 |
| 1597 | 49552 | -82 | I-DAVT | ATI | 08/06/89 |
| 1598 | 49820 | -81 | JA8294 | Japan Air System | 16/06/89 |
| 1599 | 49813 | -88 | N940DL | Delta Air Lines | 17/06/89 |
| 1600 | 49794 | -82 | I-DAWU | ATI | 20/06/89 |
| 1601 | 49854 | -83 | D-ALLL | Aero Lloyd | 19/06/89 |
| 1602 | 49814 | -88 | N941DL | Delta Air Lines | 12/07/89 |
| 1603 | 49632 | -83 | 9Y-THV | BWIA International | 11/07/89 |
| 1604 | 49465 | -87 | JA8279 | Japan Air System | 28/07/89 |
| 1605 | 49815 | -88 | N942DL | Delta Air Lines | 19/07/89 |
| 1606 | 49759 | -88 | N156PL | Midway Airlines | 21/12/89 |
| 1607 | 49733 | -82 | N495AA | American Airlines | 12/07/89 |
| 1608 | 49816 | -88 | N943DL | Delta Air Lines | 02/08/89 |
| 1609 | 49515 | -82 | B2131 | SAIC 16/China Eastern | 12/12/89 |
| 1610 | 49726 | -87 | N803ML | Midway Airlines | 19/07/89 |
| 1611 | 49618 | -83 | F-GGMD | Minerve | 21/07/89 |
| 1612 | 49817 | -88 | N944DL | Delta Air Lines | 12/08/89 |
| 1613 | 49818 | -88 | N945DL | Delta Air Lines | 23/08/89 |
| 1614 | 49706 | -87 | SE-DHI | Transwede Airways | 05/09/89 |
| 1615 | 49821 | -81 | JA8295 | Japan Air System | 12/08/89 |
| 1616 | 49925 | -82 | N941AS | Alaska Airlines | 16/08/89 |
| 1617 | 49641 | -87 | HB-IUD | CTA | 18/08/89 |
| 1618 | 49740 | -82 | I-SMEP | Alisarda | 21/08/89 |
| 1619 | 49734 | -82 | N496AA | American Airlines | 18/08/89 |
| 1620 | 49760 | -88 | N157PL | Midwest Express | 01/12/89 |
| 1621 | 49727 | -87 | N804ML | Midway Airlines | 01/09/89 |
| 1622 | 49516 | -82 | B | SAIC 17/China Northern | 27/02/90 |
| 1623 | 49761 | -88 | N158PL | Aeromexico | 30/11/89 |
| 1624 | 49762 | -88 | N601ME | Midwest Express | 17/11/89 |
| 1625 | 49909 | -81 | SE-DII | SAS | 30/08/89 |
| 1626 | 49763 | -88 | N160PL | Aeromexico | 30/11/89 |
| 1627 | 49784 | -83 | N509MD | Austral Lineas Aereas | 05/09/89 |
| 1628 | 49785 | -83 | HL7271 | Korean Air Lines | 14/09/89 |
| 1629 | 49819 | -88 | N946DL | Delta Air Lines | 20/09/89 |
| 1630 | 49741 | -83 | OH-LMU | Finnair | 23/09/89 |
| 1631 | 49786 | -83 | 9Y-THW | BWIA International | 19/09/89 |
| 1632 | 49764 | -88 | N161PL | Aeromexico | 30/11/89 |
| 1633 | 49517 | -82 | B | SAIC 18/ | |
| 1634 | 49777 | -87 | N805ML | Midway Airlines | 27/09/89 |
| 1635 | 49735 | -82 | N497AA | American Airlines | 26/09/89 |
| 1636 | 49787 | -83 | HL7274 | Korean Air Lines | 28/09/89 |
| 1637 | 49663 | -83 | G-PATD | Paramount Airways | 29/09/89 |
| 1638 | 49910 | -81 | OY-KHH | SAS | 29/09/89 |
| 1639 | 49795 | -82 | I-DAVV | Alitalia | 12/10/89 |
| 1640 | 49736 | -82 | N498AA | American Airlines | 06/10/89 |
| 1641 | 49737 | -82 | N499AA | American Airlines | 12/10/89 |
| 1642 | 49789 | -83 | 9Y-THX | BWIA International | 20/10/89 |
| 1643 | 49790 | -83 | EC-307 | Spanair | 24/10/89 |
| 1644 | 49791 | -83 | F-ODTN | Aerocancun | 30/10/89 |
| 1645 | 49765 | -88 | N162PL | Aeromexico | 06/12/89 |
| 1646 | 49778 | -87 | N806ML | Midway Airlines | 09/11/89 |
| 1647 | 49518 | -82 | B | SAIC 19/China Northern | 03/04/90 |
| 1648 | 49738 | -82 | N501AA | American Airlines | 30/10/89 |
| 1649 | 49739 | -82 | N33502 | American Airlines | 31/10/89 |
| 1650 | 49797 | -82 | N44503 | American Airlines | 07/11/89 |

| Fuselage Number | Serial Number | Model | Registration | Operator | Delivery Date |
|---|---|---|---|---|---|
| 1651 | 49798 | -82 | N70504 | American Airlines | 31/10/89 |
| 1652 | 49799 | -82 | N505AA | American Airlines | 09/11/89 |
| 1653 | 49911 | -81 | OY-KHL | SAS | 17/11/89 |
| 1654 | 49827 | -87 | EC-290 | Iberia | 06/04/90 |
| 1655 | 49792 | -83 | XA-RPH | Aerocancun | 22/11/89 |
| 1656 | 49793 | -82 | C-GKMV | Minerve Canada | 01/12/89 |
| 1657 | 49766 | -88 | N163PL | Midway Airlines | 21/12/89 |
| 1658 | 49519 | -82 | B | SAIC 20/China Eastern | 05/06/90 |
| 1659 | 49912 | -81 | LN-RMJ | SAS | 01/12/89 |
| 1660 | 49800 | -82 | N7506 | American Airlines | 04/12/89 |
| 1661 | 49801 | -82 | N3507A | American Airlines | 04/12/89 |
| 1662 | 49802 | -82 | N7608 | American Airlines | 20/12/89 |
| 1663 | 49803 | -82 | N7509 | American Airlines | 11/12/89 |
| 1664 | 49878 | -88 | N947DL | Delta Air Lines | 21/12/89 |
| 1665 | 49913 | -81 | SE-DIL | SAS | 15/12/89 |
| 1666 | 49879 | -88 | N948DL | Delta Air Lines | 29/12/89 |
| 1667 | 49828 | -87 | EC-EUD | Iberia | 04/04/90 |
| 1668 | 49968 | -83 | F-GHEI | Air Liberté | 26/02/90 |
| 1669 | 49804 | -82 | N510AM | American Airlines. | 15/12/89 |
| 1670 | 49779 | -87 | N807ML | Midway Airlines | 27/12/89 |
| 1671 | 49520 | -82 | B | SAIC 21/ | 17/09/90 |
| 1672 | 49805 | -82 | N90511 | American Airlines | 27/12/89 |
| 1673 | 49806 | -82 | N7512A | American Airlines | 27/12/89 |
| 1674 | 49780 | -87 | N808ML | Midway Airlines | 10/01/90 |
| 1675 | 49856 | -83 | D-ALLM | Aero Lloyd | 06/02/90 |
| 1676 | 49880 | -88 | N949DL | Delta Air Lines | 09/02/90 |
| 1677 | 49881 | -88 | N950DL | Delta Air Lines | 21/02/90 |
| 1678 | 49829 | -87 | EC-EUC | Iberia | 04/90 |
| 1679 | 49882 | -88 | N951DL | Delta Air Lines | 23/02/90 |
| 1680 | 49904 | -83 | OH-LMV | Finnair | 23/02/90 |
| 1681 | 49413 | -87 | OE-LMM | Austrian Airlines | /90 |
| 1682 | 49414 | -87 | OE-LMN | Austrian Airlines | /90 |
| 1683 | 49883 | -88 | N952DL | Delta Air Lines | 09/03/90 |
| 1684 | 49830 | -87 | EC-EUL | Iberia | 12/04/90 |
| 1685 | 49884 | -88 | N953DL | Delta Air Lines | 21/03/90 |
| 1686 | 49890 | -82 | N513AA | American Airlines | 08/03/90 |
| 1687 | 49857 | -83 | D-ALLN | Aero Lloyd | 30/03/90 |
| 1688 | 49831 | -87 | EC-EVB | Iberia | 27/04/90 |
| 1689 | 49885 | -88 | N954DL | Delta Air Lines | 28/03/90 |
| 1690 | 49521 | -82 | B | SAIC 22/ | 05/09/90 |
| 1691 | 49886 | -88 | N955DL | Delta Air Lines | 31/03/90 |
| 1692 | 49888 | -87 | OE-LMO | Austrian Airlines | /90 |
| 1693 | 44914 | -81 | OY-KHM | SAS | /90 |
| 1694 | 49891 | -82 | N7514A | American Airlines | 27/03/90 |
| 1695 | 49892 | -82 | N3515 | American Airlines | 31/03/90 |
| 1696 | 49893 | -82 | N5116AM | American Airlines | 31/03/90 |
| 1697 | 49894 | -82 | N7517A | American Airlines | 30/03/90 |
| 1698 | 49895 | -82 | N7518A | American Airlines | 30/03/90 |
| 1699 | 49887 | -88 | N956DL | Delta Air Lines | 27/04/90 |
| 1700 | 49976 | -88 | N957DL | Delta Air Lines | 28/04/90 |
| 1701 | 49977 | -88 | N958DL | Delta Air Lines | 03/05/90 |
| 1702 | 49522 | -82 | B- | SAIC 23/ | 03/10/90 |
| 1703 | 49832 | -87 | EC-EXF | Iberia | 31/05/90 |
| 1704 | 53050 | -83 | EC-EUZ | Aviaco | 07/05/90 |
| 1705 | 49610 | -87 | LN-RMK | SAS | |
| 1706 | 49833 | -87 | EC-EXG | Iberia | 29/05/90 |
| 1707 | 49896 | -82 | N7519A | American Airlines | 14/05/90 |
| 1708 | 49897 | -82 | N7520A | American Airlines | 10/05/90 |
| 1709 | 49898 | -82 | N7521A | American Airlines | 17/05/90 |
| 1710 | 49978 | -88 | N959DL | Delta Air Lines | 24/05/90 |
| 1711 | 49979 | -88 | N960DL | Delta Air Lines | 15/06/90 |
| 1712 | 49980 | -88 | N961DL | Delta Air Lines | 31/05/90 |
| 1713 | 49796 | -82 | I-DAVW | ATI | 29/05/90 |
| 1714 | 49834 | -87 | EC-EXR | Iberia | 20/06/90 |
| 1715 | 49926 | -88 | XA-AMS | Aeromexico | 31/05/90 |
| 1716 | 49927 | -88 | XA-AMT | Aeromexico | 31/05/90 |
| 1717 | 49835 | -87 | EC-EXM | Iberia | 22/06/90 |
| 1718 | 53051 | -83 | EC-EVU | Aviaco | 14/06/90 |
| 1719 | 49969 | -82 | I-DAVX | Alitalia | 14/06/90 |
| 1720 | 49930 | -83 | HB-ISZ | Balair | 20/06/90 |
| 1721 | 49836 | -87 | EC-EXN | Iberia | 02/07/90 |
| 1722 | 49899 | -82 | N7522A | American Airlines | 20/06/90 |
| 1723 | 49915 | -82 | N59523 | American Airlines | 21/06/90 |
| 1724 | 49523 | -82 | B- | SAIC 24/ | 04/12/90 |
| 1725 | 49981 | -88 | N962DL | Delta Air Lines | 27/06/90 |
| 1726 | 49982 | -88 | N963DL | Delta Air Lines | 28/06/90 |
| 1727 | 49466 | -87 | JA8280 | Japan Air System | 29/06/90 |
| 1728 | 49855 | -83 | F-GGME | Minerve | 29/06/90 |
| 1729 | 49916 | -82 | N70524 | American Airlines | 28/06/90 |
| 1730 | 49837 | -87 | EC-EXT | Iberia | 24/07/90 |
| 1731 | 53052 | -83 | N942AS | Alaska Airlines | 18/07/90 |
| 1732 | 49928 | -88 | XA-AMU | Aeromexico | 20/07/90 |
| 1733 | 49838 | -87 | EC-EYB | Iberia | 06/08/90 |
| 1734 | 49907 | -81 | JA8296 | Japan Air System | 20/07/90 |
| 1735 | 49917 | -82 | N7525A | American Airlines | 26/07/90 |
| 1736 | 53012 | -83 | D-ALLO | Aero Lloyd | 28/07/90 |
| 1737 | 49970 | -82 | I-DAVZ | ATI | 31/07/90 |
| 1738 | 53013 | -83 | D-ALLP | Aero Lloyd | 30/07/90 |
| 1739 | 49839 | -87 | EC-EYX | Iberia | 16/08/90 |
| 1740 | 53014 | -83 | D-ALLQ | Aero Lloyd | 13/08/90 |
| 1741 | 49929 | -88 | XA-AMV | Aeromexico | 10/08/90 |
| 1742 | | | | | |
| 1743 | 49918 | -82 | N7526A | American Airlines | 16/08/90 |
| 1744 | 49919 | -82 | N7527A | American Airlines | 22/08/90 |
| 1745 | 49840 | -87 | EC-EYY | Iberia | 30/08/90 |
| 1746 | 49524 | -82 | B | SAIC 25/ | 08/01/91 |
| 1747 | 49983 | -88 | N964DL | Delta Air Lines | 14/09/90 |
| 1748 | 49984 | -88 | N965DL | Delta Air Lines | 24/08/90 |
| 1749 | 49908 | -81 | JA8297 | Japan Air System | 28/08/90 |
| 1750 | 49920 | -82 | N7528A | American Airlines | 05/09/90 |
| 1751 | 49841 | -87 | EC-EYZ | Iberia | 26/09/90 |
| 1752 | 49921 | -82 | N70529 | American Airlines | 04/09/90 |
| 1753 | 49922 | -82 | N7530 | American Airlines | 12/09/90 |
| 1754 | 49931 | -82 | N809ML | Midway Airlines | 12/09/90 |
| 1755 | 49971 | -82 | I-DACM | ATI | 15/09/90 |
| 1756 | 49932 | -82 | N810ML | Midway Airlines | 24/09/90 |
| 1757 | 49972 | -82 | I-DACN | ATI | 14/09/90 |
| 1758 | 49923 | -82 | N7531A | American Airlines | 19/09/90 |
| 1759 | 49924 | -82 | N7532A | American Airlines | 24/09/90 |
| 1760 | 49987 | -82 | N7533A | American Airlines | 26/09/90 |
| 1761 | 49889 | -82 | N811ML | Midway Airlines | 27/09/90 |
| 1762 | 49973 | -82 | I-DACP | ATI | 27/09/90 |
| 1763 | 49842 | -87 | EC-EZA | Iberia | 30/09/90 |
| 1764 | 49934 | -83 | N907MD | Austral | 29/09/90 |
| 1765 | 49900 | -82 | N6202D | Unifly | 28/09/90 |
| 1766 | 49901 | -82 | N6202S | Unifly | 28/09/90 |
| 1767 | 49905 | -82 | OH-LMW | Finnair | 02/10/90 |
| 1768 | 49988 | -82 | N7534A | American Airlines | 30/09/90 |
| 1769 | 49989 | -82 | N7535A | American Airlines | 22/10/90 |
| 1770 | 49990 | -82 | N7536A | American Airlines | 23/10/90 |
| 1771 | 49843 | -87 | EC-EZS | Iberia | 31/10/90 |
| 1772 | | | | | |
| 1773 | 49935 | -83 | G-DCAC | Airtours International | 19/11/90 |
| 1774 | 49974 | -82 | I-DACQ | ATI | 26/10/90 |
| 1775 | 49975 | -82 | I-DACR | ATI | 31/10/90 |
| 1776 | 53044 | -83 | N905ML | Midway Airlines | 30/10/90 |
| 1777 | 53045 | -83 | N906ML | Midway Airlines | 31/10/90 |
| 1778 | 49936 | -83 | G-HCRP | Airtours International | 19/11/90 |
| 1779 | 53018 | -83 | N943AS | Alaska Airlines | 05/11/90 |
| 1780 | 49991 | -82 | N7537A | American Airlines | 31/10/90 |
| 1781 | 49992 | -82 | N7538A | American Airlines | 08/11/90 |
| 1782 | 49993 | -82 | N7539A | American Airlines | 13/11/90 |
| 1783 | 53019 | -82 | N944AS | Alaska Airlines | 13/11/90 |
| 1784 | 49937 | -83 | G-COES | Airtours International | 21/01/90 |
| 1785 | 49938 | -83 | XA-RTK | La Tur | 18/12/90 |
| 1786 | 49906 | -82 | OH-LMX | Finnair | 15/11/90 |
| 1787 | 49939 | -83 | EI-CBR | Irish Aerospace | 03/12/90 |
| 1788 | 49940 | -83 | G-TTPT | Airtours International | 28/12/90 |
| 1789 | 53020 | -82 | N94/AS | Alaska Airlines | 07/12/90 |
| 1790 | 49994 | -82 | N7540A | American Airlines | 04/12/90 |
| 1791 | 49995 | -82 | N7541A | American Airlines | 05/12/90 |
| 1792 | 49996 | -82 | N7542A | American Airlines | 10/12/90 |
| 1793 | 49941 | -83 | G-JSMC | Airtours International | 14/12/90 |
| 1794 | 53046 | -83 | N907ML | Midway Airlines | 03/12/90 |
| 1795 | 53115 | -88 | N966DL | Delta Air Lines | 12/12/90 |
| 1796 | 53116 | -88 | N967DL | Delta Air Lines | 14/12/90 |
| 1797 | 53017 | -82 | N812ML | Midway Airlines | 14/12/90 |
| 1798 | | | | | |
| 1799 | 49942 | -83 | EI-CBS | Irish Aerospace | 04/12/90 |
| 1800 | 49998 | -81 | SE-DIX | SAS | 18/12/90 |
| 1801 | 53021 | -83 | N948AS | Alaska Airlines | 21/12/90 |
| 1802 | 53025 | -82 | N7543A | American Airlines | 18/12/90 |
| 1803 | 49999 | -81 | SE-DIN | SAS | 21/12/90 |
| 1804 | 53026 | -82 | N7544A | American Airlines | 19/12/90 |
| 1805 | 53027 | -82 | N16545 | American Airlines | 18/12/90 |
| 1806 | 53053 | -82 | I-DACS | Alitalia | 21/12/90 |

NOTE: Companies shown in the production lists are the first operators only of each aircraft produced. This does not automatically confer ownership as, especially since the middle 1980s, large quantities of aircraft have been and are being purchased by specialist leasing companies such as ILFC, Polaris Leasing and the GPA Group, for immediate onward lease to airlines, often retaining their original registrations.

# 6 DC-9/MD-80 ACCIDENTS

Aircraft are written off in many different ways, not all resulting in the loss of life. While the DC-9 list may appear long, it must be put in that context and related to the number of aircraft built and the length of service. Unfortunately, when a spectacular accident does happen, it remains in the memory for many years. One such occurrence was the mid-air collision on 10 September 1976 over Vrbovec in Yugoslavia involving a British Airways Trident 3 and an Inex-Adria Airways DC-9. One of the most tragic air accidents, it resulted in the loss of 176 lives and was blamed on an error by the Zagreb Air Traffic Control Centre. With rapid technological advances, incidences of mechanical failures are diminishing, but with more and more people flying, overloaded ATC and overworked controllers are still with us. Accidents will always happen, but this should not detract from the excellence of the product.

| Fuselage Number | Serial Number | Model | Registration | Operator and scene of accident | Date |
|---|---|---|---|---|---|
| 11 | 45700 | -14 | N3305L | Delta Air Lines Forth Worth, Texas, USA | 30/05/72 |
| 22 | 45724 | -15 | I-TIGI | Itavia Tyrrhenian Sea | 27/06/80 |
| 36 | 45726 | -14 | N626TX | Continental Airlines Denver, Colorado, USA | 15/11/87 |
| 52 | 45794 | -14 | N9101 | West Coast Airlines Portland, Oregon, USA | 01/10/66 |
| 58 | 45771 | -14 | N8910E | Eastern Air Lines Miami, Florida, USA | 09/02/79 |
| 74 | 45796 | -14 | N9103 | Texas International Baton Rouge, Louisiana, USA | 17/03/80 |
| 80 | 45777 | -15 | N1063T | Trans World Airlines Urbano, Ohio, USA | 09/03/67 |
| 89 | 47056 | -14 | YV-C-AVM | Avensa Maturin, Venezuela | 22/12/74 |
| 105 | 47002 | -15 | N926AX | Airborne Express Philadelphia, Pennsylvania, USA | 06/02/85 |
| 106 | 47025 | -32 | YV-67C | Avensa Barquisimeto, Venezuela | 11/03/83 |
| 148 | 47077 | -32 | EC-BII | Iberia La Trauche, France | 05/03/73 |
| 153 | 47100 | -15 | XA-SOC | Aeromexico Puerto Vallarta, Mexico | 20/06/73 |
| 155 | 47081 | -14 | N9104 | Texas International Denver, Colorado, USA | 16/11/76 |
| 162 | 47034 | -15 | N974Z | Ozark Air Lines Sioux City, Iowa, USA | 27/12/68 |
| 166 | 47075 | -31 | N975NE | Delta Air Lines Boston, Massachusetts, USA | 31/07/73 |
| 196 | 47118 | -32 | I-DIKB | Alitalia Rome, Italy | 07/01/80 |
| 204 | 47032 | -32 | N3323L | Delta Air Lines Chattanooga, Tennessee, USA | 27/11/73 |
| 231 | 47159 | -31 | N954N | North Central Airlines Chicago, Illinois, USA | 20/12/72 |
| 254 | 47124 | -15 | XA-SOF | Aeromexico Leon, Mexico | 02/09/76 |
| 288 | 47196 | -32 | CF-TLU | Air Canada Cincinnati, Ohio, USA | 02/06/83 |
| 289 | 47197 | -32 | CF-TLV | Air Canada Toronto, Canada | 26/06/78 |
| 332 | 45870 | -31 | N8961E | Eastern Air Lines Ft. Lauderdale, Florida, USA | 18/05/72 |
| 334 | 47227 | -32 | I-DIKQ | Alitalia Palermo, Sicily, Italy | 23/12/78 |
| 338 | 47200 | -32 | CF-TLY | Air Canada Montreal, Canada | 02/06/82 |
| 346 | 47240 | -15F | N565PC | Emery Worldwide Cleveland, Ohio, USA | 17/02/91 |
| 357 | 47211 | -31 | N988VJ | Allegheny Airlines Shelbyville, Indiana, USA | 09/09/69 |
| 358 | 47213 | -32 | TC-JAC | Turkish Airlines Adana, Turkey | 21/01/72 |
| 361 | 47267 | -31 | N8967E | Eastern Air Lines Akron, Ohio, USA | 28/11/73 |
| 362 | 47296 | -32C9 | 67-2258 | United States Air Force Scott AFB, Illinois, USA | 16/09/71 |
| 393 | 47309 | -14 | N100ME | Midwest Express Milwaukee, Wisconsin, USA | 06/09/85 |
| 440 | 47304 | -21 | LN-RLM | SAS Oslo, Norway | 30/01/73 |
| 443 | 47400 | -31 | N8984E | Eastern Air Lines Charlotte, North Carolina, USA | 11/09/74 |
| 448 | 47243 | -32 | YV-C-AVD | Avensa Maracaibo, Venezuela | 16/03/69 |
| 457 | 47407 | -33CF | N935F | Overseas National Airways St. Croix, US Virgin Islands | 02/05/70 |
| 470 | 47356 | -32 | XA-JED | Aeromexico Cerritos, California, USA | 31/08/86 |
| 481 | 47333 | -31 | N994VJ | Allegheny Airlines Philadelphia, Pennsylvania, USA | 23/06/76 |
| 503 | 47441 | -31 | N9345 | Hughes Airwest Duarte, California, USA | 06/06/71 |
| 510 | 47245 | -31 | N975 | Southern Airways Huntingdon, West Virginia, USA | 14/11/70 |
| 546 | 47500 | -32 | HI-177 | Dominicana Santo Domingo, Dominican Republic | 15/02/70 |
| 587 | 47503 | -32 | YU-AHR | Inex-Adria Airways Aden, South Yemen | 19/03/72 |
| 588 | 47506 | -31 | N961VJ | USAir Erie, Pennsylvania, USA | 02/04/86 |
| 592 | 47482 | -32 | YU-AHT | JAT-Yugoslav Airlines Prague, Czechoslovakia | 26/01/72 |
| 608 | 43393 | -31 | N1335U | Southern Airways Atlanta, Georgia, USA | 04/04/77 |
| 620 | 47451 | -32 | YU-AJO | Inex-Adria Airways Prague, Czechoslovakia | 30/10/75 |
| 649 | 47463 | -32 | PK-GND | Garuda Banjarmasin, Indonesia | 13/01/80 |
| 674 | 47561 | -32 | PK-GNE | Gardua Kemayoran, Indonesia | 13/06/84 |
| 693 | 47579 | -32 | YU-AJN | JAT-Yugoslav Airlines Belgrade, Yugoslavia | 23/11/74 |
| 729 | 47621 | -32 | XA-DEN | Aeromexico Chihuahua, Mexico | 27/07/81 |
| 741 | 47649 | -32 | YU-AJR | Inex-Adria Airways Zagreb, Yugoslavia | 10/09/76 |
| 746 | 47641 | -32 | I-ATJA | Alitalia Zürich, Switzerland | 14/11/90 |
| 753 | 47622 | -32 | XA-DEO | Aeromexico Altamirano, Mexico | 08/11/81 |
| 758 | 47636 | -32 | PK-GNI | Garuda Denpasar, Bali, Indonesia | 30/12/74 |
| 766 | 47667 | -32 | I-ATJC | ATI Cagliari, Italy | 14/09/79 |
| 770 | 47645 | -32 | EC-CGS | Aviaco Madrid, Spain | 07/12/83 |
| 836 | 47741 | -32 | PK-GNQ | Garuda Medan, Indonesia | 04/04/87 |

## MD-80 ACCIDENTS

| Fuselage Number | Serial Number | Model | Registration | Operator and scene of accident | Date |
|---|---|---|---|---|---|
| 917 | 48001 | -81 | N1002G | Douglas Aircraft Yuma, Arizona, USA | 19/06/80 |
| 989 | 48050 | -81 | N1003G | Austral Lineas Aereas Posadas, Argentina | 12/06/88 |
| 998 | 48047 | -82 | YU-ANA | INEX-Adria Airways Ajaccio, Corsica | 01/12/81 |
| 1040 | 48090 | -82 | N312RC | Northwest Airlines Detroit, Michigan, USA | 16/08/87 |

*Below:*
**A Southern Airways DC-9-14 being worked on.**